1ST_1982

The Castle in Medieval England and Wales

The Castle in Medieval England and Wales

COLIN PLATT

Charles Scribner's Sons
New York

I dedicate this book to my daughter Emma
of whom, as I write, I have cause to be especially proud

Printed in Great Britain.
Library of Congress Catalog Card Number 82-60228
ISBN 0-684-17799-4

Contents

List of Illustrations

Preface and Acknowledgements

A castle is a building, and a book about castles must be a book about buildings, however we might wish to view them. But whereas the emphasis in fortress studies, in the past, has usually been placed on the architectural evolution of the castle and on the discussion of its military role in particular, the many different roles that the castle was called upon to play are now receiving greater attention. It may be perfectly correct, for example, to identify a decline in castle-building practice in England after its 'apogee' during the reign of Edward I. Yet the castle, demonstrably, was at least as much alive in the later Middle Ages as it had been in the final decades of the thirteenth century. Circumstances had changed, but just as one principal purpose had determined the form of the castle in the earlier period, another dictated a new emphasis in the later.

In this book, I have rarely aspired to reach judgements of any kind on the military effectiveness of the castle. My own experience as a soldier was brief and not especially apposite, and the reader will find little here to inform him about fields of fire, about siege techniques, or about the more intricate technicalities of defence. In their place I have concentrated, as I truly believe the historian ought to do, on the castle in the context of events. From the Norman Conquest onwards, the castle was an expression of personal aspirations; it was a visible demonstration—and perhaps the most visible—of wealth and of a man's status in society. Of course, the castle had its purpose in defence. And it would be perfectly proper, as others have seen it, to focus on this purpose exclusively. Significantly, though, when the military engineers of the sixteenth century, having entered a new era of efficient siege artillery, lowered the castle's profile or even dug their forts deep into the ground, the private patron, with other interests to promote, very rapidly lost his enthusiasm for such buildings. And who, indeed, would choose to make his home in a battery or a pill-box if he had the wealth to live anywhere else?

It is not my belief that the true character of a building can be conveyed in words alone. Accordingly, I have made every effort throughout this book to illustrate the castles I discuss. For help in doing this, I am indebted to Alan Burn, of the Southampton University Cartographic Unit, and to his skilled and resourceful staff. They have been responsible for every drawing in this book. With the kind permission of individual officers of the Inspectorate of Ancient Monuments and Historic Buildings and of the Director of Publishing at Her Majesty's Stationery Office, we have been able to base our plans of Queenborough and of the Edwardian castles in Wales on plans previously published in H. M. Colvin's *The History of the King's Works* (volumes I and II). Similarly, our plan and section of Orford and the plans we reproduce here of Cilgerran, Carreg Cennen, Goodrich, Nunney, and St Mawes, are re-drawn from the originals in the Department of the Environment guides to those castles. I am particularly obliged to Beric Morley, of the Inspectorate, for his consent, freely and promptly given, to our re-drawing (with amendments suggested by himself) of his reconstruction of the Hylton façade (Fig. 164).

For the plates, in each case remaining the copyright of the original photographer, I am grateful to Christopher Dalton for Fig. 123; to John Wright Photography for Fig. 136 (originally passed on to me by Mr M. J. M. Westwood, general manager of Warwick Castle); to the Committee for Aerial Photography, Cambridge, for Figs. 1 and 19; to Anthony Kemp for Figs. 21 and 52; to Quentin Hughes for Figs. 35, 57, and 173; to B. T. Batsford Ltd for Figs. 18, 49, and 109; to Hallam Ashley for Figs. 9, 30, 46, 92, 119, 130, 139, 158, 159, and 161; to Olive Smith, widow of the late Edwin Smith, for Figs. 23, 26, 77, 97, 121, 141, 151, and 170; to A. F. Kersting for Figs. 44, 51, 65, 66, 134, 149, 150, 160, 168, 171, and 176; to the Bodleian Library, Oxford, for jacket illustrations and Figs. 88, 89, 108, 129, 133, 138, and 165; to the Welsh Office, Cardiff, for Figs. 12, 56, 58, 59, 60, 67, 69, 70, 72, 73, 75, 80, 86, 99, 100, and 142; to the Royal Commission on Historical Monuments (National Monuments Record) for Figs. 4, 5, 6, 8, 22, 24, 25, 36, 45, 78, 93, 95, 98, 101, 104, 114, 115, 118, 124, 125, 146, 155, and 157; to the Property Services Agency (Photographic Library) for Figs. 2, 7, 10, 15, 17, 28, 31, 32, 39, 43, 47, 48, 79, 91, 103, 111, 116, 117, 131, 143, 148, 152, 153, 154, 172, 174, and 180; to Aerofilms Ltd for Figs. 3, 11, 13, 14, 20, 27, 29, 34, 38, 40, 42, 54, 55, 62, 64, 68, 71, 82, 84, 85, 87, 90, 94, 96, 107, 110, 120, 122, 127, 128, 132, 135, 137, 140, 145, 166, 177, 178, and 181. The following plates, obtained from IPC Magazines Ltd and the copyright of *Country Life*, are published here with the permission of the individual owners of the buildings: 16 (Cardiff), 105 (Scotney), 106 (Saltwood), 112 (Dudley), 144 (Borthwick), 156 (Buckden), 162 (Belsay), 163 (Chipchase), 167 (Thornbury), 169 (Hoghton). I am much obliged to Sir Bernard de Hoghton for information used in the caption of Fig. 169. Illustrations provided by the Property Services Agency are reproduced with permission of the Controller of Her Majesty's Stationery Office. I am also indebted to HMSO for permission to reproduce illustrations provided by the Welsh Office.

Glossary

Ante-chapel   a chamber or lobby, usually small, opening into a chapel

Ashlar   a stone worked square before its use in building

Bailey   the defended outer court of a castle

Barbican   an outer work, usually an enclosure but quite commonly also a gated bridge or ramp, before the main gate of a castle

Bartisan   a battlemented turret projecting at roof-level from the corner of a tower

Bastion   an earthwork or walled projection from the line of an artillery fortification, intended to provide flanking fire; hence 'angle-bastion'

Bergfried   a fighting-tower, being one of the earliest elements of the castle

Blind arcade   the decorative treatment of a wall, characteristically Norman, by setting blank arches, carried on columns, against it

Bridge-pit   the pit into which the heel of the drawbridge descends when the bridge itself is raised

Burh   an Anglo-Saxon fortified town or other major defended place not necessarily urban

Corbel   a stone or timber projection from the face of a wall intended to support the end of a beam or to help carry a platform

Crosslet loophole   an arrow-slit in the form of a cross

Curtain (wall)   the wall, usually free-standing and with interval or angle towers, which encloses a castle courtyard

Diaper work   the use of different coloured bricks to achieve an all-over decorative pattern of repeated lozenges or squares; also seen in stonework and in painting

Donjon   the keep, or great tower, of a castle

Draw-bar   the bar, securing the castle gate on the inside, which might be drawn back into the porter's lodge before opening the gate

Drawbridge   a hinged or pivoted bridge which might be raised on the approach of an enemy

Drum tower   a circular tower (i.e. shaped like a drum), usually a mural tower of some kind

Embrasure   a splayed opening in a wall or a parapet to take a window or a gun

Fenestration   the windows of a building and their arrangement

Flanker   a gun emplacement commanding a curtain wall or rampart from a recess in the flank of a bastion

Forebuilding   a covered stair, sometimes including a chapel on its upper storey, protecting the first-floor entrance of a tower keep

Garderobe   a privy or lavatory, though the word is sometimes also used to denote a private bedchamber or a store

Interval tower   a mural tower, or one of a number of towers set along the length of a curtain wall

Machicolation   an opening in the floor of a projecting parapet or fighting gallery, through which missiles could be directed at an enemy; frequently applied also to the entire projecting structure

Mangonel   a stone-casting engine-of-war

Motte   a castle mound, characteristically shaped like an upturned basin

Mullion   the vertical bar between the lights of a window

Murder hole   a hole, often called a *meurtrière*, contrived in the vault of an entrance passage, through which missiles could be rained on an assailant

Newel stair   a circular stair winding round the newel, or central pillar

Orillons   the two spurs of an arrow-head bastion, protecting the flankers

Pentice   a covered way, lean-to shed, or gallery

Pilaster buttress   a shallow vertical buttress frequently used with other such buttresses to achieve an ornamental effect

Portcullis   a heavy grating designed to close off an entrance passage, sliding vertically in grooves cut on either side to receive it

Ringwork   a defensive bank and ditch, circular or oval in plan, surrounding a hall or other housing

Sally-port   the secondary entrance, or postern, of a castle, intended to help the garrison make a swift sortie against the besiegers

Shell keep   a tower contrived by circling the top of a castle mound with a stone curtain wall

Solar   a private chamber, often placed at the dais end of the hall

String course   a projecting horizontal band, usually moulded and intended for decorative effect, across the surface of a façade

Talus   the slope of a wall outwards towards the base; also called a glacis

Transom   the horizontal bar between the lights of a window

Trebuchet   a stone-casting engine-of-war

Wall-walk   the passage or fighting platform behind the parapet of a curtain wall

Ward   the court or bailey of a castle

Chapter 1

Castles of Conquest and Settlement

When the Normans came to England in 1066, few of them would have known much about the country they had invaded. Many had campaigned successfully already under the command of Duke William, and they knew him as a man who had never lost a battle. Nevertheless, Norman arms neither had been in the past, nor would be in the future, invariably victorious. The Conquest was a gamble, and it was recognized as such. Its success depended—and this was the importance of the victory at Hastings—on the winning of the time in which a strategy of settlement might develop. There might be little, as Hastings showed, to distinguish the Anglo-Saxons from the Normans in military prowess. But it was the Normans, in the longer term, who had the advantage. For what they understood, having practised those techniques elsewhere, was that the first rule of successful appropriation was to make sure of the territories they held. To this end, they had developed the castle.

In every Conquest narrative, the role of the castle is central. When Duke William landed at Pevensey, his first action was to build a temporary castle for himself in what remained of the original Roman fort. At Hastings, he built himself another one to follow this, immediately after the battle, with a re-fortification of the earthworks at Dover. London, before the end of the year, was to be secured by castles 'against the fickleness of the vast and fierce populace', while systematic programmes of castle-building then accompanied each successive campaign—at Exeter in the West Country, at York and at Durham in the north, at Warwick and at Nottingham in the Midlands, at Lincoln, Huntingdon, and Cambridge towards the east, and many more.

Significantly, in these early stages of the Conquest, when the Normans built a castle at an existing town, they did so not to protect the inhabitants of that centre but to overawe them. And in just the same way, during the subjection of the countryside, the castle's essential purpose was as forward-base and refuge, the fighting hub of an appropriated estate. Every castle in later years would have functions other than military; it would be a residence, a treasury, a centre of administration, and a prison. But while the Conquest itself was under way, the castle was part of the process. One of the pioneers of the method was Roger de Montgomery, earl of Shrewsbury (1074–94), builder of the great motte at Hen Domen. And it was Orderic Vitalis, the English-born son of Roger's man Odelerius d'Orléans, who passed the most often-quoted judgement on the Conquest. The English, he said, though brave and warlike, had very few of those fortifications which the French call 'castles' in their land. It was this that had made their resistance to their conquerors so feeble.[1]

Orderic Vitalis lived at a time when the private castle was at its most familiar, and he felt no need to make the distinction between communal and private fortifications—between public and private war—over which historians sometimes stumble. Similarly, while the English, under their relatively strong central government, had

1 Surviving earthworks of the former motte and bailey castle at Hen Domen, raised soon after the Conquest: a tree-lined ditch outlines the bailey (right), while another ditch (left), also overgrown, separates the motte from the bailey

preserved the tradition by which communal fortifications like the burhs remained essentially the responsibility of the state, a man of Roger de Montgomery's background would have grown up with different ideas altogether. Certainly, when Roger de Montgomery raised the motte at Hen Domen, on the Welsh border, as early as 1070–71, he was clearly no novice at castle-building, any more than was the Conqueror, his cousin. He had been fighting alongside Duke William since the early 1050s, and although William had had his successes in pulling together the Norman duchy in a way it had never been before, both knew their fellow-countrymen, under a looser rein, as 'eager for rebellion, ripe for tumults, and ready for every sort of crime' (Orderic Vitalis), 'a race inured to war' who could 'hardly live without it, fierce in attacking their enemies, and when force fails, ready to use guile or to corrupt by bribery' (William of Malmesbury). It was in this turbulent and unruly society in western France, already old when Duke William took ship for England, that the two essential preconditions for castle-building had been brought together, setting a new pattern for the West. First of these was a breakdown of public order resulting from the disappearance of any sort of central authority that might prohibit, as the Carolingians in their day had tried to do, the waging of private war. Second, and in the long term even more important, for it kept the castle in being for another five centuries at least, was the recognition of the castle, whatever other purposes it might have, as the most appropriate symbol of lordship.

The scholars' quest for the remote origins of the private castle continues today as actively as it has always done. Nevertheless, it is already clear that private fortifications, in one form or another, were beginning to develop alongside the larger communal works from as far back as the second half of the ninth century, perhaps earlier. References to such fortresses, increasingly known as 'towers', become common in the tenth century, while it seems that even the larger public fortifications, at about this time, were becoming equipped with some strongpoint or individual retreat for the lord. For a while, certainly, strongpoint and residence remained apart, as the lord continued to live, except in times of emergency, in his adjoining manor-house or palace. But when, in due course, strongpoint and residence merged in one, the private castle as we know it was born.[2]

Something of this process can be seen at Fécamp, where recent excavations have demonstrated a significant re-planning of the fortified area in the early eleventh century, cutting down its size as Duke Richard II, styled 'the Good', converted what had been essentially a communal fortification into a private castle.[3] But Richard of Normandy was no more than following in the wake of the wicked Fulk Nerra, count of Anjou (987–1040), who for some decades already had been a pioneer in the development of a castle strategy that would become the model for the more active of his neighbours. Thus it was Fulk of Anjou's deliberately planned chain of fortresses, splitting the dominions of the rival counts of Blois, that showed the way towards a new use of the castle in conquest. Two generations later, the Norman conquerors, Duke William in England and Count Roger in Sicily, would travel this road in their turn.

2 Old Sarum: a Norman ringwork centrally placed in an Iron Age hill fort, with the outline of the twelfth-century cathedral in the foreground

Fulk Nerra was a pioneer castle-builder in other directions also. The evidence, it has been pointed out often enough, can be read in different ways. Nevertheless, his name has been associated with the raising of what may well have been one of the first great mottes in 1032–7 at Montglonne. And while Fulk's stone keep at Langeais, now that a similar building at Doué-la-Fontaine has been claimed to pre-date it, may not be the earliest such rectangular *donjon* in France, it remains undoubtedly the most remarkable survival from such an early date.[4] Very probably, most castles in western France, whether private or comital, would have remained for the best part of the eleventh century no more than smaller, more defendable, versions of the great linear earthworks familiar from much earlier times. However, variety in castle-building, even at this date, is its most obvious characteristic, and if the earthwork ring (now usually known as the 'ringwork') was one sort of defence, the piled-up mound (sometimes complementary and called a 'motte') was plainly another. By the second half of the eleventh century in Normandy, and rather earlier in the region of the Loire, the motte, on linguistic evidence alone, had developed as a common form of castle, very well adapted to low-lying lands where no natural defences were available.[5] Like the ringwork, it suited ideally a feudal society, only comparatively recently developed, where the individual estate was the unit to be protected, rather than the trading settlement, the centre of government, or the frontier.

It was a great mound, like an upturned basin, that Roger de Montgomery raised at Hen Domen within a few years of the Conquest on what, before this, had been virgin ploughland.[6] And it seems likely that the motte at Hen Domen was associated from the beginning with an enclosed bailey, or lower great court, from which it was separated by a defensive ditch, spanned by a wide flying bridge resembling those shown at Dol, Dinan, and Bayeux in the near-contemporary Bayeux Tapestry.[7] Roger de Montgomery, as a great Norman landowner second only in wealth to the duke himself, is very likely to have built his castle in the latest and most sophisticated style. However, it should not be thought that even the duke-king William, while the Conquest was in progress, had always the leisure or the means to do the same. Indeed, the castle of classic 'motte and bailey' plan, although very common in England from the late eleventh century and still being built through much of the twelfth, was the exception rather than the rule at the Conquest. Other temporary expedients were usually tried first.

The terrain of England, unlike much of Germany and Italy and even parts of western France, does not usually lend itself to natural fortification. Nevertheless, the promontory castles now recognized as pre-Conquest in Normandy have their parallels in England in the first improvised fortifications at such castles as Corfe in Dorset, Lydford in Devonshire, and Scarborough and Richmond in Yorkshire. Moreover, if naturally defendable sites were rare, other opportunities were there for the taking in the earlier defence works that scattered the land. Prehistoric and Anglo-Saxon earthworks, sometimes one and the same, were refortified by the Normans at Thetford (Norfolk), at Castle Neroche (Somerset), at Old Sarum (Wiltshire), at Oxford, and at Dover. The Conqueror had taken immediate advantage of the Roman defences at Pevensey, his landing point, and either he or his followers and successors were to do the same in London and Cardiff, at Carisbrooke (Isle of Wight), at Rochester (Kent), and at Brough and Brougham in Westmorland.

Obviously, the very different defensive potential of each one of these sites

3 The Roman coastal fort at Pevensey, re-used by William the Conqueror as his forward base in 1066 and subsequently fortified more permanently by Robert of Mortain in the south-east corner of the enclosure

suggested very different solutions, and the variety of the fortifications raised in England by Duke William and his followers was hardly less than the mixed origins of the invaders themselves would have suggested. William's army, although certainly built up around a core of his own Norman vassals, included Bretons and Flemings, Lorrainers and men of Anjou. All of these would probably have experienced castle warfare in one form or another, but they would have seen it carried out in very different terrains and might have applied the lessons of this experience very variously.

It is not always easy to identify the primary fortifications on a site subsequently refortified many times. However, the excavations at Castle Neroche, in Somerset, have demonstrated a sequence beginning with a large 'communal' promontory fort, possibly Anglo-Saxon, and continuing through the refortification of the site on a smaller scale with a ringwork (immediately post-Conquest) to the construction, not very much later, of the great motte.[8] The first Norman fortifications at Castle Neroche belong, their excavator suggests, to the period of the western rebellion of 1067–9, when they might have served as a temporary strong-point for the invaders. They were not considered adequate for permanent defence, and seem to have been rebuilt within a generation to a conventional motte-and-bailey plan on a larger and more defendable scale. In precisely the same way, and perhaps even by the same person, Robert of Mortain, half-brother of the Conqueror, the earliest Norman fortifications at Pevensey were adapted within a very few years, as Duke William's temporary defence of the Roman west gate was abandoned and as a new castle was established in one corner of the over-large Saxon Shore fort.[9] Certainly, the Conqueror's initial bank and ditch at Dover would later be overlaid by one of the greatest stone castles in England, equalled only by the Tower of London where much the same processes occurred.

Temporary campaign fortifications are one thing, permanent castles obviously another. And yet there was variety in these as well. Alan the Red, the builder of Richmond Castle, although a kinsman of the Norman Duke William, was himself a Breton, and both there at Richmond and on his Lincolnshire estates was inclined to surround himself with colonists from his native Brittany. Perhaps as a consequence of his own background, the castle he built at Richmond in the 1070s was quite unlike anything else that was being put up in England at the time. Like Hen Domen, Richmond was a true castle of the Conquest, designed specifically to protect the new settlers and to take possession effectively of an estate. It had no further strategic purpose, for it lay well away from all the major lines of communication of the day, and it had clearly been sited where it was for one reason alone: to take advantage of the lie of the land. Count Alan made use of a natural triangular platform, already adequately defended on its southern side by the fall of the land towards the River Swale. On the other two sides of the triangle, he built strong stone walls with interval towers, three on the east and a fourth at the south-west corner. At the apex of the triangle, on the north, was a great stone gate-tower, later to be converted into a keep.[10]

5 The keep at Richmond, formerly the gate-house of Alan the Red's castle but later rebuilt before the end of the twelfth century as a tower keep

4 *Opposite* The south front of Richmond Castle, overlooking the River Swale

6 *Right* The former gate-tower and later tower keep at Ludlow, converted by blocking and re-siting the gate passage next to it

In many respects, and in particular in the scale of the great enclosure which seems to belong to earlier days of essentially communal fortification, the castle at Richmond is unique. But it shares the defensive emphasis on the gate-tower with a contemporary building like Rougemont Castle (Exeter) and with the slightly later Ludlow Castle, in Shropshire, and it is this that links it most interestingly with a whole class of curtain-wall-and-gatehouse castles, associated with the post-Conquest settlement but very different in character from the contemporary keep-centred fortresses. Richmond, and castles like it, translate into stone the distinction between the two basic castle plans of eleventh-century western France—the ringwork and the motte. Its stone equivalent in the motte-style castle is the Conqueror's great keep at the White Tower (London) or the still larger contemporary royal fortress at Colchester.

Significantly, Bishop Gundulf of Rochester (d. 1108), who supervised the building of William's White Tower and who may also have had a hand in designing it, chose another style in the curtain-wall-and-gatehouse plan when he came to build a castle of his own. At Rochester, the first Norman castle, on Boley Hill outside the former Roman enclosure, had probably been a motte. However, Gundulf's fortress, on which work began soon after the accession in 1087 of William II, was re-sited in the adjoining south-west corner of the Roman town where it could take advantage, at one point at least, of the existing Roman foundations. Bishop Gundulf's castle, as he laid it out anew, was a large irregular oval, surrounded on all sides by a strong stone wall and entered by a gate towards the town. In effect, what Gundulf had built—no doubt for reasons of economy and in direct contrast to the Conqueror's grandiose and costly keep at the White Tower—was a ringwork in stone not unlike Richmond. It was not until towards the end of the next reign that another cleric, William of Corbeil (archbishop of Canterbury 1123–36) brought Rochester back within the tower-keep tradition by building there the 'noble tower' which remains that castle's most spectacular monument (below, pp. 23–5).[11]

7 *Left* Decorative blind arcading and pilaster buttresses on the south front of the White Tower, London

8 *Below* The Chapel of St John in the Conqueror's White Tower

9 William I's fortress-palace at Colchester, showing the chapel apse (right) projecting from the main bulk of the keep

Like Richmond again, Gundulf's Rochester is one of the earliest stone castles in England, and the circumstances of its building are full of interest. Following in the footsteps of another pioneer castle-builder, Fulk of Anjou, Gundulf had made a pilgrimage to the Holy Land early in his life, no doubt visiting Rome on the way. Furthermore, he had been a monk at the important and highly regarded Norman abbey of Bec where one later archbishop of Canterbury, Anselm, was his direct contemporary, while another, Lanfranc, was then prior. He had moved with Lanfranc to Caen in 1063 and had subsequently accompanied the archbishop-elect to Canterbury in 1070, still his close associate and already, in all likelihood, something of a specialist in building. Certainly, the lessons learnt at St Stephen's (Caen) and elsewhere were very soon to be applied in England, both by Gundulf's patron and by himself. One of the ways in which Lanfranc is said to have pacified his rebellious English monks was by building them a fine new cathedral. And in just the same way Gundulf, immediately after his elevation to the See of Rochester in 1077, began work at once on the rebuilding of the cathedral at that ancient Anglo-Saxon episcopal seat to be engaged contemporaneously on the work at the White Tower and to confirm in these years his reputation as 'very competent and skilful at building in stone'. Among Anglo-Norman clerics of his day, Bishop Gundulf was probably unique. However, many of his contemporaries in England, including Lanfranc himself, were as ready to find the finance for large-scale building projects, and he had moreover an exact equivalent in the German, Bishop Benno of Osnabrück. Like Gundulf, Benno could turn his hand to military architecture as readily as he could build for the Church. As master mason to the German king-emperors Henry III and Henry IV, he built the great Harzburg and many other fortresses, while designing and being responsible for laying out the late-eleventh-century cathedral at Speyer. Between the two of them, Gundulf and Benno demonstrate very clearly the close association of castle- and church-building in western Europe that would become especially important during the course of the twelfth century but which was already, with the use of stone in military architecture, recognizably an essential partnership. Nor is there any building in which this is more evident than in the White Tower (London) itself.

Work on the White Tower is thought to have begun about a decade before the

10 The motte at Carisbrooke Castle, raised by the fitzOsberns soon after the Conquest and later (probably by the 1130s) crowned with a stone shell keep

Conqueror's death, and the qualities of this extraordinary building (unique except for the one very close parallel at Colchester) are only to be understood if it is viewed in the context of the immediate post-Conquest settlement. For almost a century, since Doué-la-Fontaine and Langeais (above, p. 4), stone tower keeps had been known in the West, while there are some comparisons to be made between the White Tower and such other more nearly contemporary keeps as Loches, in Touraine, and Aderno, in the Norman kingdom of Sicily. But what sets the White Tower and Colchester so much in a class of their own is that they stand not as fortified towers but as palaces, containing within them in vertical sequence all the accommodation that in the more normal palaces of the period would have been laid out horizontally on the ground. Both castles have their store-rooms, their service rooms, their halls, their chambers, and their chapels. In each case, the keep is completely self-contained, and it is built on a scale and to a degree of sophistication appropriate to one of the richest princes of his day. At London especially, the Conqueror's purpose seems to have been as much to broadcast his wealth and authority as to secure his person and his court. The White Tower is decorated externally with pilaster buttresses and with blind arcading more appropriate to a major ecclesiastical building than to a fortress. And although this form of decoration is not repeated at Colchester, both buildings are equipped with projecting chapels at the south-east corner which are clearly a vital element in the whole concept of the building and have done much to determine its plan. Remote origins for these buildings have been suggested in the Carolingian fortress-palaces which, for the most part, have yet to be investigated.[12] However, it seems very much more likely that both the White Tower and Colchester were purpose-built (just as Richmond and Rochester certainly were) to meet the special needs of the Conquest and Settlement. Very likely, before either was complete, those special needs had changed. Neither castle, to be sure, was repeated.

One reason for this, of course, was expense; another, that whereas there was only one king-duke, there were many among his friends and associates who had quite

11 The great ringwork and bailey at Castle Acre, raised in the twelfth century to take the place of the light defences of William de Warenne's post-Conquest stone hall

different needs and aspirations to be met. One of the very few other stone castles in England to be securely datable to the reign of the Conqueror himself is Exeter, and here, although it was William (so Orderic Vitalis wrote) who chose the site, he left the building of the castle in 1068 to Baldwin de Meules, one of his closest associates in the highly profitable adventure of the Conquest. Baldwin's solution to the problem of fortifying Exeter was the familiar one of cutting off a corner of the Roman defences with a ditch and bank of his own. However, he added to this a feature of particular interest in a unique stone-built gatehouse of passageway form, perhaps matched originally at other castles of this kind at Pevensey, Rochester, and London, but the only such building to survive. Triangular-headed window openings over the outer arch, finished with stone strips in the Anglo-Saxon manner, suggest (with other contemporary architectural details) that this was a work on which native craftsmen were employed.[13] Yet it is evident that the total concept of the castle was Norman, not pre-Conquest; furthermore, that it belonged from the first to the ringwork-and-gatehouse plan to which a keep, neither then nor later, was essential.

12 William fitzOsbern's stone hall on the ridge at Chepstow, built before 1071 and one of the most important architectural survivals from the immediately post-Conquest settlement period

13 Corfe: a ridge-top fortress of the Conquest and Settlement period, subsequently equipped with a stone tower keep (centre) and bailey wall as early as the first decade of the twelfth century

Contemporaneously at Carisbrooke, on the Isle of Wight, another close friend and kinsman of William the Conqueror was re-using the remains of a former Roman fortification in quite a different way. It was probably William fitzOsbern (d. 1071), although it could have been William's son Roger, who piled the great Norman banks on the line of the Roman walls at Carisbrooke to form an unusually regularly planned enclosure.[14] And it would have been one or other of these magnates again who raised the very considerable conical motte which still occupies the north-east corner of what became then the lower enclosure, or bailey, of the finished castle. William fitzOsbern, Baldwin de Meules, Alan the Red (builder of Richmond Castle), and indeed the Conqueror himself, were all kinsmen, companions-at-arms of some years' standing, and members of a very tight circle. Nevertheless, each chose a different plan for at least one of the castles for which he was responsible, mirroring the confusions of a society to which the castle as yet was a comparative newcomer and where every man pleased himself as to what he made of it.

Some indeed, even within the Conqueror's own circle, were not prepared to make anything of it at all. William de Warenne, later earl of Surrey, was as much a member of this inner group as were William fitzOsbern, Baldwin de Meules, and Alan the Red. Yet his first stone buildings on his newly acquired estates at Castle Acre, in Norfolk, did not add up to a castle in any true sense, being no more than lightly defended. Certainly, not so very much later, a more intensive fortification of Castle Acre was to be undertaken, to be seen still in the impressive earthworks and other remnants of today. But the original hall at Castle Acre, as recent excavations have made clear, was a two-storied stone building 'of palatial dimensions', entered by a wide door at ground-floor level and defended only, so far as can be judged, by a low surrounding

14 The motte and bailey earthworks, later strengthened with stone walls, at Berkhamsted, one of the better-preserved of the post-Conquest earthwork castles

bank and palisade.[15] At Chepstow, in Monmouthshire, William fitzOsbern (the builder of Carisbrooke) had raised a great hall, or 'tower', for himself before 1071 which has some of the characteristics, including an accessible ground floor, of Castle Acre.[16] And at Corfe Castle, too, on the vulnerable south coast, what seems to have been the great hall of this important royal castle was placed some way distant from the stone-walled Inner Bailey of the first post-Conquest fortress, in what was only much later to be strongly walled as the West Bailey of the concentrically planned castle of King John.[17]

Primitive fortifications and false starts of one sort or another are only to be expected of the Conquest. And, inevitably, the re-modelling of many of the earliest campaign fortifications followed their first building within decades, sometimes less. One obvious example of this very common sequence is, of course, the White Tower itself, strengthening the first post-Conquest fortification which it then largely filled.[18] But there are others as clear, up and down the country, which tell the story of a shaking-

15 A vertical air-photograph of the motte, with surrounding ditch and bailey, at Pickering Castle

down of settlement as the conquerors dug in for good. Robert of Mortain's great motte at Castle Neroche, although raised within a few years of the Conquest, was already a secondary re-fortification of this important Somerset site (above, p. 5). And it was probably Robert of Mortain again who, in the systematic settlement of the rebellious West Country, rebuilt the first post-Conquest rampart at Launceston (Cornwall), facing it with timber on either side to make a more formidable permanent defence.[19] At Winchester, a motte seems to have been added to the first earthwork castle as early as 1071–2, to be levelled not much more than a generation later on the building of the early-twelfth-century stone keep.[20] Corfe's stone keep may be a few years earlier, being dated now to *circa* 1105, and its building coincided with the construction of a stone bailey wall at least doubling the area defended.[21]

Certainly, there is a good case for arguing that it was in this period principally, and not very much before, that the 'motte and bailey' and other castles of 'classic' post-Conquest plan first gained general acceptance. Castle Acre (Norfolk), at first so lightly defended as to be scarcely a castle at all, was shortly to become a most sophisticated fortress and one of the greatest ringwork-and-bailey castles in the land. And there is little doubt that, within a generation of the Conquest, the model of such early mottes and baileys as Castle Neroche (Somerset), Carisbrooke (Isle of Wight), and Hen Domen (Montgomery) was well known to all with a professional interest in fortification, encouraging a legion of imitators. Still, in many surviving stone castles of today, the motte-and-bailey earthworks of the first Norman settlement fortress are clearly visible as the main plan determinant in later generations. They are most obvious, of course, in castles where subsequent re-fortifications consisted of little more than the conversion of timber palisades into stone walls. And, among many examples of this practice, the outstanding survivals are Berkhamsted (Hertfordshire), Pickering (North Yorkshire), and Trematon and Launceston (both in Cornwall). But the same motte-and-bailey skeleton is there again, plain to see, in more sophisticated later fortresses like Windsor (Berkshire), Arundel (Sussex), Warkworth and Norham (Northumberland), Berkeley (Gloucestershire), Rockingham (Northamptonshire), Dudley (Staffordshire), and Caldicott (Monmouthshire). So uniform is the plan, and so widespread, that it can only belong to a relatively short period of construction, beginning no earlier than the middle, or even the later, years of William the Conqueror, and already over in almost every region before the reign of Henry II.

What had promoted the earthwork castle had been private war, to which it was clearly well suited. And what brought it down in the end was partly the expense of providing a permanent substitute in stone, but even more the outlawing of the private war that had provided both milieu and justification in the first place. From an early date, the Anglo-Norman kings had done what they could to discipline the more violent of their subjects. Prominent in the agreement at Caen of 1091, being a settlement of differences between William Rufus of England and Duke Robert of Normandy, the Conqueror's warring sons, were clauses limiting private war, even if they did not specifically prohibit it. And it was at this time too that clear restraints were placed on fortification, even by bank and ditch, with an absolute prohibition on castle-building.[22] Fortifications 'consisting of three walls' were reserved to the king in a compilation of laws datable to *circa* 1115, near the middle of Henry I's reign, nor was any fortification (*castellatio*) to be constructed by Henry's subjects without the king's specific permission.[23] What laws of this kind meant by a 'fortification' it is not easy to say. However, it is plain that so long as the king's writ ran in the land—which it did under Henry I and then failed so lamentably to do during the 'nineteen long winters' of Stephen's reign—no man might expect to build himself a fortress and get away with it. If he did go ahead without the sanction of the king, both he and his heirs would always be at risk of dispossession.

A clear consequence of the king's power to limit private fortification was that the practice of castle-building in England either advanced or stagnated in close harmony with the waning or waxing of royal government. Thus at Abinger, in Surrey, the little motte that had carried fortifications in the relatively troubled reign of William Rufus and during the succession dispute that followed it, lost them again when Henry I then tightened his grip on the kingdom. Only in the reign of Stephen (1135–54) was the castle at Abinger once again rebuilt, to be abandoned for a second and final time when order returned with the Angevin Henry II.[24] If this were the experience of Abinger, it was no less the case at other more important castles in every English county. However, there was one area in particular where the laws of the king, in castle-building as in much else, yielded to a stronger local custom. In the Welsh March, no practical distinction could yet be drawn between 'public' and 'private' war. The castle and annexed 'castlery' was as much the fighting unit in the conquest and settlement of Wales as it had been in the Norman penetration of England. With every lordship went the right to build a fortress.[25]

The special importance, then, of the Welsh evidence is that it allows us to follow through the practice of private castle-building as it developed unchecked through one of its most crucial periods at the turn of the eleventh and the twelfth centuries. And what has emerged most clearly in the recent archaeology of the region has been the continuing role in such fortifications of the ringwork. Of course, mottes also were common in the March, one particularly interesting group of twelve, on the Shropshire–Montgomery border, being associated with the first Norman settlement of the area under Roger de Montgomery, builder of Hen Domen, and his successors, Hugh and Robert.[26] Nevertheless, there are marked concentrations of ringworks in both Glamorgan and Gower, and two important excavations in the former, at Dinas Powys and Penmaen, with a third only slightly less so at Llantrithyd in the same county, have begun to define the form that these ringworks of the post-Conquest settlement usually took. Dinas Powys is a complex site, with a long prehistory of occupation before its two-phase re-fortification by the Normans. Yet here, without doubt, it was the Normans who built a wide rampart, revetted externally in stone, to enclose a roughly oval area. And it was here not much later—most probably in response to the immediate threat of a Welsh rebellion—that they strengthened their rampart with two further banks on the most vulnerable south-east quarter, to make an improvised multivallate fortification more Iron Age than Norman in character.[27]

The ringwork at Dinas Powys, in its second-phase re-fortification, reflects the pressures of the over-rapid conquest and uneasy settlement of South Wales in the early 1090s. And probably more characteristic of the castles by which the Normans, after 1097, established a permanent hold on Glamorgan was Castle Tower, Penmaen, another ringwork not unlike Dinas Powys in its general plan but supplied with what would seem to have been a timber gatehouse tower, perhaps with accommodation over the gate-passage and with a fighting-platform and look-out at the top.[28] A similar timber tower may well have guarded the entrance of the early-twelfth-century ringwork at Llantrithyd,[29] not is it unlikely that ringworks of this period should very commonly have been supplied with such tower-defended entrances, the modest equivalent of the great gate towers of such stone-built magnate castles as the immediately post-Conquest Richmond (Yorkshire) or the more nearly contemporary Ludlow (Shropshire). Ringworks, for the most part unexcavated but probably of this type, cluster especially thickly in coastal Glamorgan and peninsular Gower, both areas of permanent Norman settlement.[30] And it is certainly the case that by the time they were built there, generally early in the twelfth century or in the very last years of the eleventh, the plan had had plenty of opportunity to develop. So, indeed, had the motte and bailey, one particularly fine example of a motte being preserved at the *caput*, or headquarters, of the Glamorgan lordship of Cardiff, where it is located rather incongruously in the north-west corner of the former Roman fortress. At Cardiff, the entire great enclosure of the Roman coastal fort was converted by Robert fitzHamon, the Norman conqueror of Glamorgan, into the regularly planned bailey of his up-to-date castle, in very much the same way as, during the first conquest and settlement of England, William fitzOsbern had made use of the Roman defences at Carisbrooke, on the Isle of Wight (above, p. 12). Some twenty years after the Carisbrooke works, the method of re-fortification at Cardiff again involved the re-excavation on a larger scale of the original Roman defensive ditch, piling up the spoil over what was left of the Roman circuit walls to raise the Norman rampart. Techniques had been refined in the generation since the Conquest, and Cardiff is undoubtedly a text-book motte and bailey, the work of a man thoroughly at home in the plan. But they had not essentially changed.

The ringworks and mottes of the conquest and containment of Wales are among the latest of their type, and, continuing as they do over an unusually long period when castle-building was freely sanctioned by the king, they are especially thick on the ground. However, so far did they spread down through the land-holding classes in the conquered and frontier regions that many of them remained of the very simplest construction, innovation and experiment in castle-building being more common in areas where the process was always less of a routine. Certainly, one of the most interesting of the post-Conquest castles of ringwork type is the unusually early stone

16 Cardiff: a Roman coastal fort subsequently re-fortified by Robert fitzHamon, the Norman conqueror of Glamorgan

17 The stone curtain wall, datable to *circa* 1100, at Eynsford, seen from the south-west, with the foundations of the hall and chamber block of the twelfth-century rebuildings immediately in front of it, where the original timber watch-tower once stood

castle at Eynsford, in Kent, within a few miles of Bishop Gundulf's larger stone ring at the fortress of Rochester and not far to the north of another important castle at Tonbridge, the main feature of which was its motte. Eynsford was one of the archbishop of Canterbury's castles, and it most probably owed its unusual strength to the financial support of the archbishop. Nevertheless, the final form it took is more likely to have resulted from the military experience of the first William de Eynsford, a devout knight, very useful to the Church, who took a prominent part in local administration and who must certainly have known Bishop Gundulf of Rochester well. There are, indeed, some parallels to be found in the building technique of the curtain walls at Eynsford and Rochester, as well as in the general plan of both castles. At Eynsford, as at Rochester (above, p. 7), the main emphasis in the defence was on the curtain wall, massively constructed of flint although comparatively low on first building. Within the irregular oval of the wall there was a timber-built watch-tower, sited off-centre towards the north-east quarter of the enclosure, the ground-level being built up round its base in the form of a low broad motte.[31]

Eynsford is of interest as an early castle type, comparatively rare in England but powerfully reminiscent of the most common German plan of this period, where the fighting-tower, or *bergfried*, was the central element in the design and where the great curtain wall was the other main component of the defence. However, Eynsford is important in another way too, for it is one of the earliest examples of a technique of motte-building in which the castle tower was founded on the original ground-level

18 *Left* St George's Tower, Oxford: a late-eleventh-century stone perimeter tower on the former castle site

19 *Opposite below* The tree-covered motte and its accompanying bailey within a ringwork at Mileham, Norfolk, illustrating a not uncommon confusion of styles at earth-work castles of twelfth-century date

and the mound then piled up round about it. Recent work on a number of early castle sites has led to the identification of substructures of this kind, sometimes of considerable sophistication. At its simplest, such a structure might be no more than a strong timber frame, built on the ground-level before the raising of the mound and intended to carry the weight of a tower on the soft, unconsolidated surface. A frame of this kind was identified, although never fully described, at the excavations on the motte at Burgh Castle, in Suffolk.[32] And it is clear that at Burgh Castle, as at other mottes of its type including Abinger (above, p. 15), the essential characteristic of the castle was the mound itself, to which the tower on the top of it was secondary. The tradition of earthwork defences in eleventh-century Normandy was strong. When it was brought to England, it could result in castles like Carisbrooke and Cardiff, at both of which the earlier stone walls were concealed in the ramparts and a high conical motte was built as the strongpoint of each fortress. But of equal importance, and of perhaps even greater antiquity in the smaller private fortresses of the West, was the free-standing defensive tower—the *bergfried* of Germany and the *turris* of the tenth-century documentary record in northern France.[33] Eynsford, obviously, is one good example of such a tower, where the mound surrounding it was certainly an afterthought. Another, although sited on the circuit of the defences rather than, as at Eynsford, at their centre, is the remarkable stone St George's Tower, on the castle site at Oxford, attributable to the late eleventh century.[34] And there was a timber-built version of the Oxford tower, approximately contemporary, serving as a small keep, watch-tower, and refuge of last resort, on the rampart of the ringwork at Sulgrave

(Northamptonshire).[35] What is of particular interest in fortifications of this type is that they reflect and continue a strong continental tradition which has seldom, until now, been given much attention in England but which the evidence of archaeology has brought into focus for the first time.

One crucial site in this new investigation of the castle mound has been South Mimms, in Hertfordshire, to all appearances a conventional motte-and-bailey fortress which has usually been dated to the early 1140s and identified with the castle which Geoffrey de Mandeville, first earl of Essex, is known to have built in the area. But South Mimms was not a conventional motte and bailey at all. As the excavations of the early 1960s showed, the main feature of the motte at South Mimms, around which it had been built up, was a tall timber tower, set on flint footings on the original ground surface, and rather like a belfry in its form. Only after the building of the tower, which seems to have been plastered internally and which may have been roofed in lead, was the mound then piled up around it, using the upcast from the encircling ditch and concealing a lower basement chamber to which a passage through the mound still gave access.[36]

If Geoffrey de Mandeville was indeed the builder of South Mimms, he did not live long to enjoy it. But, in any event, a timber structure of this kind, for all its sophistication and careful founding, could not have lasted long buried in the body of a mound, and stone towers, to be discussed in the next chapter in the wider context of the stone tower keep in general, were already taking its place. What they confirm is that the tower, with or without a mound, remained the crucial element in the building of the twelfth-century castle, to the extent that it became, as we shall continue to observe it in later centuries, a symbol of dominion and lordship. There are many more mottes and baileys in England and the Welsh March than there are ringworks, and undoubtedly the principal recommendation of the motte-and-bailey plan was that it gave the lord's tower special prominence. At Aldingham (Lancashire), during the course of the twelfth century, the original ringwork of the post-Conquest settlement was first filled in at the centre to form a motte and then, within a generation or so, revetted in timber and heightened by a stage yet again.[37] Even in south Glamorgan, where ringworks were especially familiar, the relatively sophisticated ringwork at Rumney, with its stone built entrance tower, was later filled to make a castle mound.[38] Whatever the special circumstances of each of these conversions, the obvious virtue of the final product lay in nothing of more importance than its height.

Chapter 2

The Transition to Stone

In castle-building, the choice of stone over timber as the preferred building material was nowhere made very lightly. The great outer wards of many stone castles—among them Framlingham, in Suffolk, and Helmsley and Pickering, in Yorkshire—continued to be protected by ditch and palisade defences right through into the fourteenth century, and might never have been walled in stone. Clearly, too, a comprehensive re-fortification in stone was beyond the means of all but a few of those who had raised their mottes quite freely in the past. Nevertheless, so rapid had been the advance of building techniques in the decades on either side of 1100 that a project which might have seemed impossible in one man's generation was yet well within the reach of his grandson. While true most particularly of ecclesiastical building, where cathedrals, monasteries, and parish churches were everywhere being reconstructed in stone, the fashion for stone-building had spread to domestic architecture before the end of the twelfth century at latest, and long before that had come to be accepted in the castle.

20 The stone castle at Framlingham and its outer earthwork-protected baileys

21 The tower keep at Houdan (Ile-de-France), cylindrical in plan with four angle turrets; believed to date to *circa* 1120 and one of the most advanced military buildings of its time

Of course, there were good military reasons for such a conversion as well, proceeding especially from the developing science of siegecraft in which many were making themselves expert. However, it is still difficult, early in the twelfth century, to detect a change in the fundamental principles of castle-building such as would certainly be evident before the century was over. The great stone keep at Houdan (Ile-de-France), datable to 1110–25, is a very remarkable cylindrical building, equipped with four 'angle' towers and far in advance of its contemporaries. Nevertheless, it is plain that, in the design of such a building, the provision of flanking fire, although considered, had not been understood. The continuing curve of the keep's main wall hid large areas of its base from view.[1]

22 Farnham: the stone square visible at the centre of the motte preserves the plan of Bishop Henry's tower keep, round which the mound was piled as building proceeded; the tower dates to *circa* 1138, the stone casing of the mound being added before the end of the century

23 Decorative blind arcading on Henry I's great keep at Norwich, restored in the nineteenth century but faithful to the original design

In a different but still a significant way, the transition to stone may be illustrated at a castle like Farnham, in Surrey. At Farnham, Henry of Blois, bishop of Winchester (1129–71), was to build himself a great stone tower, square in plan, the lower part of which he encased in the castle mound. Such towers had been built in timber before, and it is very likely that the men the bishop hired for this particular project had learnt their trade principally as carpenters. Required to use stone at Farnham, they built a strong stone support designed to run up through the core of the mound and to hold the weight of the tower that crowned it. Then, having piled up the mound around this core, they constructed a stone platform on the surface of the mound which oversailed its well-founded base on all four sides. In timber, such a technique would have been perfectly acceptable; the tower could have rested on the larger frame adequately supported below. In stone, where the weight of the tower now fell, at least in part, on the edges of the oversailing platform, the method invited collapse.[2]

By the time that Bishop Henry built his tower at Farnham, in 1138 or thereabouts, tower keeps of its kind, although certainly more common later in the century, were already becoming familiar. He himself, through the troubled years of his brother Stephen's reign, continued to be a great builder of castles, including at least one other strong stone tower at his palace at Wolvesey, in Winchester.[3] And we now know too of other massive stone towers, again attributable to the Anarchy years, partly buried in their mottes at Ascot Doilly, in Oxfordshire, and at Aldingbourne ('Tote Copse Castle'), in Sussex, being the stone equivalents of Geoffrey de Mandeville's timber keep at South Mimms.[4] But the ancestry of these buildings is longer than this. Although probably not to be sought in the exceptional palace-fortresses of William the Conqueror (above, pp. 9–10), it seems more traceable to such precedents as Loches and Aderno, Beaugency, Grand Presigny, and Falaise.

Of these, the great stone keep at Falaise (Normandy), put up in the 1120s, was the work of the Anglo-Norman Henry I, and its closest equivalent in Henry's English kingdom was the even grander building at Norwich. Here, as at contemporary Rochester and Hedingham, the early-twelfth-century rectangular keep is already a very sophisticated building. Like the Conqueror's White Tower, and with the same purposeful display, Henry's keep at Norwich was richly decorated externally with blind arcading, reminiscent of the work of the master masons who were busy just then on the building of Norwich Cathedral. Yet this decorative treatment—largely absent at Falaise, at Rochester, and at Hedingham—only superficially disguises the purpose of a fortress which, in every other way, was an up-to-date instrument of war. Even the handsome windows of the principal residential floor at Norwich have their purpose in the defence of the castle, for they are backed internally by a continuous fighting gallery, running round every side of the building and fashioned in the thickness of the wall. Equally, in a wall massive enough to take such a gallery lay the main weight of the castle's defences.[5]

For Henry, and for other princes of his time, the stone castle was much too powerful a weapon to be let slip into the hands of the aristocracy. And restrictions on building in stone, repeating the contemporary view of such castles as very much more dangerous than timber, are quite frequent in the legislation of the period.[6] How effective these fortresses could be in war is demonstrated by yet another of Henry's castles, built for the king by William of Corbeil, archbishop of Canterbury (1123–36), and severely tested almost a century later in a celebrated siege by King John. The archbishop's 'noble tower' at Rochester was sited within the irregular oval of Bishop Gundulf's late-eleventh-century fortress, converting it at once from a castle of ringwork type into one in which the tower keep was dominant. As was always to be the case with the stone keeps of the period, Rochester's strength lay principally in the great width of its outside walls. However, another important element in Rochester's design, which it shared with some other great keeps of its time, was the strong internal cross-wall, dividing it centrally on the east-west axis and giving the whole structure particular rigidity. Behind this wall, the defenders of the castle in 1215 were able to continue their resistance even after John's miners had brought down the south-east angle of the keep. To this day, it remains one of the principal supports of the tower.

24 The residential tower keep at Rochester, built for Henry I by William of Corbeil, archbishop of Canterbury

Strong though the keep at Rochester was, it had also been designed as a comfortable residence for the archbishop. The massive cross-wall, dividing the building from top to bottom, very largely dictated its internal plan. But a finely constructed arcade pierced it at second-floor level, linking the two principal apartments. And there are many details, both on this floor and the next, to establish that the chambers they carried were indeed intended for the constable of the castle, being quite adequate too for the archbishop's occasional visits. Certainly, each of the principal chambers had its own handsome fireplace; it was well supplied with windows in two stages, one above the other; and had at least one lavatory (or *garderobe*) fashioned in the thickness of the outside wall. The third floor, although of only one stage, was similarly equipped with fireplaces and fine windows, having its own well-head even at this level to draw water up through the ingenious well, accessible from all the floors of the keep, which is a feature of the central cross-wall. On this floor also, at the eastern end of the southern chamber where the collapse of 1215 occurred, there is some evidence to suggest the former presence of a large chapel, almost certainly the chapel that William of Corbeil would have built for his personal use. As in the much later 'castle' at Acton Burnell (Shropshire), similarly built for a prince of the Church (below, p. 103), the whole top floor of the keep at Rochester might very well have been reserved for the archbishop.

Such exclusive use is further implied by the provision of another fine chapel at second-floor level, where it could serve the principal 'public' apartments of the keep, in the uppermost storey of the rectangular forebuilding attached to the north-east angle of the main tower. A forebuilding of this kind had not been a feature of castles like the White Tower or Colchester, designed only a few decades before. Yet it was usual already in keeps of the first half of the twelfth century, and such growing emphasis on the defence of the approaches was to be a characteristic of military engineering in this period. At Rochester, where a particularly handsome example of the genre survives virtually intact, the forebuilding was itself entered only at first-floor level. It was approached by a stair beginning its ascent on the west face of the keep and turning towards the forebuilding at the north-west angle where it was further protected by a small tower. Any assailant who got this far had still to cross a

25 The arcade at second-floor level at Rochester, linking the two principal chambers on this floor

26 The tower keep at Hedingham, built for the de Vere family and similar in design to Rochester

wide bridge-pit, normally spanned by a drawbridge, before reaching the main entrance of the castle. If he broke through the door, itself stoutly secured with a draw-bar, he would at once meet the portcullis behind it.[7]

To the north of Rochester, the remarkable tower keep at Hedingham (Essex) may well be the work of the same gifted military engineer, for there are many points of comparison between them. Hedingham has lost all but a few traces of its forebuilding. However, at both castles angle turrets still rise above the level of the battlements, there are flat pilaster buttresses central to the external walls, and the main feature of the internal design is the carrying of the second floor up through two stages to make an impressive galleried residential space which at Hedingham (without the massive internal cross-wall of Rochester) was clearly designed as a single great hall.[8]

Better preserved than Rochester, especially in the detail of its fenestration, Hedingham was evidently a costly work, providing comfortable accommodation for a man of high rank while appropriately celebrating his dignity. From its first building, indeed, and throughout the Middle Ages, Hedingham remained a valued possession and the principal seat of one of the longest-lasting dynasties of medieval England, the de Vere earls of Oxford. And it is plain that the keep at Hedingham owed its exceptional quality and scale to the great wealth accumulated first by the original Aubrey de Vere (from Ver in Normandy, near Bayeux), companion of the Conqueror, then by his son or grandson, the second Aubrey, sheriff of eleven counties for Henry I in 1130 and shortly afterwards great chamberlain of England. Aubrey II died in 1141, and it may have been his son Aubrey III, later created earl of Oxford, who

27 William d'Aubigny's residential tower keep at Castle Rising, built within a great ringwork of post-Conquest date

completed the work on the keep. In any event, the family fortress could only have been raised on the scale it was if there had been unusual resources to back it. Furthermore, Henry I would not have encouraged such massive investment in private fortifications had he not been confident of the loyalty of his servant, whose fortune he had himself helped to build.

How others in Henry's confidence might also be allowed to fortify their residences is illustrated by two of the works of Roger of Salisbury, bishop of Salisbury through the better part of Henry's reign and, as justiciar of England, second only in power to the king. One of Roger of Salisbury's many responsibilities was the abbacy of Sherborne, in Dorset, which he held until 1122 and which gave him great estates in the area. It was at Sherborne, accordingly, that he built himself an impressive fortified palace, the principal features of which were a massive earthwork of ringwork type with, centrally placed within it, a stone courtyard residence equipped at its south-west corner with a great strong tower, or keep. In much the same way, at his own episcopal seat at Old Sarum, Bishop Roger again built a fine courtyard residence, although the pre-existing Norman ringwork was already so strong that he had less need to strengthen the tower he nevertheless attached to it. Both buildings anticipate Henry of Blois' work at Wolvesey Palace, in Winchester (above, p. 22), and together they

28 The forebuilding at Castle Rising, richly decorated with blind arcading and protecting the stairway approach to the first-floor hall and chamber

illustrate at least one of the many plan possibilities now open to the more wealthy of the castle-builders in this period of transition to stone.

An interesting, and at the same time rather bizarre, solution to the problem was that adopted by William d'Aubigny (d. 1176) at Castle Rising, in Norfolk. William d'Aubigny, created earl of Arundel in *circa* 1139, was again a very wealthy man, and the keep he built at Castle Rising in the mid-century was among the most ornate and the largest in the kingdom. Particularly memorable for its richly decorated forebuilding and the staircase approach to it, Castle Rising is a hall keep of the Norwich type rather than a tower keep like Rochester and Hedingham, being planned on only two main floors, the upper of which was the residential space, with hall, kitchen, chapel, and 'gallery'. Yet this expensive and sophisticated palace-keep stands four-square in the middle of a great post-Conquest ringwork, duplicating the defensive strength of an existing keep by merely building another one inside it. If the principle of concentric defences had been considered at Castle Rising at all, it had certainly been misapplied, making of this fortress as much a transitional piece in its own way as had been the still earlier experimental cylinder keep at Houdan, in the Ile-de-France (above, p. 21).

Somewhat similar in its final effect was the Warenne earls of Surrey's re-fortification of their estate centre at Castle Acre, in the same county, where the original ringwork was greatly enlarged and the stone hall it enclosed was rebuilt in the form of a tower.[9] But a more common adaptation of pre-existing earthworks, if only because the earthwork type was itself more general through the kingdom, was the straightforward replacement of the timber defences of a motte and bailey with their exact equivalent in stone. A castle like Hedingham, although known about and admired by many, could be built by only a few. Plain conversions like Trematon, in Cornwall, or Pickering, in Yorkshire, were obviously much more accessible.

At the earliest examples of stone-building on artificial castle mounds, ground-slip and subsidence had clearly presented the builders with serious, sometimes insuperable, problems. One solution, as we have seen, might be to found the central tower on the original ground surface and to raise the mound about it. Another, also adopted at Farnham when a circuit wall was needed, was to case the entire mound in stone.[10] At Lewes, in Sussex, there is evidence of timber reinforcements built into the stone wall which, as early as the late eleventh century, circled the top of the motte. And here, too, the subsequent collapse of the wall at one of the points where such reinforcement had been introduced, confirms the original misgivings of the builders.[11] However, whereas the curtain wall at Lewes, one of our earliest 'shell' keeps, was built within just a few decades of the raising of the mound, at most other castles similarly re-fortified in later years, at least a century or more had elapsed. The circular shell keep on the castle mound at Pickering is unlikely to date any earlier than the 1180s, at which time the inner bailey was walled in stone, and its major strengthening, to take the form that survives to this day, was delayed for another generation.[12] At Berkhamsted (Hertfordshire), the first stone fortifications of mound and bailey very probably date to Thomas Becket's work of the early 1160s, but the motte is thought to be one of the earlier post-Conquest examples of this form and had been up for almost a century.[13] Tonbridge (Kent) seems to have acquired its shell keep no earlier than the first half of the thirteenth century, and this seems to have been the date of the systematic re-fortification in stone—with shell keep on the mound, a curtain wall round the bailey, and a good three-storeyed projecting gatehouse—of the little motte and bailey at Trematon (Cornwall) which is now perhaps the finest unaltered example of the plan.

29 Trematon: a twelfth-century motte and bailey strengthened in the thirteenth century by the addition of a shell keep (left), a bailey wall, and a strong gate-tower (top centre)

30 The motte at Berkeley Castle, later cased in stone and rebuilt as a keep

A rebuilding in this form was comparatively economical, and though it could certainly have been undertaken at some major fortresses—Windsor (Berkshire) is one royal example and Berkeley (Gloucestershire) a baronial—it was unlikely to have been left subsequently untouched by later improvers except at castles of minor importance. Pickering undoubtedly was one of those. Always one of the lesser castles in a region of northern Yorkshire well known for its concentration of major fortresses, Pickering was slow to acquire its stone fortifications and, even as modified in the 1320s, retained its primitive plan. However, this is not to say that the shell keep plan, in certain circumstances, might not be adaptable to more sophisticated theories of defence. Launceston, as the county town of Cornwall right through until the nineteenth century, had particular importance as an administrative centre and as the heart of a rich royal earldom (later, from the mid-fourteenth century, a duchy). And it is not therefore surprising that Earl Richard (1209–72), brother of Henry III, should have spent large sums on the modernization of its castle. Unusually, one of the improvements he made to the defences at Launceston was to build a strong stone tower, as he may have done contemporaneously at Berkhamsted too, in the middle of the earlier shell keep. His tower rises still, like a Henrician coastal fort of the early artillery age, a full storey above the level of the outer curtain wall; between it and this wall, a wide fighting platform was constructed, while the whole was approached by a covered stone staircase up the side of the mound, itself defended at the foot by its own gatehouse.[14]

It may be no more than the purest chance, but there are other good examples of the continued use of, and improvement on, the shell keep plan also to be found in the West Country. The castle at Restormel (Cornwall), formerly a fortress of the wealthy

31 The twelfth-century castle mound at Pickering with thirteenth-century stone additions

Cardinham family, came into Earl Richard's hands shortly before his death in 1272, and it was probably his son and successor, Edmund 'of Almaine' (d. 1300), who undertook the new works on the existing shell keep, converting it into a residence for himself of a very remarkable plan. In addition to what appears to have been a full set of the normal domestic buildings (hall, chambers, chapel, and kitchen) in the bailey at Restormel, Earl Edmund transformed the shell keep into what became, in effect, a residential tower, with central courtyard surrounded by a ring of two-storeyed accommodation, very much in the manner of Frederick II's celebrated hunting-lodge at Castel del Monte, in Apulia, which Edmund or his architect might well have known. At Restormel, the earl's private accommodation in the keep was served by its own great kitchen, sited between the gatehouse on the west and the hall on the east, being the only apartment within the shell that rose through the full height of the building. On the other side of the gate, there was a guardroom under what was probably the guest chamber, and the remainder of the ground floor round the rest of the circuit was taken up with store-rooms. On the first floor, the hall was a large and

32 Launceston: Richard of Cornwall's tower rises centrally in the shell keep, being approached by a strongly fortified stone stair up the face of the mound

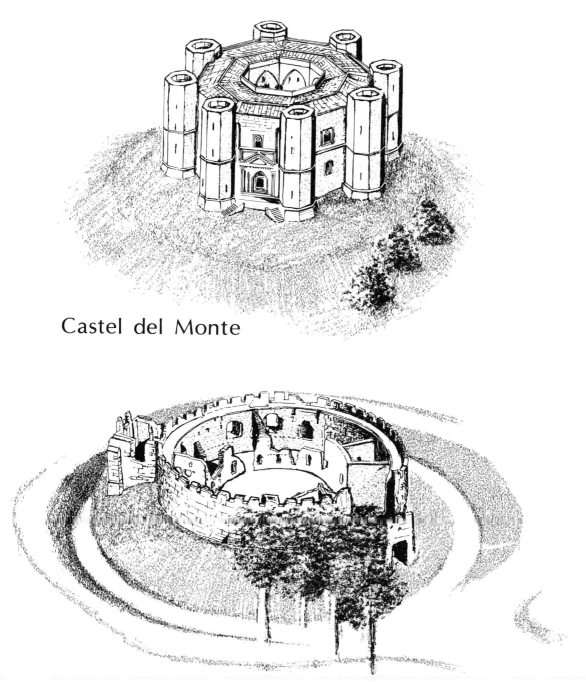

Castel del Monte

Restormel

33 Royal hunting-lodges at Castel del Monte and Restormel, both equipped as substantial and luxurious tower-houses

comfortable apartment, with windows cut through the curtain wall on either side of
the fireplace and with other windows, and perhaps a gallery, facing the courtyard.
Similarly lit and warmed, there was a solar next round the circuit to the north, with
an ante-chapel and projecting private chapel to the north again, and beyond it the
earl's private bedchamber. As at Castel del Monte, one of the features of Earl
Edmund's castle at Restormel was an abundant supply of fresh water: in the words of
the survey of 1337, '... there is there a certain water-conduit made of lead by means
of which water is brought into the castle to every domestic office.' And closely
paralleling the situation at Castel del Monte again, Restormel was set in a great deer
park of its own—a familiar feature of an increasing number of thirteenth-century
castles and manor-houses—where the earl would have sought his recreation.[15]

Restormel, as the plaything of an exceptionally rich man, has a quality all of its own.
And although its success may have contributed to what has been described as the
'archaizing' rebuilding in the early fourteenth century of another shell keep at
Totnes, in the adjoining county of Devon, Restormel itself was in no sense archaic nor
was it ever widely taken up as a model.[16] The main feature of Restormel, for which
there is no parallel evidence at Totnes, is the lavish scale of its domestic
accommodation. But this is accommodation that has been deliberately clustered
within a private tower, and the true precedents for the keep at Restormel are already
to be found more than a century before in the increasingly sophisticated and 'private'
tower keeps of the Capetian and Angevin dynasties.

34 Edmund of Almaine's tower at Restormel, seen from the air

35 Frederick II's Castel del Monte, the most elegant of the emperor's many castles

Not the first of these fortresses but among the most interesting, for it brings several distinct elements together, is Gisors, in Normandy, where the original late-eleventh-century motte was in due course to be crowned by a massive but conventional shell keep to which Henry II subsequently added his great tower. Later, but still within the twelfth century, Gisors fell to the crown of France, and it was Philip Augustus, the chief rival of Henry II and his sons, who built yet another tower keep at Gisors—the so-called Tour du Prisonnier—well away from the motte where it could command the main entrance and itself lavishly fitted internally, with a lofty vaulted hall on the principal floor, and with two similarly vaulted chambers on the floors below it, the lowest of these being the prison.[17]

Tower keeps of this kind, for Philip Augustus and his contemporaries, were to serve a particular purpose as a record and symbol of the victory of the Capetian line of kings. And the expansion of French arms at just this time, for the most part at the expense of the short-lived Angevin empire, is one of the reasons for the proliferation of tower keeps—among them Dourdan and Falaise, Rouen, Issoudun (La Tour Blanche), and Villeneuve-sur-Yonne[18]—of great size and of ever mounting sophistication in design. Indeed, it was with these keeps that Philip Augustus

36 *Above* The anachronistic early-fourteenth-century shell keep at Totnes, possibly modelled on Restormel

37 *Right* The great cylinder keep at Villeneuve-sur-Yonne, built for Philip Augustus in 1205–11 and one of a whole class of similar tower keeps, as much residential as military in purpose

(d. 1223) took his place among the greatest castle-builders, including Frederick II, Holy Roman Emperor (1220–50), in the next generation, and our own Edward I, before the end of the same century, during the conquest and settlement of North Wales. However, the tower keep itself, despite continuing popularity in France, belonged already to a fading tradition, increasingly out-dated as other concepts of defence and of attack intervened. In many of the tower keeps of the later twelfth century, as well as of the opening decades of the thirteenth, there is visibly an experimental quality in the design which marks them out as buildings of an age of transition. Alongside square and rectangular keeps hardly varying the plan of their early-twelfth-century prototypes, there were towers of quatrefoil design, cylinders, triangles, and polygons. Furthermore, a good many of these towers are already to be found associated with the elements of systematic concentric defence—the curtain walls and interval towers, the gatehouses, water defences, and barbicans—which in the course of time would reduce the keep itself to a luxury. The remarkable cylindrical keep at Conisborough (Yorkshire), built for Hamelin, second husband of Isabel, the Warenne heiress, and illegitimate brother of Henry II, was probably the first part of the original earthwork castle to be rebuilt in the new material, stone. It is a fine residential tower in the French style, with well-equipped rooms, reserved to

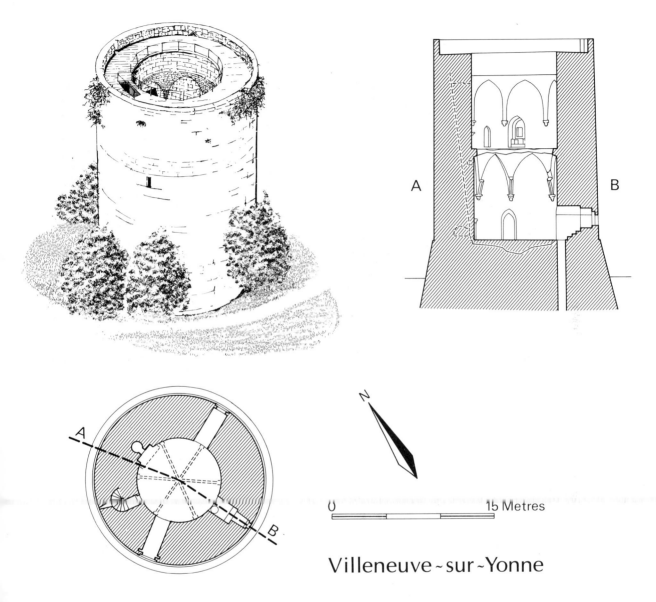

Villeneuve ~ sur ~ Yonne

the lord, on the second and third (top) floors, including a chapel and garderobe, and with storage chambers below. But the keep was never intended to stand on its own, and scarcely later in date is the curtain wall of the inner ward, or bailey, splayed strongly at the base like the tower keep itself, and equipped along all except its less vulnerable northern face with solid interval towers, or turrets, rising clear above the line of the wall-walk and opening up the field of fire of the defenders.[19]

Conisborough is datable to the 1180s, and Hamelin's half-brother, fully a decade before, had already built a tower keep at Orford, in Suffolk, which was the equal of any contemporary building in the Angevin dominions in France. Orford is a castle full of interest, not least because it had an important part to play in restraining the ambitions of the over-mighty earls of Norfolk and in implementing the royal castle policy which Henry II made so very much his own.[20] Furthermore, the keep at Orford, although very obviously belonging within the general class of such buildings, has many individual and experimental features, appropriate to a king who, both in England and in France, was a connoisseur in the construction of such towers. Orford, in its total cost, was one of the most expensive of Henry's castles, and by far the greatest element in the overall expense was the building of the impressive tower keep which is now the only part of the fortress that survives. The keep is thought to have been completed within two years (1165–7), and its unique design, with forebuilding and two other projecting rectangular turrets, makes it internally a building of unusual complexity and sophistication. Particularly individual is the way in which the two principal residential floors of the tower are planned as distinct and self-contained apartments: a lower hall with kitchen, chambers, and garderobe of its own, connected by a fine newel staircase to a similar but even grander suite on the second storey of the keep, fully equipped as before and probably intended for the use of the king himself. The chapel, in the usual position for a keep of this date, was placed on the upper floor of the forebuilding, over the entrance. A passage, contrived in the thickness of the wall, connected it on one side with the newel stair, on the other to the chaplain's own private chamber and garderobe on the first floor of the south-west turret.[21]

38 The sophisticated tower keep and surrounding bailey at Conisborough, built in the 1180s for Hamelin, half-brother of Henry II

39 *Above* Interior view of the principal residential floor in the keep at Conisborough, showing the large side-wall fireplace at this level

40 *Right* Henry II's residential tower keep at Orford, with the earthwork remains of the stone curtain wall and other buildings that surrounded it

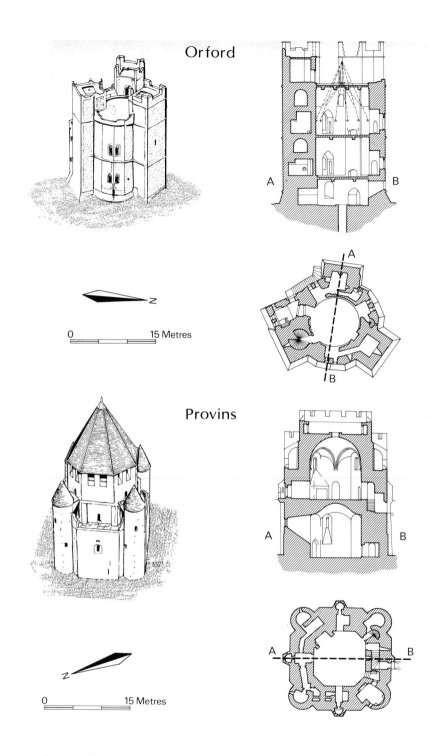

Orford

Provins

0   15 Metres

0   15 Metres

41 The tower keeps at Orford and Provins as they are now (left), shown in plan and
    section (right) with the original roof-lines restored

Like other tower keeps of its period, Orford is basically cylindrical in plan. However, the addition of the three turrets (one of them enlarged into a forebuilding) had given its internal design unusual flexibility, and the tower plan, as a general rule, was very much less accommodating. One contemporary tower, the so-called 'Tour de César' at Provins (Champagne), is at least as remarkable as Orford, being symmetrically planned with four angle turrets, each holding chambers, and being fully equipped with intra-mural passageways and stairs.[22] But the more smoothly cylindrical the tower became, and thus the better able it was to resist assault by deflecting the missiles of the attackers, the less opportunity it gave the designer to vary the accommodation within it. William Marshal's keep at Pembroke, built at the turn of the twelfth and thirteenth centuries, dominates the inner ward of the castle and was clearly, throughout the fighting life of the fortress, a crucial element in its defences. Yet the great hollow cylinder of the keep, with its massively solid walls continued at the same thickness throughout its height, is uncompromisingly military in purpose. Only the newel stair has been contrived in the thickness of the wall. Otherwise, the rooms on the three residential floors above the basement are simple circular apartments, two of them with fireplaces and one of these (on the second floor) with a handsome two-light window and window-seats, but the third planned more obviously as a 'fighting-deck', although still with a good window of its own. From the quality of their fittings, it is obvious that these rooms were intended for the personal occupation of the earl and his family, at least when forced to resort to them in an emergency. But the keep is without garderobes and lacks even that other essential, a well. It might do as a retreat, but would never have been acceptable as the permanent residence of one of the wealthiest men of his time.[23]

42 William Marshal's great cylinder keep (left centre) dominating the approaches to the inner ward at Pembroke

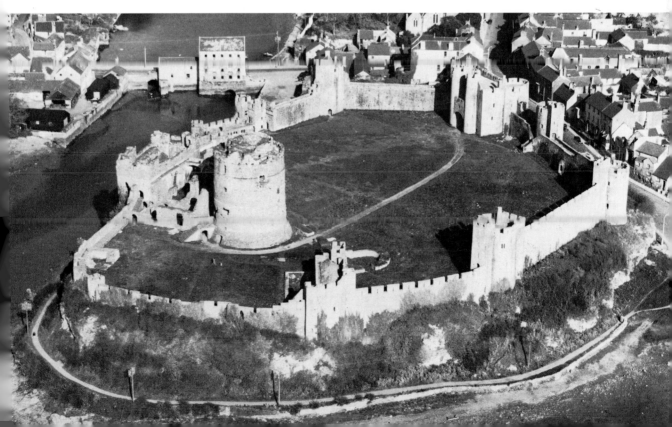

Accordingly, so long as the keep continued to be thought of as the lord's private residence, the more convenient and adaptable rectangular plan had obviously a good deal to recommend it. Henry II, as Orford demonstrates, was right up among the leaders of the tower-keep builders of his day. And indeed in the 1170s he continued to build other polygonal keeps, although neither of comparable sophistication, at Tickhill (Yorkshire) and Chilham (Kent), both of which cost him a good deal of money.[24] Nevertheless, he is better known still for the rectangular tower keeps which, characteristically lofty, have their own distinctive 'Angevin' profile. It was not Henry II but Philip Augustus, in the early thirteenth century, who added the cylindrical tower to the great rectangular mass of the Anglo-Norman fortress at Falaise. The last and the most expensive of Henry's keeps, being the work of Maurice 'the Engineer' who had also been responsible during the previous decade for a comparable but smaller royal tower keep at Newcastle, was the bulky tower at Dover, on the vulnerable south coast, sophisticated in detail but entirely conventional in its overall rectangular design.

Dover is the culmination of a long tradition, and the way to it is lined by a whole series of other similarly massive stone fortresses with which Henry II and his more trusted magnates equipped the land following the troubles under Stephen. It was at least partly by means of these castles, as is now well known, that Henry II and his sons, Richard and John, altered the balance of power between their barons and themselves decisively in favour of the crown.[25] But the deliberate castle policy that contributed to this result was never such as to prohibit baronial castle-building altogether, and many of the tower keeps of the Angevin era had little to do with the king. When Henry II's masons were busy on the royal keep at Newcastle, near the mouth of the Tyne, Hugh du Puiset, bishop of Durham (1153–95), was likewise engaged in transforming his own motte and bailey at Norham (Northumberland) into a stone fortress, the principal feature of which was a great three-storey rectangular tower keep.[26] It was at approximately this date too that Conan the Little, son of Alan

43   The tower keep on the former motte at Norham, built for Bishop Hugh du Puiset in the late twelfth century

44 Middleham: a strong rectangular residential keep of the late twelfth century is here surrounded by a similarly rectangular outer enclosure later heightened and extensively re-modelled by the Nevilles

the Red, began the rebuilding of his father's late-eleventh-century stone gatehouse at Richmond (Yorkshire) as the strong new tower which Henry II, after Conan's death in 1171, completed in its present form.[27] Meanwhile at Middleham, just a few miles to the south of Richmond, Conan's relative, Robert fitzRalph, had abandoned the original earthwork castle and was beginning the building of the substantial tower keep which continued thereafter, throughout the life of the fortress, to provide the bulk of its domestic accommodation. The plan of Middleham, which is one of the largest of the English rectangular keeps, is simple but entirely effective. Approached by a long stair on the eastern face of the keep leading to the usual first-floor entrance, it provides on that floor a great hall, with pantry and buttery at its south end, divided by a strong central spine wall from the great chamber and 'chamber of presence' on the west. On the ground floor, approached from the hall by a circular newel stair in the south-east corner of the keep, was the kitchen, with its cellar and other stores. A small chapel had been contrived in the north-east angle of the first floor, at the upper end of the hall. But this, in the next century, was clearly considered inadequate on its own, and a larger chapel was then built as a tower-like addition, tacked onto the keep towards its south-east angle, between it and the eastern curtain wall.[28]

Middleham's keep is on two floors only, and it was certainly more usual for the royal keeps of this period to be planned on three floors at least. This was true, for example, of the keep at Scarborough (Yorkshire), built on three storeys over a basement, and completed at considerable cost during the 1160s.[29] And if the great keep at Kenilworth (Warwickshire) was of only two floors effectively, that was because the normal basement area was in this instance earth-filled, being probably the bulk of the earlier sliced-down motte, cased in stone when the castle was rebuilt for Henry II in the 1170s.[30] The impressive tower keep at Portchester (Hampshire), as originally planned, was of just two storeys, the upper of which housed the hall and great chamber, separated from each other by the central spine wall which had also been a feature of Middleham. Yet significantly enough, soon after its construction, the keep at Portchester, now one of the king's, was raised by another two stages.[31]

45 *Left* The royal tower keep at Scarborough, built in the 1160s and very clearly residential in purpose

46 *Below* The south-east angle of Henry II's great keep at Kenilworth, with re-cut windows of the same period as Robert Dudley's late-sixteenth-century gatehouse (right)

Although there is nothing to establish when precisely this happened, it must certainly have occurred by quite early in the thirteenth century, thus bringing the castle up to date.

Both as up to date as it could be and yet curiously old-fashioned as soon as other

defensive rings left it stranded without purpose in the middle, was the keep that Henry II, towards the end of his reign, raised for the protection of the narrow straits of Dover. Works like Scarborough and Newcastle had prepared the way, but there is nothing to equal, in Henry's English dominions, the strength and complexity of the keep at Dover, built during the last decade of his reign. Approached by way of a three-towered forebuilding which is as much the culmination of this particular tradition as is the bulk of the keep itself, the accommodation of Henry's tower at Dover is arranged on three floors, the lowest of which is a basement store, with two separate suites of apartments (in the manner of Orford) on each of the floors above it. Like Orford again, the great thickness of the walls is made full use of, higher in the castle, for intra-mural chambers, passageways, and staircases, giving the designer of the castle the flexibility he needed to introduce every possible 'modern' improvement. William Marshal's almost contemporary cylinder keep at Pembroke, for all its military effectiveness, was to have few of these refinements, lacking even such a necessity as a well (above, p. 39). In contrast, Henry's keep at Dover had both the well, serving all floors, that had been known in such castles since Rochester, and a piped water supply linking separate chambers with the well-head. At Dover, too, the garderobes are exceptionally numerous and well-planned, frequently with common shutes and pits, and with facilities for cleaning these pits from the outside. There were fireplaces serving the principal chambers on both of the main residential floors of the castle. And each of these levels (of which the top and the grander was the king's) had a fine self-contained chapel of its own.[32]

47 The tower keep at Portchester, originally planned on two floors only but subsequently raised by a further two stages within a few decades of its first building

Not so very long after Henry's rebuilding of Dover Castle, its defences were tested in Prince Louis' siege of 1216. However, the keep itself was never more than threatened during the siege, and it is obvious that the purpose of a building of this kind was not exclusively military. Like the palace-keeps of the Conqueror at London and at Colchester, Dover had its function as a royal residence, for which it had to be appropriately equipped. Moreover, it had clearly been conceived at least as much as a symbol of Angevin power as Philip Augustus's tower keeps were themselves a celebration of the rival Capetians. Both dynastic lines, just as soon as they were in the position to do so, imposed severe restrictions on castle-building by those whom they had any reason to distrust. Systematically, they captured and destroyed the castles of their enemies; they introduced their own garrisons where they left a castle standing; they licensed castle-building on condition that the crown might resume a fortress when it wished; and they neutralized areas, including some frontiers, by means of anti-castle pacts. Moreover, in their own castle-building they had the advantages of unprecedented wealth and of a new building technology which, while it owed something to the model of castles overseas, was still more the product of local circumstances and of the ambitious contemporary building programmes of many of the princes of the Church. Gothic vaults and buttresses in the new manner might be expensive. But they could, if properly applied, immensely improve the accommodation within a building while weakening it not in the slightest. Within the twelfth century, techniques of quarrying, of transport, of cutting and working the stone, and of lifting it securely into place, all experienced improvements. The rivalries of dynasties and the perennial contest between king and aristocracy in which the advantage lay increasingly with the former—these were the circumstances for the introduction of a golden age in castle-building for which resources were available in an expanding economy and for which the engineers, having learnt their trade on other projects, were already very adequately prepared.

48 *Left* Henry II's great residential keep at Dover: the most ambitious and extravagant of Henry's castle-building works and one of the quickest to become out of date

49 *Right* The upper chapel in the keep at Dover

Chapter 3

Growing Sophistication

The native ingenuity of the Western European military engineer is undoubtedly the best explanation for the technical advances so obvious in the castles of twelfth-century England and France. Nevertheless, there are certain characteristics of castle-building in the latter part of the century which seem to derive from another source altogether, being more surely the product of the crusaders' experience in the Holy Land and along the western seaboard of Byzantine and Islamic Asia Minor. Most commonly cited among these innovations are the stone-built machicolated wall-walks and projecting galleries, supplied with openings in the floor through which missiles could be dropped, which began to be furnished to some of the greater royal castles of the period, in particular to towers and gatehouses. Related to these were the walls splayed at the base (the talus or glacis) which helped project missiles outwards when dropped through the machicolations above, as well as lending extra strength to the entire structure. But more important than either was the principle, witnessed in Asia Minor and deriving from Antiquity, of the regularly spaced flanking or mural tower. It was the exploitation of this mural tower in the West, greatly improving the fire-power of the garrison, that was the outstanding development in castle architecture, introducing the decline of the traditional tower keep in favour of concentric defence.

The fourteen mural towers, four of them gate towers, of Henry II's inner bailey at Dover, built in the 1180s, are among the earliest examples in the West of regularly spaced systematic provision of this kind.[1] And of course, at Earl Hamelin's innovatory castle at Conisborough, in Yorkshire, exactly contemporary with Dover, both the glacis and the mural tower were included in the design, even though executed on a much smaller scale.[2] However, there was certainly nothing in the West to compare as yet with the geometrically regular planning of a castle like Belvoir (Kaukab al-Hawa) in the Holy Land, sold to the Hospitallers in 1168 and entirely rebuilt by them within the following two decades. Belvoir preserves the precise rectangular plan of the Roman *castrum*, with square towers at the angles in the Roman manner and with a great gate tower centrally placed on the western wall, just as the Romans would have had it. But it adds to these too an outer enclosure, almost as regular, with interval towers along the line of the curtain, connected behind by a wide fighting-platform which backed the whole circuit of the defences. Belvoir, strictly speaking, has no central keep, being a castle of two curtain walls, the inner of which backed and dominated the outer. It was an instrument of offensive war, at least as much as a retreat. With its four sally-ports in the outer curtain, in addition to the strongly defended main gate, it was as easy to get out of as the traditional tower keep, once surrounded, was difficult to leave. It had been designed for counter-attack.[3]

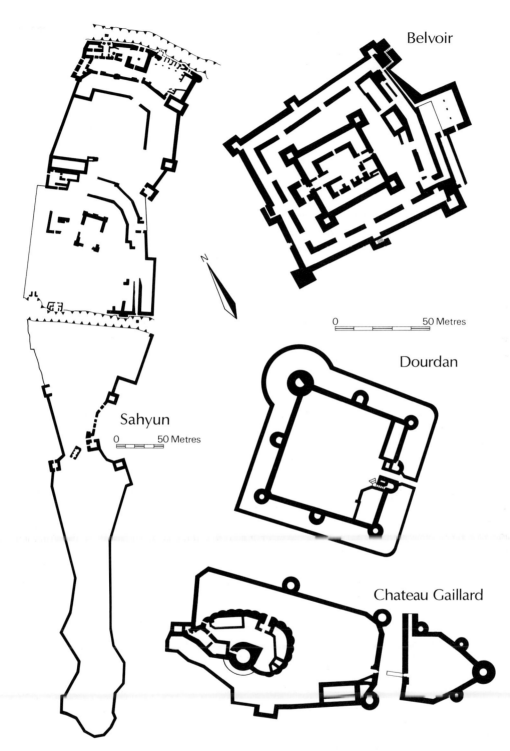

Belvoir

Dourdan

Sahyun

0   50 Metres

0   50 Metres

Chateau Gaillard

50 Contemporary variety in castle-planning: Sahyun influenced by pre-existing Byzantine defences, Belvoir and Dourdan showing dependence on Roman models, Château-Gaillard employ-
ing every new defensive technique know to the best military engineers of the late twelfth century

Undoubtedly, castle-builders by the late twelfth century were familiar, in the West as well as in the Near East, with the writings of some of the better military theorists of Antiquity. They knew a good deal, both from this source and from their own practical experience, about siegecraft, and they could study the elements of Roman defences in the stone-walled forts and other enclosures that everywhere survived on the ground. But this is not to say that they very commonly adapted their own practice to the principles with which they were acquainted from the past. The remarkable town wall at Avila, in central Spain, with its many interval towers modelled directly on parallel Roman works, has been dated as early as the last decades of the eleventh century. Yet neither from this nor from the still more impressive Greek defences of Constantinople, seen by numerous crusaders in just those years, did the castle-builders of western Christendom absorb the lessons of the interval tower, which it might take them another full century to apply. In castle architecture generally, the keep or strong tower has always been the preferred focus of defence. And when the crusaders themselves reached the Holy Land, one of the first things they did to defend their new territories was to build tower keeps of their own. Many of these survive today in Palestine and Syria, where they might have

51 The main entrance front at Sahyun, as re-fortified by the crusaders in the twelfth century with interval towers and with a central keep, commanding the gate beyond

been added, as at the fortress of Sahyun, to existing defences of considerable sophistication and complexity. However, whereas the Franks at Sahyun largely ignored the Byzantine fortifications of their predecessors on the site, they were not completely untouched by what they found there. The isolation of the mural towers at Sahyun, cut off from any access to the wall-walk, is a well-known Byzantine device, although not an especially good one. Better was the defence of the gate by a strong adjoining tower, also applied at Sahyun, and better still was the development, of which we begin to hear by the mid-twelfth century, of both the corner and the interval tower. Four-square castles with towers at the corners, one of them perhaps strengthened into a tower keep, are known in the crusader states from the 1160s and before.[4] Two generations later, they were being built in France, where the castles of Philip Augustus at Dourdan and Yèvre-le-Chatel, although making characteristic use of the new circular or drum tower form, must otherwise have evolved from the plan of the Roman *castrum* as developed and applied by the crusaders.[5]

Anticipating these, and even more directly influenced by castle-building practice in the Holy Land from which Richard I had only recently returned, was the English king's 'Fair Castle of the Rock' at Château-Gaillard (Normandy), completed within two years between 1196 and 1198 and one of the most remarkable innovatory fortresses of all time. Richard retained the tower keep of his period as the final strongpoint of the castle, even if he gave it all the latest refinements, including the beaked plan then finding favour in France, with the strongly splayed base and the prominent machicolations (now gone and perhaps never completed) which he must have observed in the Near East. However, where castle design advanced furthest at Château-Gaillard was not in the keep but in its protection by three successive lines of defences, crossing the promontory on which the castle was sited and enclosing in turn an outer, a middle, and an inner bailey. The outer bailey was in effect a barbican, protected by a great cylindrical tower at its most vulnerable point and itself blocking the approaches of the middle bailey which could be entered only over the bridge it controlled. Both outer and middle curtain walls had prominent drum towers to reinforce them, while the inner curtain was finished off on the exterior with a completely individual series of large-scale 'corrugations' no doubt intended to improve covering fire from the wall-walk. Richard himself took a lively and continuous interest in the works at Château-Gaillard, on which he spent more even than his father, Henry II, had had to find for Dover.[6] And it was Richard's personal concern in the building process that both brought it at the time to a swift conclusion and now gives the castle its peculiar importance. At Château-Gaillard, one of the most highly regarded military leaders of the day gave himself, unmindful of the expense, to the problem of constructing an impregnable fortress which might stand as a gesture of defiance to the Capetians and as a protection of those Norman lands which Richard had lately regained for the Angevins. These ambitions were to be frustrated in the siege of 1203–4, concluding with its capture by Philip Augustus. But the French king himself was to re-use ideas first satisfactorily developed in the West at Château-Gaillard. One of these, very obviously, was the beak-shaped tower, three of which were later used on the outer curtain of Philip's early-thirteenth-century re-fortification of Loches, a former Angevin castle. Yet of greater importance were the more general characteristics of Richard's fortress—its pioneering development of concentric defences and its refinement of the mural tower. No great castle after this date would be erected in ignorance of these lessons.

52 Two of the seventeen drum towers, lacking their upper stages, at the French royal fortress of Angers

The major royal castles were, of course, among the first to be modernized extensively in the new fashion. Saumur, later transformed into a romantic fortress of chivalry by Louis of Anjou, was another of Philip Augustus's castles in the Roman manner, with great towers at each of its four corners, while perhaps the most impressive of all contemporary defended circuits was the curtain wall, with seventeen drum towers, of the royal fortress of Angers, on the River Maine, for the most part completed in the 1230s during the early years of the long reign of Philip's grandson, Louis IX. In England, Kenilworth (Warwickshire) got its outer defensive ring, largely towerless, to the order of John and Henry III. Windsor (Berkshire), Dover (Kent), and the Tower of London were each of them to be equipped before the end of Henry's reign

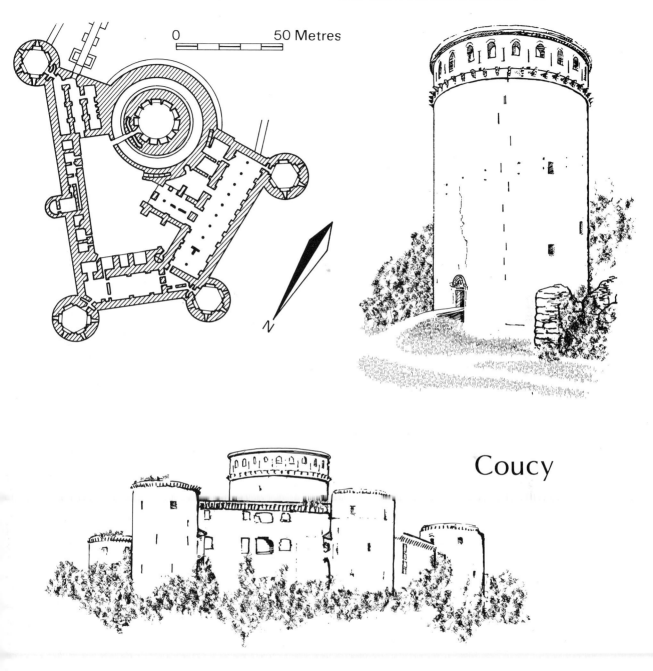

Coucy

53 Enguerrand III's great fortress at Coucy, built in 1220–40; the keep at Coucy was demolished by the
German army in 1917–18, and has been sketched here from an earlier photograph

with additional strong stone circuits, further defended along their lines by regular interval towers. However, the impact of the new fashions is perhaps best judged, in England as it is in France, at single-date castles like the Marcher fortresses at Montgomery, Grosmont, and Skenfrith, or at that extraordinary pile at Coucy, west of Laon, which remains to this day one of the greatest private fortresses ever built.

Coucy, constructed in the 1220s and 1230s for Enguerrand III ('Sire de Coucy'), was a castle designed in the very latest mode to match anything yet built by the king. Enguerrand himself had ambitions for the crown of France. His castle, like those of Philip Augustus, was deliberately designed to reinforce his dynasty with a residence fit for a prince. Again following Philip, the Sire de Coucy's fortress was equipped both with a great cylinder keep on its most vulnerable southern face and with prominent drum towers in the latest manner at each of the four angles of the irregular trapeze-shaped bailey, the plan of which had been dictated by the fall of the land on the promontory. And yet, unlike other castles of the period, including William Marshal's near-contemporary Pembroke (above, p. 39), where keep and bailey seem to have been conceived as independent units, the two main elements of Enguerrand's fortress are integrated with a new precision. At Coucy, too, another new element is the emphasis now placed on the systematic planning of the domestic accommodation, lining the walls of the inner bailey to make a courtyard residence of considerable convenience and splendour.[7] Still the keep, protected by its own moat and curtain wall, remained both a strongpoint and a retreat, dominating the main gate (as did the tower at Pembroke) and providing accommodation of a standard certainly adequate for the use of the lord's family in an emergency. However, the keep essentially was no more than the largest of five great towers on the bailey circuit, each of them with a similar role in the defence. It was part of a unified defensive system as carefully worked out as at Richard's Château-Gaillard. It was no longer, as such a building might usually have been scarcely more than a generation earlier, the unique central residence of the lord.

On a smaller scale, the same general principles were beginning to be applied to the building of new castles in the Welsh Marches. Pembroke itself, of course, was one of the earlier of those, and the great personal wealth of William Marshal, combined with

54 Dover: Henry II's keep (centre) is surrounded by concentric rings of fortifications, the inner contemporary with the keep while the outer dates largely to the reigns of John and Henry III; the main gate of the castle (bottom right), known as the Constable's Tower, was re-sited by Hubert de Burgh

55 Montgomery Castle from the air, showing Hubert de Burgh's inner ward (top left) and the outer ward (right) completed later in the thirteenth century

the extensive military experience he had acquired both in France and in Syria, had already made it one of the pioneer buildings of its time. But it was another great figure, Hubert de Burgh (d. 1234), justiciar of England and earl of Kent, who, during the long minority of Henry III, became especially important as the introducer of the new castle architecture into England. Hubert de Burgh, like William Marshal, was a thoroughly experienced soldier, having held Chinon, on the Vienne, against Philip Augustus's armies in 1204, and having further extended his reputation in siege warfare by the heroic defence of Dover in 1216, when under assault by Prince Louis. And it was the weakness of the main outer gate at Dover, which nearly lost the castle to the French, that must have persuaded Hubert de Burgh in later years to place so much emphasis on the strengthening of the gatehouses at the castles he built anew or re-modelled. At Dover, after the siege, Hubert de Burgh's works included the complete re-design of the castle approaches, the most important elements of which were the sealing of the old gate, the building of a new entrance at the Constable's Tower, and the provision of elaborate underground works at the Norfolk Towers and Fitzwilliam Gate designed to facilitate the exit of the defenders at points crucial to the castle's defence.[8] However, at Dover much of the character of the thirteenth-century re-fortification was already dictated by works of the twelfth century and later, and of more interest in the context of the new castle architecture is the fortress Hubert built from nothing at Montgomery.

Montgomery had been defended originally by the motte at Hen Domen (above, p. 4), one of the earliest of the permanent castles of the Conquest. But in the autumn of 1223, as part of a programme of resettlement against the Welsh, the decision was taken to rebuild the fortress on a new site altogether, about a mile from the old, taking advantage of a natural rocky eminence. To a large extent, the unusually narrow plan

56 The gate passage of Hubert de Burgh's great gatehouse at Montgomery

of the castle was dictated by the constraints of its site. Nevertheless, the outstanding feature of the inner ward at Montgomery, as built for Hubert de Burgh before his fall from power in 1232, was the great gatehouse tower, closing the entire southern end of the ward like the jaws of a magnet, with two drum towers on its outer face and with the long entrance passage of the period. All but the ground floor of the gatehouse is now lost, demolished in 1649. Yet enough evidence remains on the site and in the records to establish that Hubert de Burgh's gatehouse was planned as a tower of four floors, with three great chambers running the full width of the building on each of the floors above the entrance passage, and with a guardroom placed on the right of the entrance from which the draw-bar of the gate could be operated. At Montgomery, as was usually the case, the inner ward of the castle was completed first, being already sufficiently formidable by 1231 to fend off an attack by Llywelyn ap Iorwerth ('the Great'), who in that year burnt the town. Twenty years later, another major programme of works at the castle, which had reverted to the crown on Hubert's fall in 1232, led to the replacement of the temporary timber outer defences and to the walling of the middle ward in stone. In its final form, the castle promontory at Montgomery was protected on its most vulnerable southern quarter by successive lines of defence, including the outermost rock-cut ditch and barbican, with another ditch in front of the mid-thirteenth-century gatehouse of the middle ward, and a third crossing the approaches of Hubert de Burgh's already formidable keep-gatehouse.[9] Like other fortresses similarly placed on a naturally defendable site, a genuinely concentric defence was neither practicable nor necessary at Montgomery, there being more to gain by multiplying the obstacles along the length of the promontory.

Flexibility in design practice is the mark of every great castle-builder. There is little real resemblance, for example, between Frederick II's Italian fortresses at Lucera and Catania, at Termoli, Bari, Syracuse, and Castel del Monte, although all were built in the 1230s or 1240s and each reflected, at least in some degree, the emperor's personal taste.[10] Similarly, Hubert de Burgh, while he built another keep-less castle at Grosmont (Monmouthshire), where the defensive strength was concentrated chiefly on the gatehouse and on the strong drum towers of the curtain,[11] could equally retain (if he needed it) the less fashionable cylinder keep, as he did for example at the neighbouring Skenfrith, and as Frederick would do, in a more sophisticated fashion, at his fortresses at Termoli and Lucera. Skenfrith, although on a comparatively small scale, has many of the characteristics of the most 'modern' castles of its period, including prominent drum towers at each of the angles and even the strong cylinder of the keep itself, still finding favour in France. With the exception of the solid half-round tower built in the 1260s against the west curtain, Skenfrith is a single-date castle, probably completed between 1228 and 1232 as one of Hubert de Burgh's final works. The gatehouse is now lost, giving the castle a defenceless look. Nevertheless, the curtain wall on each side of the gate, and on every quarter of the castle, is overlooked by prominent drum towers at the angles, while the keep itself, placed slightly off-centre, rises well above the line of the wall-walk which it oversees and effectively commands. Plainly, the keep at Skenfrith was still thought of as residential; there is a comfortable chamber on the second floor, with two windows, a fireplace, and a garderobe. However, one of the advantages of the relatively open geometric planning of the castle as a whole was that there was plenty of room within the outer curtain for accommodation of a suitable standard for the lord. Skenfrith is not a fortress-palace of courtyard plan like Enguerrand's Coucy or Frederick II's Bari or Catania. Yet it has a fine range of domestic buildings, probably including the great hall and at least one chamber, next to the tower and against the

57 Frederick II's symmetrically planned Sicilian fortress at Catania, with prominent drum towers at the angles

58 The cylinder keep at Skenfrith, set on a mound where it could oversee and command the curtain wall of Hubert de Burgh's castle, built in 1228–32

inner face of the west curtain. And although another range against the east curtain was never built, very probably because of problems of flooding, it seems certain that more accommodation on this side of the ward was projected in Hubert de Burgh's original plan.[12]

Skenfrith, with its neighbours, Grosmont and White Castle, and with Hadleigh Castle, in Essex, are known (by the account of the contemporary chronicler Matthew Paris) to have ranked as Earl Hubert's dearest possessions, on which he spent great sums. Much of this would have gone on improving the fortifications. However, a good part went too into the new accommodation which castles of this date were increasingly expected to provide. At Grosmont, the entire eastern side of the castle courtyard is taken up by an exceptionally substantial and strongly built hall and chamber block. This had been the first part of the castle to be rebuilt by Hubert de Burgh, and it dates to about 1210. Only after the completion of the residential element at Grosmont were the defences re-modelled in a second programme of work, datable no earlier than the 1220s.[13]

59 Grosmont: another of Hubert de Burgh's castles where the residential quality of the building (hall and chamber block on the left) has been given as much emphasis as defence

60 A thirteenth-century cylinder keep at Tretower, replacing earlier domestic accommodation and sited centrally within a curtain wall of mid-twelfth-century date

Increasingly, then, in castles of the new style, the changing function (and even disappearance) of the keep was placing greater importance on the residential quality of the buildings of the inner ward, now intended to accommodate the lord. A castle like Tretower (Brecon), not far from Grosmont, might exceptionally be rebuilt in the second quarter of the thirteenth century as a great cylinder keep, planned as the lord's residence and replacing the buildings which, in the previous century, had lined the surviving outer curtain.[14] However, much more usual would have been such a replanning as occurred contemporaneously at Cilgerran (Pembrokeshire), a former Welsh castle which in 1223 came permanently into the possession of the English. The outstanding characteristics of Cilgerran still are the two great drum towers on the most exposed face of the inner curtain which are so much a mark of the period. With the strongly constructed two-storey gatehouse and linking curtain wall on the south and east, they cut off the promontory and secured it successfully against any further counter-attack by the Welsh. Plainly, though, while both towers had some residential function, being supplied with fireplaces in three out of their six upper chambers, they could never have been intended as more than supplementary in this way to the more comfortable quarters of the inner ward, sheltering behind their bulk. These quarters were probably timber-built, and they have disappeared almost completely. However, enough remains to suggest that they must have included a hall and kitchen, with a great chamber and perhaps other lodgings and storehouses as well.[15] Without them, certainly, Cilgerran would have been barely inhabitable, even by the comparatively austere standards of its day.

Those standards, in any event, were changing rapidly. Cilgerran's rebuilders had been William Marshal's sons, successively earls of Pembroke until the extinction of their line on the deaths of Walter and Anselm within weeks of each other in the last

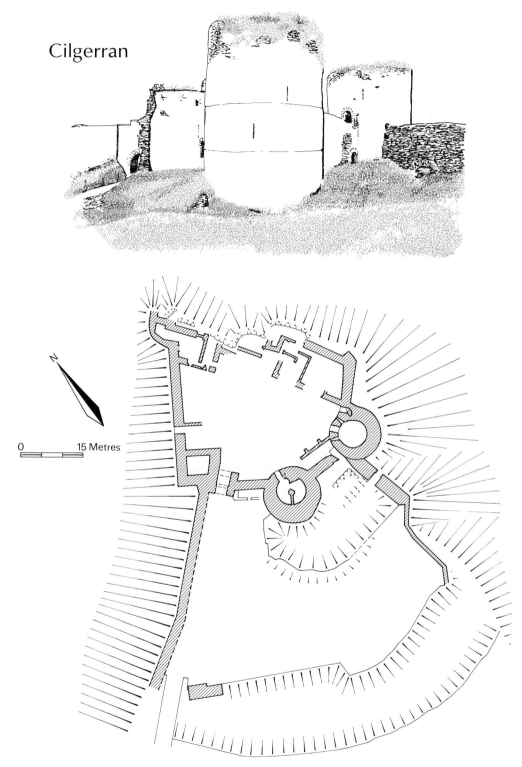

Cilgerran

0   15 Metres

61 Cilgerran: illustrating the use of drum towers and a strong gatehouse to replace a keep at this promontory castle of the second quarter of the thirteenth century

months of 1245. And one of the finest examples of what was likely to happen to many family fortresses of the period is provided by the works they themselves began at Chepstow, in Monmouthshire, subsequently continued by the Bigod inheritors of this estate. Both the Marshal earls of Pembroke and their successors, the Bigod earls of Norfolk, were to make their contribution to the defensive capability of Chepstow Castle. But at least as important in the works they completed there was the entire rebuilding of the domestic accommodation of the castle to a new and more comfortable standard. William fitzOsbern's original stone keep, exceptional though it may have been when first built shortly following the Conquest (above, p. 13), was clearly out-moded a century and a half later. What the Marshals did to it was to rebuild the upper levels of the tower, inserting large new windows at first-floor level on the more secure northern face, and adding another storey over the western third of the building to carry an additional chamber, again with large windows of its own. By the time they had finished, the austere stone tower of the first castle on the site had become a hall-and-chamber block of palatial dimensions, comparable to the contemporary domestic arrangements of the king. Yet even this for Roger Bigod III, who inherited the castle in 1270 and who held it thereafter for the next thirty years, was not to be considered enough. The Marshal earls, with their other extensions and re-fortifications at Chepstow, including the strongly defended west barbican, had added the lower bailey at the east end of the ridge which Roger Bigod was to make the focus of his own activity at the castle. It was here, against the north curtain wall of the lower bailey, that Roger Bigod built himself a great domestic range in the late 1270s and early 1280s, adding not just one hall to the castle's accommodation but two. During the next eight years (1285–93), he also built a strong tower (Marten's Tower) at the south-east angle of the bailey, clearly designed as a private lodging for his own personal use. It is one of the earliest of the great tower-houses which became such an accepted and familiar element of the late-medieval fortress.

Roger Bigod, like other Marcher lords of his day, collected substantial revenues from his Welsh inheritance which were certainly sufficient to support his activity as a builder. These were the years, beginning in 1271, when Gilbert de Clare, earl of Gloucester, was building his great private fortress at Caerphilly, in Glamorgan. And both earls were exceptionally powerful men, accustomed to private war as much as to the service of the king, with whom they not infrequently took issue. Accordingly Chepstow, like Caerphilly (below, pp. 86–9), had to function repeatedly as a barracks for the earl's personal army; it had to provide comfortable lodgings on many occasions for Roger Bigod's principal supporters; it had to accommodate the administrators of the earl's Marcher lands, as well as serving as a residence for Roger himself. It was this great (and accumulating) personal retinue of the lord, giving him the authority to stand up against Edward I as one of the two principal leaders of the baronial opposition in the 1290s, that had to be lodged whenever necessary at Chepstow. In effect, Chepstow had already become by the late thirteenth century a 'castle of livery and maintenance', related more closely to such fortresses of chivalry as Warwick, Kenilworth, and Arundel (all a hundred years later in date) than to any earlier model.

As such, of course, the quality of the accommodation that Roger Bigod added to Chepstow is very much easier to understand. Clearly, the immediate need was to provide adequate accommodation somewhere within the fortress for the men entering the earl's service. In the Marshal era, during the first half of the thirteenth century, the middle and lower baileys at Chepstow had been successively developed, their curtain walls strengthened with fine drum towers, and a great double-towered gatehouse built at the enclosure's easternmost limit. Each of these towers would have provided its own suite of lodgings, as indeed it continued to do. But whatever other arrangements were made to house the Marshal retainers at Chepstow, the state that Roger Bigod intended to keep there required another standard of accommodation altogether. To the neglect of the great tower in the upper bailey, which hitherto had been the residential focus of the castle, Roger Bigod developed the lower bailey with a great and a lesser hall, ingeniously planned as a single unit so that the pantry and buttery of the more important hall should be sited immediately above the same offices of the lesser one. There was a fine linking stair, and comfortable private chambers at the east ends of both halls, each of them equipped with its own garderobe.

Work on the two new halls at Chepstow is thought to have begun in 1278, to be finished some seven years later. And it was followed almost immediately by the complete rebuilding of the great tower at the crucial south-east angle of the lower bailey, probably between 1287 and 1293. A tower of three storeys over a basement, Marten's Tower was entered at ground-floor level by a door from the bailey, itself strongly defended by its own portcullis. To the left of this door, a circular stair rose to the first-floor hall, ascending again the full height of the building to the second-floor chamber and the chapel. The detailing of the stonework throughout the tower is of high quality, especially in the finely ornamented chapel, and there are window seats, fireplaces, and private latrines, one on each residential floor. Such a standard of fittings can only mean that the south-east tower at Chepstow was intended to accommodate Earl Roger himself. And its relative isolation from the other lodgings in the castle is an important indicator of a contemporary shift in taste. Earl Roger's own expenditure on the two halls at Chepstow, with his final building campaign, undertaken in the 1290s, to complete the upper storey of the great tower, are enough to show that the day had not yet come when Piers Plowman could lament:

> Desolate is the hall each day in the week
> Where neither lord nor lady delights to sit.
> Now has each rich man a rule to eat by himself
> In a privy parlour, because of poor men,
> Or in a chamber with a chimney and leave the chief hall
> That was made for meals and men to eat in,
> And all to spare from spilling what spend shall another.[16]

But already in the 1240s Bishop Grosseteste of Lincoln had remarked on the practice, in at least one noble household, of taking meals to private places, eating them away from the hall.[17] And Piers Plowman, in the 1370s, is less than a century removed from Earl Roger.

In practice, what Chepstow demonstrates so well is the division of the typical late-medieval magnate establishment into a number of separate households. Each of these households had its individual function, whether civil or military, and it was natural enough for the castle architect, even in a new building, to perpetuate these divisions in the way he disposed the residential suites and in such barriers as he introduced between them.[18] At Chepstow, the lord's desire for privacy—and perhaps for a

62 Chepstow: already important in the immediately post-Conquest period when the Great Tower (centre) was built, Chepstow was progressively extended and improved during the thirteenth century by its Marshal and Bigod owners. It was Roger Bigod III (d. 1306) who developed the accommodation in the lower bailey (right) with adjoining halls on the river front and with a personal tower (bottom right), known as Marten's Tower, on the bailey's most vulnerable quarter

treasury and strongpoint as well—was met by the building of Marten's Tower, its final defensive role neatly emphasized by the courtyard-facing portcullis. However, it should be remembered that Earl Roger's contribution to Chepstow was not so much in the modification of the castle's defences, already recently transformed by his Marshal predecessors, as in the provision there of handsome new suites of residential accommodation, suitably styled for his rank. In much the same way, one of Henry III's most important building projects at Windsor, completed at huge expense in the 1240s, had been the construction of a whole new set of royal apartments in the lower ward, away from the great tower as at Chepstow.[19] And Henry similarly, throughout his long reign, had continued to spend lavishly on the modernization of his castles, transforming many of them into comfortable residences. Winchester and the Tower of London, Nottingham, Marlborough, Bristol, and Gloucester were all treated in this way, to be equipped with new lodgings for the king and queen, with chapels, wardrobes, and privy-chambers, with new halls roofed in the latest manner, floored with ornamental encaustic tiles, and splendidly painted and glazed.[20]

Most of these comforts, including the use of floor-tiles and the practice of wainscoting and glazing, were innovations of the thirteenth century, many of them pioneered in secular building by the king himself and all of them spreading, in the next few decades, down through the wealthier social classes.[21] Before 1300, the characteristic austerity of the twelfth-century castle had come to be disguised, in almost every instance, by successive additions and improvements. Carisbrooke Castle, on the Isle of Wight, had been a large but straightforward motte and bailey, one of the earliest in the land (above, p. 12). Under Isabella de Forz, countess of Aumale, who supervised improvements there from 1270 until she sold it to the crown in 1293, the entire character of Carisbrooke was transformed. She built a chapel at Carisbrooke and at least two chambers, one of them her own private apartment; she re-modelled the kitchen, linking it to the hall with a covered way, or pentice; she extended the great gatehouse, laid out a new garden, and saw to the digging of a new well. By 1299, when a survey was taken for the crown, the accommodation at Carisbrooke was said to include no fewer than three chapels, one of them Isabella's personal chapel of St Peter, another no longer in use; there was the hall and the kitchen, with larder, bakehouse, and brewhouse, with cellars, a granary, stables, and a forge; and there were many separate chambers—a great chamber and four other chambers probably annexed to the hall, with the constable's chamber over its own cellar, and with other chambers on the upper floor of the gatehouse and in the several storeys of the towers.[22]

While Carisbrooke, we know, was the favourite residence of a rich and a long-lived noblewoman, there is little reason to suppose that the accommodation it offered was exceptional within its own class. Outside England, in France and in Germany, there had been an identical move within the thirteenth century towards the provision of greater domestic comfort in the castle, even at the cost of some weakening of its defences. And although this was the period too, as we shall see in the next chapter, of the final perfection of the medieval fortress as an instrument of conquest and settlement, the residential role of the castle in less threatened areas was always more likely to be dominant. Carisbrooke Castle and its kindred fortresses offered a secure setting, in a rich and self-confident generation, for a life of dignity and affluence. As, shortly afterwards, the economy collapsed, as social patterns disintegrated, and as public order everywhere was at risk, such security appeared still more desirable in late-medieval Europe—the castle more necessary, not less so.

Chapter 4

A Time for Professionals

Edward I's great chain of fortresses in North Wales is usually recognized as a high point in castle-building in the West, and it was here, in castles like Harlech and Beaumaris, that a new perfection in symmetrical planning was achieved. Nevertheless, many of the principles applied so successfully in North Wales by Edward and by his architect-engineer Master James of St George already had a long history in castle-building. The regularly spaced mural tower, as we have seen, may be found at Dover a full century before Edward employed it as normal building practice in the castles with which he enforced English settlement in North Wales. Similarly, the double enclosure and geometric plan have their origins in Antiquity, while both were in use at Belvoir, in the Holy Land, no later than the 1170s and 1180s (above, p. 47). The tower keep, never wholly abandoned even by Edward, had for some decades now been a form of extravagance with a purpose as much social as military. The near-impregnable gatehouse which is so characteristic a feature of the Edwardian fortress, has its antecedents in the Constable's Tower, built by Hubert de Burgh at Dover after Prince Louis' siege (above, p. 53), or in the elaborate approaches, certainly completed before 1271, of the great Hospitaller castle at Krak des Chevaliers, in Syria.

Accordingly, Edward's castles need to be seen in context. Individually, they could be matched and even exceeded by great contemporary baronial fortresses like Gilbert de Clare's Caerphilly (Glamorgan). And it is obvious that there is very little in them that had not been anticipated, somewhere or another, before. Yet their importance rests in their quality as a group, where within a few decades the latest thinking in military engineering had come to be focused on a whole series of major buildings, driven on by the king's personal enthusiasm and by the threat of rebellion, and supported by unparalleled investment. Against Gilbert de Clare's Caerphilly or Henry of Lancaster's Kidwelly (Carmarthenshire), Edward I could set six (and more) great fortresses of his own.

Edward's six major castles were Flint and Rhuddlan, both begun in 1277, Conway, Caernarvon, and Harlech, all started in 1283, and Beaumaris (1295). In addition, he encouraged and even directly subsidized the castle-building programmes of his loyal knights, while finding the funds for modernizations elsewhere at the royal castles, including the completion of his father's inner curtain wall at the Tower of London and the provision of yet another strong stone circuit and moat beyond it. For all of these works, both he and his men were well prepared. As a very young man, Edward had fought already in Wales; besides other military experience at home during the baronial wars and the contest with Simon de Montfort, he had spent much time in France and in Spain, had travelled through Italy, and had stayed for prolonged periods in Sicily, from which he left and to which he returned from crusade. He had

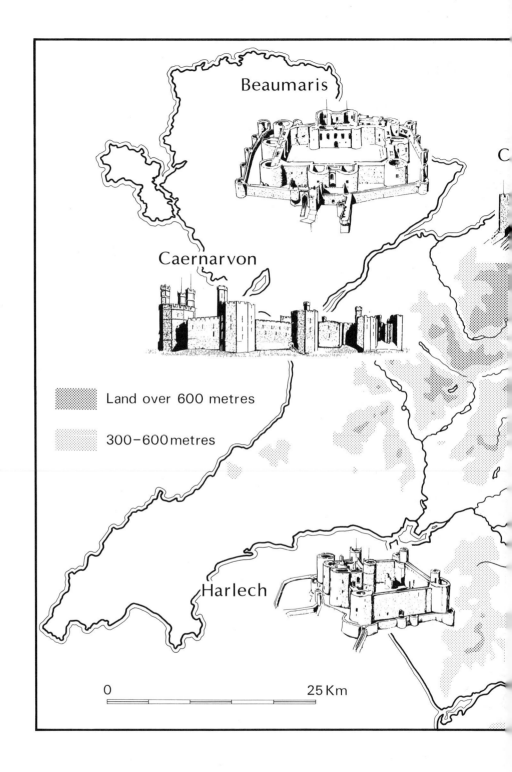

Beaumaris

Caernarvon

Land over 600 metres

300-600 metres

Harlech

0   25 Km

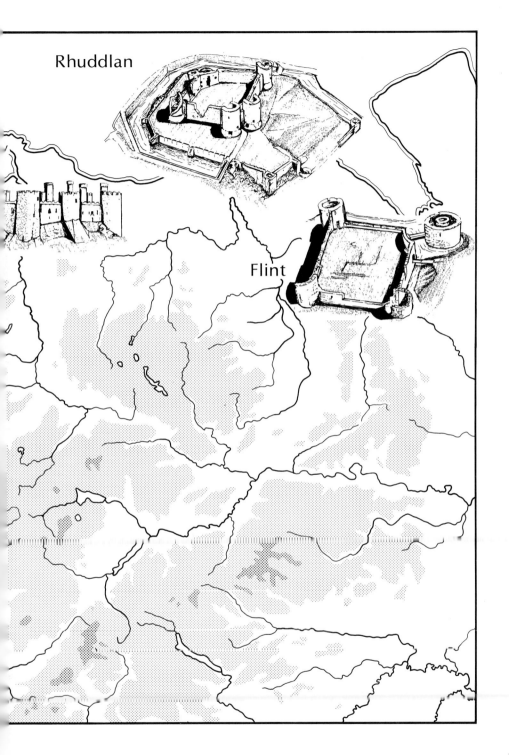

63 Edward I's castles of conquest and settlement in North Wales, showing their primarily coastal distribution

Rhuddlan

Flint

65

visited Cyprus on the way to the Holy Land in 1271, had fought with some success in Syria and Palestine before his return in 1272, and even if he did not know personally the castle at Krak des Chevaliers, which had fallen to the Mamluks in 1271, would have been well acquainted with the principles of its defences, many of which he would have seen repeated in the castles he had visited elsewhere. In effect, Edward's extensive military experience, built up over the long years during which he had waited for his father, the old king, to die, equipped him with a knowledge of contemporary fortification probably unequalled in his time throughout Europe. He would have seen the great castle and fortified town at Carcassonne which, as completed by Louis IX and Philip III, was to remain the most ambitious complex of concentric fortifications ever built in the medieval West. And his acquaintanceship with Louis IX's other great urban enterprise at Aigues-Mortes, on the south coast of France, was influential in more than one way in his own programme of conquest and settlement in Wales. Both at Aigues-Mortes and at Carcassonne, castle and town had been conceived as a single enterprise, justification and support for each other. In precisely the same way, Edward himself was to 'plant' new towns, in North Wales and in English-held Gascony, building up units of permanent settlement more viable than a fortress on its own.

Edward I built ten Welsh castles in all, and the first two major ones, at Flint and at Rhuddlan, were associated from the beginning with purpose-built towns, each supplied with its earthwork defences. Edward's later castles, as is only to be

64 Concentric fortification at the Tower of London: at the centre, the White Tower (built by William the Conqueror), with a first ring of defences (begun in their present form by Richard I, continued by Henry III, and completed by Edward I), and with a lower outer ring overlooked and commanded by the inner (begun by Edward I, completed by Edward III, and modified by Henry VIII)

65 Krak des Chevaliers, Syria: a castle of sophisticated concentric plan which became a model for castle-builders in the West

expected, were more sophisticated than either of these. Yet both Flint and Rhuddlan, in the context of the king's own experience of castles, present features of interest, and at both, at least from 1278, the hand of Master James of St George is also evident. Most strikingly, the great tower at Flint, standing at the south-east corner of the inner bailey from which it is separated by a moat, recalls Louis IX's Tour Constance at Aigues-Mortes, the port from which Edward in 1270 had set sail with his army for North Africa. Exceptionally among Edward's other works, Flint was equipped with a tower keep in the grand French manner, providing the main residential accommodation at the castle. And while there are many points of difference between the towers at Flint and at Aigues-Mortes, most particularly in their internal arrangements, the association of planned town and great tower in just this way is too close to be entirely coincidental.[1]

If Flint demonstrates an individual French influence on the castle-building of Edward I soon after he became king, the contemporary fortress at Rhuddlan, built in tandem with Flint to protect the same stretch of the North Welsh coastal plain, shows us what he had learnt in a more general way from the many castles he had seen on his

66 The entrance to Louis IX's inner fortress at the walled city of Carcassonne, restored in the last century by Viollet-le-Duc

travels. Within the constraints imposed on it by the site, Rhuddlan is a regularly planned concentric castle, with a dry moat on three sides revetted in stone, bounded by the River Clwyd on the west. However, Rhuddlan's most remarkable features are rather the almost perfect symmetry of the castle's inner ward, with the care that was taken in both the inner and outer wards to promote the fire-power and mobility of the garrison. At Rhuddlan, there was good accommodation in the many tower chambers, with other domestic buildings (including the royal apartments) lining the inner curtain wall. Nevertheless, the castle is very much a soldier's conception, planned deliberately for aggressive defence where the initiative might remain with the garrison. To this end, communication with the sea was ensured by a major work of diverting and canalizing the River Clwyd to bring deep-water shipping over two miles up-river to the docks of the castle and to those of the re-sited new town. A strong tower (Gillot's Tower) was built to protect the dock gate, while three other gates (the

Town Gate, the River Gate, and the Friary Gate) allowed the garrison, should the opportunity arise, to pick its point of exit at will. In the same spirit, each of the mural towers along the outer curtain wall was equipped initially with a flight of steps down into the dry moat, with a sally-port for the use of the defenders. Exposed to fire from the many downward-sloping arrow slits along the line of the outer curtain, and attacked on either side by the garrison, any intruder who penetrated the moat would not have found it easy to remain there.

Had he done so, and even if he had got beyond the moat into the outer ward, his problems if anything would have been intensified. The most important principle of concentric defence is that the outer defensive ring should be overseen and commanded by the garrison of the inner. At Rhuddlan, the great inner curtain— much higher and thicker than the outer—is pierced by arrow slits backing onto embrasures along its length, with drum towers and the two gatehouses to strengthen each corner, and with central turrets against the wall-walk between them. As with the outer curtain, an active and aggressive defence of the castle was made possible by the provision of three points of exit: a small sally-port in the north-west curtain and strongly defended symmetrical gatehouses in the opposing east and west corners.[2] In striking contrast to the king's other castle along the coast at Flint, there was no provision at Rhuddlan for a keep. There is no suggestion in the design of this castle of

67 Flint Castle seen from the estuary, with the north-east tower (centre) and the great tower (left), the latter probably modelled on Louis IX's Tour Constance at Aigues-Mortes

68 Rhuddlan from the air, showing the symmetry of the inner ward, with matching towers at the opposing angles, and the siting of the castle next to the navigable Clwyd

passive defence—of waiting out a siege in the expectation of the arrival of a relieving army. Rhuddlan was an instrument of Edward's on-going conquest and subjection. Only in the event of a serious and prolonged rising of the Welsh would it be expected to do duty as a retreat.

Just as Flint and Rhuddlan, laid out together in 1277, had differed very markedly in plan, so other elements in the king's past experience were drawn on six years later

69 *Below left* A view of Rhuddlan from the north, with the badly damaged north tower (centre) and the west gatehouse (right)
70 *Below right* Conway, with its eight equal-sized drum towers, those of the inner ward crowned with turrets

in the design of three further great castles—Conway, Caernarvon, and Harlech—each very different from the others. Most remarkable at Conway are the eight great towers, almost identical in plan and scale, which are the principal element in its defences. Yet at Conway, although the approaches through the west barbican are tortuous enough, there is no strong gatehouse, whereas the gatehouse especially is the dominant feature of Harlech Castle, the whole defence of which hinges upon it. Caernarvon, in many ways the most impressive of the three as a demonstration of Edward's purpose in North Wales, is distinguished by a return to the principle of the tower keep, not sited, as one might have expected, on the original castle mound but at the extreme western angle of the lower bailey.

Very probably, each of these castles had a propaganda role to play. And the lime-washing of Conway's walls, with the turreted towers of its inner ward and its decoratively pinnacled battlements, must have made it a splendid and a memorable sight. But at none was this function more important than at Caernarvon, where the supposed association of the locality with Christian Rome gave it a special importance in Edward's personal mythology. In 1283, just as work on the new castle began, the discovery was made at Caernarvon of what were thought to be the bones of Magnus Maximus, father of the first Christian emperor, Constantine. The next year, and

71 The Edwardian fortress at Harlech on its precipitous site which allowed little room for an outer bailey

certainly by design, Edward of Caernarvon, later Prince of Wales, was born there.

Much that might otherwise seem puzzling about Caernarvon is explained by these particular associations. Whereas Edward's other castles in Wales, including the later Beaumaris, were all characterized by the use of circular drum towers, the nearest parallel to the polygonal towers and distinctive banded masonry of Caernarvon is in the ancient fifth-century Theodosian land wall of Constantinople which Edward and his advisers would undoubtedly have attributed to the Emperor Constantine himself. Similarly the prominence at Caernarvon of the Eagle Tower, in addition to its more obvious imperial connotations, would have been owed to that desire, always so important in the continental castle, to equip the fortress with a building of especial dignity, appropriate to the rank of its occupant.

In point of fact, the accommodation in the Eagle Tower, with its great central apartments and its many finely vaulted octagonal and hexagonal wall-chambers including two chapels and a kitchen, was probably designed for Otto de Grandson, one of the king's most loyal Savoyard friends who had been in Edward's service since 1258 and who rose to be first justiciar of Wales. It had been Otto, so at least one story went, who had sucked the poison from the wound inflicted on Edward by an assassin in Syria; and Otto, although not as close to the king in later years as some others among the knights of his household, continued to serve him well.[3] As a Savoyard, moreover, he would have had much in common with the architect of Caernarvon, Master James of St George, whose surname derived from the palace at St Georges-d'Espéranche (Isère), similarly equipped with polygonal towers, which he had designed and built some years before for Count Philip of Savoy, the king's relative and long-time friend.[4] It is possible, indeed probable, that Edward himself had visited St Georges on his way back to England to claim his throne in the summer of 1273. And in all these ways Caernarvon stands out as an intensely personal building, reflecting the experience of the king's earlier years and the aspirations of his tenure of the crown.

72 The residential gatehouse at Harlech, viewed from the inner ward

73 Caernarvon, with Edward I's triple-turreted Eagle Tower (left); the polygonal towers and distinctive banded masonry of Caernarvon are thought to have been modelled on the fifth-century walls of Constantinople, with which the site was linked in legend

Caernarvon has all the characteristics of a great fortress of chivalry, and in that sense it looks forward to the castles of the later Middle Ages where display, even at the expense of military efficiency, might come to be of overriding importance. Nevertheless, as was always to be the case with Edward's castles, it was an instrument of war as well. Much ingenuity during the thirteenth century had gone into the development of multiple defences, especially of the castle gate and its approaches. And while Caernarvon's gatehouse is not, as at Harlech, the castle's most conspicuous feature, it is still a building of formidable complexity and strength. The so-called King's Gate at Caernarvon is a work of the second major building period at the castle, closely following the Welsh revolt of the autumn and winter of 1294–5 during which both castle and town had fallen bloodily to the rebels. Inevitably, it shows the over-reaction of a designer determined that a similar catastrophe should never be allowed to happen again. After the drawbridge, there are no fewer than five doors and six portcullises in the King's Gate, each section of the entrance corridor being commanded by arrow-loops in the side walls and 'murder holes' in the vaulting above.[5]

At Caernarvon, with the town laid out immediately to the north of the castle, there was no opportunity to elaborate the outer approaches such as had been done, for example, most effectively by the Hospitallers at Krak des Chevaliers and, more modestly, by Edward himself at Conway. Although the moat on this quarter was wide, there was no room for the barbican and strongly fortified stepped approach of

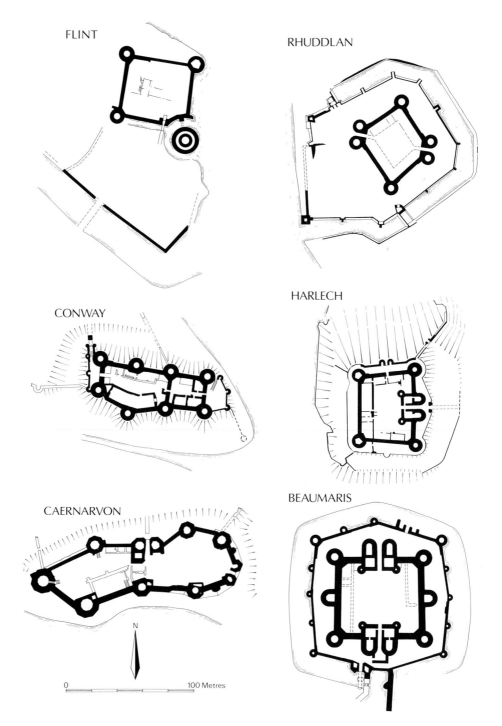

74 The major Edwardian castles in plan, demonstrating both the variety and the sophistication of their construction

Conway, nor did the level site of the castle and town at Caernarvon give any scope for the remarkable dog-legged ramp that prevented an assailant, by one defensive device after another, from reaching the main gate at Krak. When, however, Edward and his architect, shortly after the first outbreak of the Welsh rebellion in 1294, projected a new castle on Anglesey, north of Caernarvon and on the other side of the Menai Strait, they were able to select for themselves a fresh site altogether, with neither natural nor existing artificial obstacles to obstruct it. This fortress, to which Edward himself is thought to have given the name Beaumaris ('beautiful marsh'), has since frequently been described as the most perfect concentric castle of them all.

Beaumaris, with the war in Scotland to absorb Edward's energies and with other heavy expenditure in France, was never completely finished. The towers of the inner curtain wall were never taken to their full height, the southern gatehouse remained unfinished, and the projected great hall and other accommodation within the inner ward are unlikely even to have been begun. Yet the castle as we see it today is still an outstanding example of a unified single-period plan, put in operation by a king whose personal interest in the works brought him to stay at Beaumaris within a few months of their beginning, and supervised by an architect, Master James of St George, who had long practised his trade under the most enlightened and generous patronage, first at home in Savoy, until tempted to England in 1278, and then on Edward's many projects in Wales.[6]

For three years, until he joined Edward in Scotland in 1298, the building programme at Beaumaris was Master James's principal concern, and there is no doubt that the overall plan of the castle is his, as are many details of the work which dragged out over the rest of Edward's life and through much of the reign of his son. Master James had been the designer of Harlech Castle, of which for a term, from 1290 to 1293,

75 The unfinished castle at Beaumaris, seen from the air, with its great residential gatehouses to the left and right of the inner court

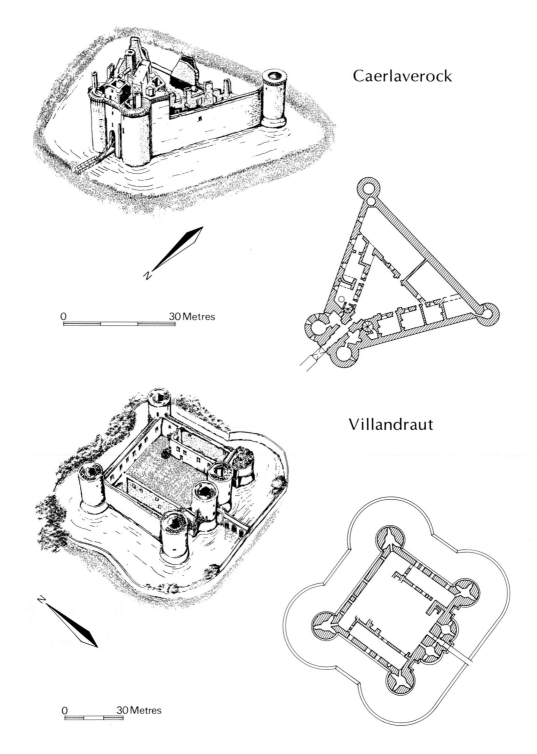

Caerlaverock

Villandraut

76 Contemporary castles at Caerlaverock (Scotland) and Villandraut (France), both thought to have been influenced by Edwardian castle-building in North Wales

he had been constable, having his residence in the great gatehouse. And at Beaumaris, the gatehouse plan of Harlech is repeated almost exactly in the two massive gatehouses which, in the absence of a keep, were to serve as the principal strongpoints of the fortress. Symmetrically placed, opposite each other, in the north and south walls of the inner ward, the gatehouses at Beaumaris were the keys to a defensive system which began on the outside with a water-filled moat and which was immensely strengthened by the many-towered perimeter of the outer ward, octagonal in plan to allow for the greater projection of the central towers and gatehouses of the inner curtain wall. At first glance, the plan of Beaumaris is the purest geometry, each tower matched and complemented by another. But a further subtlety of the design, which breaks this symmetry, is the deliberate strengthening of the towers at the most exposed north-east and north-west angles of the perimeter with, most particularly, the off-setting of the gates in the outer curtain so that they were sited not in front of the inner ward's gatehouses but away in each case to one side. Any assailant of these outer gates, even if he succeeded in breaking through them, would have had to turn an awkward corner immediately to the right, under fire from the gatehouse towers. If he survived this far, he would have found himself confronted by a further barbican, with the serried doors and portcullises of the gatehouse beyond it, preventing any further penetration.[7]

77 The south-west angle tower and what remains of the adjoining curtain wall at Caerlaverock, with the gatehouse (centre) and a later domestic range (right), added in the 1630s

Beaumaris, clearly, is a classic of its kind, the final fruit of a rich experience that had come close to bankrupting the kingdom. Nor is there any doubt that Edward I's works in Wales attracted widespread interest among his contemporaries, constituting a notable step forward in the science of fortification and inspiring a legion of imitators. Villandraut (Guyenne), built in the early fourteenth century for Clement V, the first French pope at Avignon, is one of the castles thought to have been inspired by Edward's fortresses in Wales.[8] And there are castles throughout Western Europe, including Hanstein, in Germany, Marschlins, in Switzerland, and Muiden, in the Netherlands, which if less certainly influenced by Edward's fortifications, nevertheless embody many of the principles which Master James either would, or had already, put to such practical effect in Wales.[9] It is not at all clear whether it was the Scots who built Caerlaverock Castle (Dumfriesshire) against the English, or the English against the Scots. Yet the advanced design of a castle like this, whoever ultimately was responsible for it, is an important demonstration of the degree to which the best new ideas had taken hold, at least by the 1290s in the first flurry of Edward's Scottish campaign. Caerlaverock is triangular in plan, with a great double-towered keep-gatehouse at the apex of the triangle and with prominent drum towers at each of its basal angles. Around the whole, a water-filled moat was contained by an earth rampart or bank, constituting between them an outer line of defences in accord with the best concentric principles of the day.[10] In effect, Caerlaverock embodies almost all the design features of the Edwardian castle as these had evolved over nearly a generation of continuous castle-building in Wales. It is rigidly geometric in plan; it employs concentric defences; it makes fully effective use of the angle tower; and it places the main defensive emphasis on the gatehouse (in earlier castles the most vulnerable point) which it develops, in the style of such fortresses as Harlech and Beaumaris, as residential accommodation for the lord.

If principles such as these could be so perfectly applied in Scotland at this date, it is all the more likely that they should have taken a firm hold in England wherever new

78 The fine late-thirteenth-century gatehouse, with twin drum towers, at Rockingham

79 The gatehouse and its stepped ramp approach to the barbican at Goodrich

work was called for, as they had already, of course, done in Wales. The exceptionally handsome surviving gatehouses of Rockingham (Northamptonshire) and Tonbridge (Kent) are both datable to the end of the thirteenth century, being part of contemporary modernizations of the defences. And if any English castle were to be put up or modified after this date, it would usually be the gatehouse that would be accorded particular attention. Certainly, this was to be the case at Goodrich Castle, in Herefordshire, one of the most remarkably complete late-thirteenth-century rebuildings of a private fortress, in which the king himself took an interest. Goodrich was a former Marshal castle which had come to William de Valence (d. 1296), the Poitevin half-brother of Henry III, on his marriage to Joan de Munchesney, a Marshal heiress, as early as 1247. William de Valence spent a life in the field, fighting in France, in Wales, and in the Holy Land, to which he accompanied Edward on crusade. And by the time he began the rebuilding at Goodrich, probably in the 1280s and 1290s, he would have accumulated an experience of military architecture scarcely excelled by the king, his long-time friend and companion-at-arms. Aymer de Valence (d. 1324), William's son and heir, was similarly a veteran of the less fortunate Scottish campaigns, with a good knowledge of military practice in France and in Flanders as well. Between them, they built a castle at Goodrich which became something of a model in its day.

Before the 1280s, Goodrich had already experienced at least a couple of major transformations. Originally an earthwork castle of the immediately post-Conquest

80 Carreg Cennen: the south-east corner of the inner ward and the precipitous approaches on this quarter

period, raised to protect a crossing of the River Wye, Goodrich had been equipped with a strong tower keep in the mid-twelfth century (later to survive all rebuildings) and with a stone curtain wall with angle towers perhaps a little over half a century later. It was the latter that was almost entirely rebuilt by the Valence earls of Pembroke, very probably with the advice of the royal masons and certainly with the practical support of Edward I himself in the form of grants of timber from his forest of Dean.

There are two clear stages in this rebuilding of Goodrich, the first being the completion of the inner ward, with the chapel tower and gatehouse in the north-east corner, with handsome drum towers on square spurred bases at each of the other angles, and with further comfortable accommodation, including a great hall and solar block, against the inner face of the curtain wall. Later, but not very much so, an elaborate barbican and an outer ward (on the north and west faces of the castle, where the lie of the land allowed it) were added to this, making the castle approaches at Goodrich among the most complex of their time.

Even before the addition of the outer barbican, the gatehouse at Goodrich was already a formidable obstacle. Its unusually long vaulted gatehall was equipped with two sets of gates, portcullises, and murder holes, being commanded also by arrow-loops in the walls on either side. Joined to the barbican by a narrow sloping causeway, bridging the moat and itself interrupted by a drawbridge, the gatehouse was then further protected by another gate and drawbridge, set at right angles to the first, which the attacker would have had to negotiate under fire from the chapel

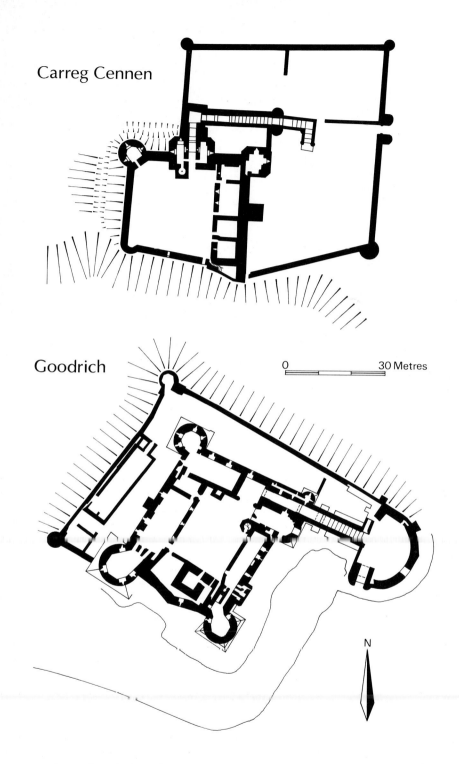

Carreg Cennen

Goodrich

0   30 Metres

N

81   Carreg Cennen and Goodrich in plan, to show the use made in each case of a naturally defendable site and the elaboration of gatehouses and barbicans characteristic of the period

tower. Approaching from the north and west, the besieger would have been confronted by the steep slope down to the River Wye, as well as by the defences (overlooked by the inner curtain) of the outer ward on these quarters. On the south and east, he would have met a broad rock-cut moat. Either way, as the castle's Valence builders had made doubly sure, he could not have gained entrance lightly.[11]

This further thinking out of the defences as work proceeded and as military expertise flowered in the hot-house atmosphere of the Welsh wars, may be illustrated also at a lesser castle like Carreg Cennen (Carmarthenshire), captured from the Welsh in Edward's first campaign and subsequently entirely rebuilt by the John Giffards, father and son, both of them veteran soldiers. John Giffard the elder (d. 1299), Baron Giffard of Bromsfield, had gained his experience initially in the Welsh wars of Henry III's reign, in the baronial revolt of 1264–5, and in Edward I's earlier Welsh campaigns. But he fought also in Gascony and in Scotland, taking a prominent part in each of Edward's many wars, and was widely known as a valiant and skilful soldier. It was either this John Giffard or Edward himself, when the castle was briefly in the crown's hands following its recapture by the Welsh in the rising of 1286, who must have undertaken the rebuilding of the inner ward at Carreg Cennen, strengthening the curtain wall with prominent towers at its more vulnerable north-west and north-east angles, and placing a typically Edwardian double-towered gatehouse midway along the same north wall.

There is nothing doctrinaire about the planning of Carreg Cennen. No tower is the same as another at the castle, and the overall plan has clearly been determined by the irregular and precipitous site. Thus when further improvements were projected for the castle, it was the peculiar characteristics of the site again which suggested where they should lie. Most sophisticated of these was the addition of a stepped ramp barbican, breaking the rush of an assailant with two left-hand corners and halting him twice before raised drawbridges which would have blocked the ramp altogether. A third drawbridge protected the main gate, with a portcullis and door behind it, and with arrow slits commanding the gatehouse passage from the guard-rooms on either side. Identical in principle with the barbican at Goodrich, Carreg Cennen's approach had been made so difficult that no besieger would have attempted to gain admittance that way. Accordingly, all that remained to be done at either castle was to supply an outer defensive line on the most threatened quarters—at Goodrich (as we have seen) on the north and west, at Carreg Cennen similarly but on the north and east where the land, although sloping, was not as precipitous as it was on the west and the south.[12] Neither regular in plan nor fully concentric, Carreg Cennen, because of the natural defensibility of the site, was as impregnable as if it were both.

Carreg Cennen, in its sensitive exploitation of the site and in the successive improvements then made there, exemplifies the high professionalism of the Edwardian castle-builder in making the best use of whatever natural advantages might assist him. However, there was little or nothing of the original Welsh fortress preserved at Carreg Cennen, and an even more striking example of Edwardian adaptability is the castle at Criccieth (Caernarvonshire), on Tremadoc Bay, where the fortifications of the last princes of North Wales were incorporated entire in the castle of their conqueror, enclosing it in a ready-made outer bailey. Here the solution of the king's mason—probably William of Drogheda who was contemporaneously at work on Harlech Castle just the other side of the bay—was both simple and entirely

82 Criccieth from the air, with the outline of the original Welsh castle on the site surrounding the Edwardian inner ward which it then came to serve as a bailey

effective. The twin-towered gatehouse of Harlech, although without its rear residential building and on an altogether less impressive scale, was re-used at Criccieth as the principal strongpoint of a new inner ward, sharing the line of the earlier Welsh defences only on the eastern side where the land dropped down sharply towards the sea. The great gatehouse faced the town (one of Edward's new English boroughs), which it still overshadows and dominates. But it was set, ingeniously, on the side of the castle furthest from the original main gate, still the only entrance to the outer ward, thus improvising economically a long and tortuous approach under fire from the high inner curtain. A concentrically planned castle, with an impregnable gatehouse, had thus been achieved with speed and at minimum cost.[13]

If there was something at Criccieth more costly than it need have been, that was, of course, the lofty gatehouse which had also to do duty as a symbol of Englishness and as a gesture of reassurance to the townspeople below. There are traces at Criccieth of the white plaster which formerly coated the walls of the entire inner ward and which, as at Conway (above, p. 71) and at White Castle (Monmouthshire), getting its name for this reason,[14] made the fortress stand out boldly in an alien land, a pledge of Edward's intention to remain there. Such a purpose for the castle, well understood in all ages, was not one that could be met by a building, however militarily effective, that failed to make its presence immediately obvious. The plastering and painting of the Edwardian castle, the carved figures and pinnacles that ornamented its battlements, the turrets and the many flags and banners on its towers—all these had

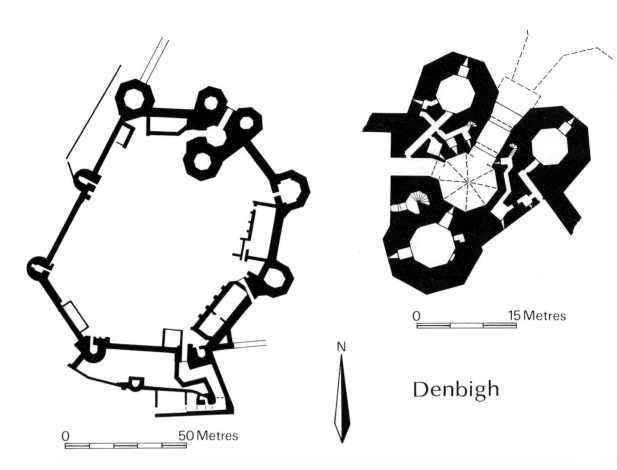

83 The gatehouse at Denbigh, seen in the context (left) of the rest of the castle, which it dominated

their function in establishing a presence, whether it was military or social reasons that were uppermost. And just as the keep in earlier days had done service as a symbol of lordship, this role would be transferred in the Edwardian castle to the towers and associated lodgings of the great gatehouse.

One of the most remarkable of these gatehouses, and still the outstanding feature of the castle, is the triple-towered gatehouse at Denbigh, in North Wales, built for Henry de Lacy (d. 1311), earl of Lincoln, very probably to the design of Master James of St George. For many years Henry de Lacy had been a close associate and counsellor of Edward I, and as one of the king's principal commanders in the first Welsh campaigns it is not surprising that he should have been granted the lordship of Denbigh in 1282, soon after the Welsh fortress was captured, nor that the king should have lent him his best architects and masons to ensure that the works made good progress. In the event, Earl Henry's many other preoccupations and the shifting focus of the king's wars away from Wales were to leave Denbigh Castle unfinished. But enough was completed to show the deliberate dominance accorded to the gatehouse in the overall master-plan of the fortress, and it was here and in the polygonal towers and banded masonry of the parts of the castle facing the new borough of Denbigh that the hand of Master James of St George (architect of the somewhat similar Caernarvon) is most obvious. The gatehouse, certainly, was a highly sophisticated building, in which the three octagonal towers—two at the front and one within the great courtyard at the rear—enclose a similarly multangular gatehouse hall with an oblique exit out into the main body of the castle. All the usual defensive devices (two portcullises, two doors, and murder holes) were employed in the gatehouse passage, but the most original feature of the building must always have been the gatehouse hall itself, vaulted over and with another great chamber of identical plan above it. A good indication of the attention given to detail in a building of this class is the careful planning of the garderobe shutes in the north-west tower, five of which are brought together at a common cesspit into which rainwater from the roof also feeds. Other professional touches are the arrow loops contrived to command the gatehouse hall from the adjoining chambers, and the passages built into the thickness of the walls to allow access from the upper storeys of the gatehouse to the fighting platforms of the curtain on either side of it.[15]

Significantly enough, when Henry of Lancaster's marriage to Matilda de Chaworth in 1298 brought Kidwelly (Carmarthenshire) securely into the hands of one of the richest baronial families in England, an important element in the modernization of the castle, in addition to a complete re-modelling of the accommodation in the inner ward, was the beginning of a great gatehouse at the southern end of the new outer enclosure—work that was not completed until the early fifteenth century but which was clearly projected much earlier. In the previous generation Payn de Chaworth, Matilda's uncle, had already begun the rebuilding of Kidwelly in the mid-1270s, shortly after returning with his brother Patrick from Edward's crusade. And the

84 Kidwelly: built originally by Payn de Chaworth as a four-square castle with drum towers at the corners and subsequently extended in the next generation by Henry of Lancaster, converting it into a castle of concentric plan by the addition of an outer curtain wall

symmetrical planning of the square inner ward, with its four great drum towers at the angles, is very much in keeping with other castle architecture of the period, including the king's own castles at Flint and Rhuddlan, at least partly inspired by the fortresses they had all seen in the East. What Henry of Lancaster now added to Kidwelly was an outer ward on all but the eastern side of the castle, well protected by a steep scarp down to the River Gwendraeth, which his own military experience in the wars in Flanders and Scotland had probably persuaded him was necessary. As largely completed before the onset of Henry's blindness and his retirement from active public life in the 1330s, Kidwelly was a major fortress of concentric plan, strongly protected by the multiple defences of its steep moat and bank, with the outer curtain wall of the Lancastrian modernization, and with its central core in Payn de Chaworth's keepless inner ward. But what is especially interesting about the Lancastrian castle at Kidwelly is the emphasis that was placed, in the absence of a keep, on the building up of the great gatehouse to the south. Of course, much of that gatehouse as we see it today is the work not of Henry of Lancaster but of the first Lancastrian kings—Henry IV and Henry V.[16] Nevertheless, there is a clear distinction, which must have been there from the beginning, between the relatively insignificant gatehouse at the north end of the enclosure, away from the town, and the very much more impressive residential gatehouse which straddled the castle's main entry to the south. Quite obviously, an important purpose of a building of this kind was to overawe at least as much as to protect.

Nowhere, of course, was this purpose more successfully achieved than at Caerphilly (Glamorgan), the greatest of all the Marcher fortresses of South Wales and one of the most remarkable defensive complexes ever completed by an individual patron in the Middle Ages. There were to be at least two stages in the building of Caerphilly, but the entire fortress has a unity of design which marks it out as the work of Gilbert de Clare (1243–95), called 'the Red', who succeeded to the great

85 Kenilworth in the setting of its formerly water-filled mere (to the left and in the foreground)

86 The north platform at Caerphilly, a fortified dam holding back the waters of the north lake

Gloucester inheritance in 1262 and to a fortune surpassed only, among the magnates of England, by those of the earls of Cornwall and of Lancaster, both of them allied to the crown. At Caerphilly, begun as early as 1271 before Edward returned from his crusade, the water defences are comparable to those at Simon de Montfort's castle at Kenilworth (Warwickshire), at the siege of which in 1266 Gilbert himself had been present. And it is most likely that Earl Gilbert's experience of that siege, in which Kenilworth's mere (now drained) had played an important part in the defence, was what determined him to spend as much as he did on achieving the same effect in Glamorgan. Caerphilly's extraordinary east front, which gives such an impression of power and impregnability to the castle's main gate on that quarter, in fact defends the dam which holds the waters of the moat in place. It seems to represent a re-thinking of the character of these defences and to be the concluding stage in the laying out of the fortress as a whole.[17]

Caerphilly was a castle without a keep. However, it developed instead—as the majority of the succeeding Edwardian castles would do—concentric defence and the reinforcement by every known device of the gatehouse. At Caerphilly, behind the already impressive screen of the fortified fighting platforms on the great dam, the castle is entered by a lesser gatehouse in the outer ward, slightly offset (although probably with no deliberate defensive purpose) from the eastern gatehouse of the inner ward which is the major individual strongpoint of the castle. An early example of the keep-gatehouse principle of defence, this building has an entrance passage closed at either end with a portcullis and door, being just as capable of being held against assault from the castle courtyard as against a besieger from outside. As at Dover, completed not so many years before and certainly known to Earl Gilbert, the

87 Caerphilly from the air, showing Earl Gilbert's great castle of concentric plan and the exceptional strength of its water defences

main gatehouse at Caerphilly was probably intended as the quarters of the constable of the castle. It had a fine well-lit chamber with adjoining chapel on the second floor, the whole comfortably clear of the portcullis apparatus which, on the first floor, had risen inconveniently through either end of the central chamber of the three apartments on that level.

Plainly, one purpose behind the height of the gatehouse at Caerphilly was to enable its defenders to overlook the outer defences, commanding the exposed and undefended back of the wide south platform, as well as the whole outer ward on that quarter. And it was the full development of this scheme of concentric defence on every side of the castle's inner core that has made Caerphilly, in one expert view, a 'concentric fortress fully worthy to be compared with Edward I's Beaumaris'.[18] However, it must not be thought that because such principles of fortification were known to all contemporaries with a professional interest in military engineering, it was open to many to apply them. Caerphilly is an exception not merely in its architecture but in the circumstances that had brought it into being. As lord of Glamorgan, Gilbert the Red was no ordinary magnate. He was privileged to operate under the law of the March, one of the freedoms of which was to build castles without licence (above, p. 15), another to wage private war. Earl Gilbert, in point of fact, was to tangle directly with Edward I on the second of these rights, and was not to come out of the struggle unscathed. However, whatever Edward may have thought of the building of Caerphilly—and he cannot have viewed it with anything but grave suspicion—there was nothing he could do to halt a project for which both the means and the right were available. Between a third and a half of Earl Gilbert's great revenues derived from Wales, the better part of this from his lands in Glamorgan.

Feeling threatened there by the prospect of a Welsh uprising, one of which was later to drive him from his estates in the very last year of his life, he was equally uncertain of the affections of the king, having made it his business after the baronial rebellion to promote the restoration of the lands of the disinherited, formerly supporters of Simon de Montfort. In Earl Gilbert, then, there was a conjunction of circumstances rare in medieval England. He had the wealth, the right, and the motives to build: one consequence of all these being Caerphilly.[19]

Chapter 5

Castles of Law and Order

When Gilbert the Red's Welsh tenants rose against him in 1294–5, there were obviously special reasons for their unhappiness. Nevertheless, the earl of Gloucester's troubles in the 1290s were not unique. Property-holders everywhere, not only in Wales, had come to feel themselves at risk by the end of the century. Over the next half century, for many different reasons, the pace of disorder would quicken.

In general terms, the expansion of the economy which until then had characterized the century had come to a halt before the end of it. There were still those, like the Clares themselves, who continued to grow in wealth. But over-population, while it suited the great landowner with a need for cheap labour, was bringing further destitution to the poor, and there are many signs on individual estates of the profound discontents this would arouse. No single explanation can account for the peasant risings that are recorded with increasing frequency in the later thirteenth century, and indeed many of these were clearly inspired as much by prosperity and by an increasing resentment of unwarranted privilege as by the hopeless rage of the destitute.[1] Nevertheless it must have been obvious to men of means before 1300 that the peace they had grown accustomed to in their own generation, and that dated back at least as far as the tightening of royal administration under King John, was not going to see out their lifetimes. Applications from them for licences to crenellate—in effect, to fortify their houses—were coming in to the king in increasing numbers from the mid-thirteenth century and would multiply still further in the next decades. Moreover, those who applied for such licences were not drawn exclusively from the magnate and baronial families, many of whom already had their castles, but from the property-owning sector as a whole.[2]

Taken on their own, of course, licences to crenellate would hardly serve as a satisfactory indicator of the effect of the new anxieties. The habit of applying for licences of this kind, and the king's practice in recording them, could both be comparatively late developments. Nor would landowners, as we shall see in the next chapter, always apply for a licence to crenellate primarily for reasons of defence. Nevertheless there is much other evidence, alongside the rising tide of such licences, to suggest a breakdown of the law and a deterioration of public order at the turn of the thirteenth and fourteenth centuries. And one of the most obvious causes of the crisis, as we see it, was the militaristic policy of the king.

Money values have changed so staggeringly since that time that it is not especially helpful—and may even be misleading—to cite figures for Edward I's expenditure on his castles in Wales and for the campaigns that led to their construction.[3] But it is certainly true that Edward's continual wars in Wales, in English-held Gascony, and in Scotland were to cost the crown many years of its revenues, and this in a kingdom

88 A besieging force conducts an assault on a town; French, 1450–1500

that was reputed at the time to be among the wealthiest and most financially secure in Christendom. Very probably, Edward's own revenues, which were much larger than his father's had been, could have borne the full cost of the once-for-always conquest of Wales.[4] However, it was the extension of the war into France and Scotland in the 1290s that not only brought Edward himself to the serious crisis of 1297–8 but committed his kingdom over the better part of two centuries to a policy of intervention beyond its borders that continued to cost it dear. The heavy subsidies to foreign allies with which Edward planned to bring France down, more costly by far even than his castles had been, had to be raised by home taxation—a six-fold rise in the export tax on wool in the *maltolt* of 1294, the exorbitant clerical subsidy of that same year, and a quickening pulse of taxation and requisitions of every kind, beginning to bite at about this time and reaching especially oppressive levels in the

89 The siege of a castle: Italian, *circa* 1460

reign of Edward's grandson in the 1330s at the opening of the Hundred Years War.[5] Datable to about 1338, the poem *Against the King's Taxes* is a contemporary lament, in a learned mixture of French and Latin, concerning the oppressions especially of the poor. It was the poet's view that—'Whoever caused him [Edward III] to cross the seas brought great ills and grievous ruin on him.' The taxation of movable goods had hitherto been an occasional impost only, but—'Now the fifteenth runs in England year after year, thus doing harm to all; by it those who were wont to sit upon the bench have come down in the world; and common folk must sell their cows, their utensils, and even clothing. It is ill-pleasing thus to pay the fifteenth to the uttermost farthing.' Furthermore, dishonest tax-gatherers had laid hands on the receipts, so that 'not half the tribute raised in the land reaches the king', nor had the king's advisers—for the king himself was not to blame, being only 'a young knight and not of an age to compass any trickery'—sought to obtain the money from those who could best afford it : 'It does not hurt the great thus to make the king a grant ; the lowly have to give all, against the will of God.' Surely, the poet argues, 'An impost like this can by no means last for long. Who can give out of emptiness or handle [what is not there]? The people are in such an ill plight that they have nothing more to give. Had they but a leader, I doubt there might be a rising. Loss of possessions often makes people foolish.'[6]

The rising, of course, failed to happen; or at least it had to wait another half-century until 1381 when a suitable leader was indeed then found in Wat Tyler. But there were tax strikes contemporaneously in several different regions of England, and there were others besides the poet to share his forebodings about trouble, including very probably the king's advisers.[7] Taxes were not the only grievance, and there were many who might have felt even graver misgivings about the intensifying climate of violence. Again the king's wars, although not exclusively to blame, had a great deal to do with the disorders.

Recruitment for the king's armies had never been easy, and in 1294 (the same year as the *maltolt* and the clerical subsidy) a dangerous precedent was set in the first proclamation of a pardon—or at any rate the prospect of a pardon—for offenders prepared to serve in the proposed Gascon campaign. Soon afterwards, the same promise was being made to recruits for Wales and for Scotland, with the result that service in Edward's armies came quickly to be recognized by criminals of all kinds, including murderers, as the best way to escape the consequences of their crimes.[8] In effect, the government that had set out at the beginning of Edward's reign to restore the law and to reform many acknowledged abuses, had now reversed its policies in the interest of the wars and was itself pointing the way to a new chaos. Such former outlaws and criminals as returned from the campaigns, hardened in violence by their experience, might have old scores to pay off and would certainly have had problems in re-establishing themselves peacefully in the communities that had been glad to be rid of them. Complaints of disorder, always to be heard in medieval England, rose to a crescendo at the end of the thirteenth century and afterwards took many decades to die down. These were the years, most particularly in the first decades of the fourteenth century, of the criminal gangs and of the birth of the legend of Robin Hood.[9] And this was the time too of the many experiments in local law-enforcement which began with the issue of special commissions of *oyer* and *terminer* (including the trailbastons after 1305) to 'hear' and 'determine' cases of violence and other felonies, and which developed into the justices of the peace.[10] 'Come to me, to the green forest,' sang the outlaw in the contemporary *Song of Trailbaston*, 'for the common law is too uncertain.' There, at least, there would be 'no annoyance but only wild animals and beautiful shade.'[11]

The uncertainty of the common law, of which the outlaw complained, had much to do with the notorious corruption of justice among the great.[12] But its principal cause must surely have been a swamping of the courts at all levels of their operation by misdemeanours and felonies of every kind, to the almost total destruction of the system. The old organization of watches and tithings, heavily dependent on the stability of communities where every man's neighbour was his policeman and informer, had come increasingly under strain as the growth of population throughout the thirteenth century had created a large class of vagrants. It was strangers who were named particularly as the criminals at the Bedford circuit court (eyre) of 1287, and it was strangers very often who must certainly have been responsible for the 'robberies, murders, burnings' which the drafters of the Statute of Westminster in 1285 considered to be 'more often committed than they have been heretofore'.[13] By 1300, felonies were said again to have increased 'immeasurably'.[14] And nothing that was to happen in the next half-century would do anything to restore order as before. A particularly serious inflation, early in the century, was to be followed disastrously by catastrophically bad harvests in 1315 and 1316, by another harvest failure in 1321, and by a series of livestock murrains.[15] In these conditions, crime followed almost exactly in the footsteps of price increases, surging as prices were forced up by scarcity, and falling as plenty returned.[16] The wars of Edward I, continued in Scotland under Edward II and exacerbated by internal disorders, frequently presented the opportunities for outbreaks of violence for which the ground was already well prepared.

Not least among the failures of Edward II as a monarch was his inability to check successfully the inclination of his magnates to resort to self-help in a crisis. In the previous reign, many had learnt to protect themselves and their estates against the assaults of the Welsh and the Scots. Indentures, or contracts, had been issued to knights, committing them to bring troops to their lord's support, sometimes in return for a money fee and occasionally, in the case of a more permanent agreement, in exchange for a grant of lands.[17] Retinues had become swollen, so that a magnate like Gilbert the Red might travel with a household of as many as two hundred if required by the occasion to demonstrate his wealth, always having his smaller war retinue of knights and bachelors to accompany him on campaign or to a tournament.[18] While the king was strong, little danger might result from the development of practices such as these. However, the mounting disorders of Edward I's later years and his single-minded pursuit of his war aims left his son with a legacy of baronial discontent and with a clutch of over-mighty subjects. It would have needed a much abler man than Edward of Caernarvon proved to be to restore the balance in favour of the crown.

One of those who, later in his life, took Edward II's part against Thomas of Lancaster, the king's most dangerous opponent, was Aymer de Valence (d. 1324), earl of Pembroke and the rebuilder, with his father, of Goodrich Castle (above, pp. 79–82). But Aymer, too, had been a leader of the baronial opposition to the king's former playmate and jumped-up Gascon favourite, Piers Gaveston, and what had made the magnates powerful enough to engineer Gaveston's fall was not any moral hold they might have had over the king but the naked force of the army they could cooperatively field. In war, the earl of Pembroke's retinue could rise to the 124 knights and men-at-arms he fielded for the king in 1315. Even in peace, he retained a permanent establishment of indentured knights seldom less than fifteen to twenty strong.[19] They were not, even under Pembroke's relatively responsible lordship, an easy group to control. Pembroke himself, towards the end of his life, became engaged in a particularly costly and unsatisfactory feud with the Berkeleys of Gloucestershire, formerly of his own retinue. His principal retainer and long-term man of business, William de Cleydon, seems also to have been, perhaps with Pembroke's connivance and certainly under his protection, a notoriously malevolent bully.[20]

These men, although normally resident on their own estates, might have had to be accommodated at any time in the household of the magnate who retained them.

90 Aymer de Valence's castle at Goodrich: both fortress and palace, with many suites of lodgings for the earl's retinue

Pembroke's lands were widely scattered, with a large concentration of manors in East Anglia and in the home counties, and with other important Gloucestershire holdings, as well as his estates in Hereford and South Wales. When he brought his retinue together at Goodrich, at a convenient half-way point between some of his major interests, many of the men who would have answered his call must have travelled a long way to get there. Thus at Goodrich there would have had to be more than the one hall of the lord and his family, including accommodation of considerable quality. Just as had already been the case at Roger Bigod's Chepstow (above, pp. 59–61), the accommodation at Goodrich had to be set out deliberately as a series of independent lodgings and suites. However here, at the later castle, advantage could be taken of the more complete rebuilding to arrange certain services in common. The chapel and great kitchen at Goodrich, both on the ground floor, are clearly intended to be communal. They are there for the benefit of the occupants of three separate hall-and-chamber blocks, all planned on a generous scale, with a further suite of first-floor hall, chamber, and attached garderobe, sited over the gate-passage and the chapel. Of these suites, the last was probably intended as the private accommodation of the constable, being the only man of high rank permanently resident at the castle. The three ground-floor halls, with their attached chambers in the adjoining corner towers, would have been shared out between the earl, his principal guests, and his

91 The dramatically sited castle at Dunstanburgh, built by Thomas of Lancaster as an estate centre in the North and as a potential retreat in times of need

retinue, each deserving to be housed in some state.[21] For a magnate of the wealth and standing of the earl of Pembroke, nothing less would have been considered appropriate.

In part, the maintenance of a great household was a demonstration of largesse, being an important element in the conspicuous consumption that was demanded of a magnate by his rank. But a large retinue might also be of some considerable political advantage. In the last years of the thirteenth century, Gilbert the Red, builder of Caerphilly, had been able to withstand the hostility of the king with the help of his loyal retainers. In very similar circumstances in the next generation, Thomas of Lancaster's inflated retinue was both his protection against the vengeance of Edward II and, in the end, his undoing.

Thomas, earl of Lancaster (d. 1322), grandson of Henry III, was the greatest nobleman of his day, with revenues at least twice as large as those of the great Clare inheritance and with a personal retinue which, in his final years, was fully equal to that of the king.[22] Hostile to Piers Gaveston from the beginning, he had been one of the principal agents of the favourite's downfall, for which Edward II never forgave him. And it was at least partly the poor welcome he could expect at court that kept him, exceptionally for a man of his rank, for long periods at home on his estates. To protect himself, as Gilbert the Red had done, Thomas of Lancaster became in his own time a great builder, spending lavishly on the many castles he owned in his major power-base, the north Midlands and south-central Yorkshire, and creating from nothing the impressive new fortress at Dunstanburgh, in Northumberland, to which he was on his way in 1322 when captured by the king's men at Boroughbridge. The circumstances of Dunstanburgh's building at this point make it a castle of particular interest, for it was the work of a man not only among the wealthiest of his time but also the most under threat.

Interestingly, Dunstanburgh is not in the least like Earl Gilbert's Caerphilly nor like any of the royal castles of that same generation which Edward I had similarly built up from nothing. It is not a concentric castle, although Thomas of Lancaster would certainly have known such castles well, and its principal feature is a massive keep-gatehouse, somewhat dwarfed by the great size of the enclosure. Such gatehouses, of course, had been a characteristic of many of the greater Edwardian fortresses. However, the best parallel to Dunstanburgh is probably the near-contemporary gatehouse of the Clare castle at Tonbridge (Kent), built for Gilbert de Clare the younger. Both are expensive and sophisticated buildings, and at both the main residential accommodation is lifted to an upper storey, away (as at Caerphilly) from the first-floor machinery of the portcullis.[23] The association of the lord's residence with the main point of defence had its obvious attractions, and although neither Dunstanburgh nor Tonbridge could compare in military effectiveness with a concentric fortress like Beaumaris, both provided a model which was more clearly attainable by the less wealthy castle-builders of the new century. In a comparatively short space of time, Thomas of Lancaster was able to build himself at Dunstanburgh an enclosure large enough to house his considerable private army, with his own personal residence controlling the gate at just the point where that enclosure was most vulnerable. A solution that had appealed to the first castle-builders in the more primitive gate-towers of Ludlow and of Richmond, was again being applied in a much later generation when the lord and his retinue, similarly beset, were re-exposed to some of the conditions of the Conquest.

92   The south curtain wall at Dunstanburgh, viewed from Earl Thomas's keep-gatehouse

Dunstanburgh was still unfinished in 1322, the year of the skirmish at Boroughbridge and of Thomas of Lancaster's execution for treason. However, its garrison that same year was already sufficiently large to supply sixty-eight horsemen for the king's invasion of Scotland. And although it was the king's constable, and not the late earl, who furnished these men, it had been precisely the extraordinary effort required of Lancaster's treasury to find the support for such soldiers that had converted the earl, despite his great wealth, into one of the most avaricious and unpopular of landowners. Lancaster's ambitious building programme, together with the mounting cost of his great retinue, had forced him to maximize the receipts from his estates just when his tenants were enduring the poor harvests, the famines, and the sheep and cattle murrains of the crisis years, 1315 to 1322. There are many examples of the oppressions of Lancaster's ministers. They ignored justice and overthrew existing rights in the interest of the earl, while some took advantage of Lancaster's prestige and military might to bully their way locally into private fortunes which were to endure a good deal longer than their patron.[24] Each new incident of violence and injustice contributed another element to the general insecurity of the times. With factional interests alive in the land, and with a king too weak to control them, each man's safety depended in the last resort on his ability to defend what he owned. He would build himself a castle if he felt he could afford it, or if that was expected of his rank. More commonly, he would raise himself a gatehouse and dig a moat.

One project in particular, characteristically mixing social with military

93   The residential keep-gatehouse at Tonbridge, as either built or re-modelled by Gilbert de Clare the younger (d. 1314)

94 Maxstoke: a rebuilding of the family manor-house by William de Clinton following his elevation, in 1337, to the earldom of Huntingdon

preoccupations, is indicative of these contemporary concerns. William de Clinton, created earl of Huntingdon in 1337 in recognition of his services to Edward III, obtained a licence to crenellate Maxstoke, his Warwickshire family home, in 1345, several years after he had started its rebuilding. With the other new earls of Salisbury, Suffolk and Northampton, similarly promoted in 1337, William de Clinton had received a substantial grant of lands from the crown to support him in a style appropriate to his rank.[25] And it was rank, revenues, and his own considerable military experience that determined the form that the new works at Maxstoke would assume. Laid out at one time and probably ready for its first occupants not later than 1344, Maxstoke perfectly demonstrates the contemporary taste for a fortified residence that was neither a castle in the conventional sense nor an open and undefended country manor-house. Planned symmetrically, it had strong octagonal towers at the four angles of the square, with an impressive three-storey gatehouse at the centre of its eastern side, standing forward from the curtain wall into the surrounding moat and approached originally over a drawbridge. For purposes of defence, it was this gatehouse, obviously, that had been planned as the hub of the fortifications. In it were the lodgings of the garrison, including two single-storey guardrooms, one on either side of the gate-passage, and separate suites of more comfortable accommodation on the first and second floors of the building, each with fireplaces, window-seats, and garderobes of its own, the lower having access to the wall-walk.

If the gatehouse held the constable and other members of the permanent garrison of Maxstoke, there was plentiful accommodation within the great court for the earl, for his guests, and for the size of retinue that William de Clinton had now to support

95 The great gatehouse at Maxstoke, being the castle's principal point of defence

as one of the more essential badges of his status. With the exception of the common accommodation of the great hall, the chapel, and the kitchen, Maxstoke was divided internally into many separate lodgings: those of the earl and of his principal guests occupying the north-west corner, well away from the main gate, while further lodgings of varying quality, very probably accompanied by another lesser hall in the east range to the north of the gate, either lined the inner face of the curtain wall or filled the vacant towers at the angles.[26] The outstanding characteristic of almost all the accommodation at Maxstoke, with the exception only of the east range, is the quality of its finish and the great comfort of the total ensemble. Maxstoke was the country retreat of a man who, unlike Thomas of Lancaster, felt himself secure in the affections of the king. If he thought it necessary to fortify his manor-house, it was partly because his status demanded such crenellation but also—and even more so—because the violence and the lawlessness endemic in his times had made such precautions no more than prudent.

To a limited extent, the earl of Huntingdon's desire to improve his life-style was shared by others of lesser rank, similarly wishing to rise in the world. But status-seeking alone on the part of the builders would be an inadequate explanation for the rash of crenellation and other fortifying works that was especially characteristic of this period. It is not, certainly, that moats and their equivalent elementary defences were unknown in previous generations, even at a relatively low level in society. In regions of tension like the Welsh Marches they had always had their purpose, and the ditching and fencing of new enclosures, in particular the homestead itself, was a perfectly natural—indeed inevitable—accompaniment of any thirteenth-century attempt to push back the limits of the forest. However, there is a growing bulk of evidence for an intensification of the fortifying drive as crime itself increased towards the end of the century, and this was to be as true of formerly unthreatened areas as it continued to be of Wales or of the fringes of the outlaw-ridden forests.

Dating a moated site is not easy. Nevertheless, such moated sites as have so far yielded satisfactory dating evidence to the archaeologists have almost all been datable to a relatively restricted period at the turn of the thirteenth and fourteenth centuries, just when violence was at its most unmanageable—when the traditional legal system had largely broken down, when the king's taxes had reached unprecedented levels of extortion, when the harvests were poor and the animals were sick, when bubonic plague had not yet pruned the excess of population over resources, and when an alternative system of law and order in the localities, administered by men of property (the justices of the peace), was still on the other side of the horizon.[27]

Clearly, if the small farmer and freeholder, with very little to protect, still found it worth his while to undertake the labour and expense of moat-digging, only the most improvident of the larger property-holders would have neglected to do the same, very probably taking it one better. We know, for example, that whereas the manor-house at Glottenham (Sussex) had always had its defences, with some form of moat dating from the eleventh century or perhaps before, it was not until the troubled decades of the early fourteenth century that the fortifications were extensively remodelled. At that time, a strong curtain wall was built within the moat at

96 Stokesay Castle: the fortified manor-house of a Ludlow clothier, formerly protected by water defences but strengthened especially, in Lawrence of Ludlow's time, by the addition of the great tower on the left

97 The late-thirteenth-century hall at Stokesay Castle

Glottenham, fortifying the inner platform, while the entrance was defended by a good gatehouse.[28]

Rather earlier, and perhaps in the context of the baronial rebellion, Roger de Somery had obtained a licence in 1264 to 'enclose with a ditch and a wall of stone and lime' his manor-house at Weoley, in Warwickshire. And although work may not have begun immediately on the transformation of the site, it was certainly within the next two generations at most that Weoley's lightly defended manor-house of less oppressive times, earlier in the century, was transformed into a minor fortress—its moat re-cut, a curtain wall built with interval towers on the raised internal platform, and the accommodation completely remodelled.[29]

One interesting surviving example of contemporary fortification on a manorial site is the massive square tower at Longthorpe, near Peterborough, built to adjoin an existing hall probably soon after 1300.[30] And it was an additional fortification very much of this kind, being another strong tower next to the pre-existing hall, that Lawrence of Ludlow built at Stokesay, in Shropshire, to give us what is certainly the most picturesque of all surviving fortified manor-houses of the period. Lawrence of Ludlow, a rich clothier well known to the king, obtained his licence to crenellate Stokesay in 1291, and it was this that enabled him to build the south tower and to give his manor-house at least the appearance of a castle. But the great external windows of the hall at Stokesay betray what was always its purpose. Lawrence of Ludlow was a man of peace, a financier rather than a soldier. It is surely unlikely that he would have had much stomach for military adventure, nor can he ever have intended his manor-house at Stokesay to stand siege or resist a large force. Stokesay was a house 'such as thieves must knock at ere they enter'—nothing more.[31]

Over the next two centuries, as the lawlessness that had brought about the improvised defences of Longthorpe and Stokesay refused to slacken, the fortified manor-house became more standardized in plan, usually developing as one or more enclosed quadrangles with a primary emphasis, as at Maxstoke, on the gatehouse. But how, in these first years, the response could still vary is best seen in the quite contrary experience of two very different buildings, at Acton Burnell (Shropshire) and Weobley (Glamorgan), both now described rather deceptively as 'castles' and both directly contemporary with Lawrence of Ludlow's Stokesay.

If Acton Burnell was ever systematically fortified beyond its central surviving building, nothing now remains of these defences. However, Chancellor Burnell, when he secured a licence in 1284 to crenellate a new mansion at his birthplace, clearly intended fortifications of some kind there. And, sure enough, the manor-house itself was to have its crenellations, with square turrets at each of the four corners of the building, one of them extended into a chapel. There are individual peculiarities of plan at Acton Burnell, most of them attributable to the special needs of Robert Burnell as Chancellor of England, with many suitors constantly in attendance, and as bishop (since 1275) of Bath and Wells, a preferment which he owed, like the chancellorship itself, to the friendship and trust of Edward I. No doubt the support of the king was enough to reassure the bishop about his personal security. And what he seems to have found adequate for his purpose was a building that relied entirely on its outward appearance for whatever military quality it possessed. Acton Burnell's most private quarter was the bishop's own suite on the third stage of the building, on the west side over the great chamber. Yet it was only

98 Acton Burnell: built in the 1280s for Chancellor Burnell as a palatial manor-house with scarcely more than token defences

from here that access could be gained to the wall-walk behind the crenellations. The several doors and generous windows of the ground floor of the manor-house, although dwarfed by the openings of the principal apartments above them, could never have been adapted for defence.[32]

More conventional in its plan, more militarily effective, and certainly more typical of the kind of building likely to have been put up in the period, was the 'castle' at Weobley, on the north coast of the Gower Peninsula. Weobley was raised, probably for a member of the de la Bere family, in no more than two building campaigns at the turn of the thirteenth and the fourteenth centuries when the threat of rebellion, although later revived, was not strongly felt in South Wales. Planned on a relatively small scale, it was a tight group of buildings with a strong tower, originally perhaps free-standing and now largely ruined, at the south-west corner of the central courtyard. To the north of the tower was the gate-passage, lacking most of the sophistications of the gatehouses of this period and closed only by a pair of stout doors. Internally, the main residential accommodation at Weobley—including a solar, a hall, a guest-chamber, and a chapel—was on the first floor, giving one extra element of security to the lord's family. On the ground floor, there were a number of stores and guardrooms supporting these apartments, with a great kitchen underlying the hall. Although impressive enough in its block-house appearance, Weobley was not so much a castle as a fortified manor-house, which is how it was described in 1410 shortly after its capture and slighting by the Welsh.[33] It would have relied for its strength largely on the south-west tower and on turning a blank face to the world. Otherwise the main emphasis of its builders had been quite consciously directed towards improving the comforts and amenities of their home.

It is this emphasis again that is most obvious at Llawhaden, the fortified manor-house (now called the 'castle') of the bishops of St David's, Pembrokeshire.

Llawhaden is not very far from Weobley, being some way inland on the other side of Carmarthen Bay, and there are many similarities in their plans. The buildings, certainly, are exactly contemporary. They are designed in each case to surround a central courtyard, and at neither was the gatehouse of exceptional importance, at least until its late-fourteenth-century rebuilding at Llawhaden. However, where they differ most particularly is in scale. The bishop of St David's household, although not so specialized as Chancellor Robert Burnell's, had its own individual requirements. With the buildings used in common—the hall, the kitchen, and the chapel—the bishop had his own very substantial private apartment at the upper, or east, end of the hall at Llawhaden. There was a chamber, with fireplace and garderobe, in the octagonal tower next to the chapel, clearly designed for the chaplain, with another chamber similarly equipped above it. Over the chapel porch, small rooms were probably intended for an archive store and writing office. Four comfortable suites or lodgings, each with an attached bedchamber and garderobe, lined the curtain wall between the chapel, on the east, and the gatehouse. They would have been used by the more important officers of the household, and could have been made available also to guests.[34]

It was either Thomas Bek, bishop from 1280 to 1293, or his successor David Martin (1296–1328) who rebuilt Llawhaden, placing such importance on the standard of the new buildings that all earlier work on the site was cleared to make room for them, the western rampart being then built over and many extensions made over the moat. Nor could the two bishops have afforded to build less if they had wished to maintain the high standing of the office that they held. Thomas Bek, under whom the fortunes of

99   The fortified manor-house at Weobley, built in the early fourteenth century for a local gentry family

St David's had revived, was himself a man of great personal wealth, a former lord treasurer and keeper of the great seal, and the elder brother of Antony Bek (d. 1310), bishop of Durham and patriarch of Jerusalem, the most splendid among the princes of the Church.

Both brothers were builders, but it was Antony, above all, who stood out in his generation as a patron without equal of new works. One of these projects was the castle at Somerton (Lincolnshire)—moated and equipped with drum towers at each angle in the common style of its day—which he built, following the licence to crenellate of 1281, on the estate which he had inherited from his mother.[35] Another was his palace at Bishop Auckland, near Durham, transformed by Antony Bek into a castle. Yet a third was the conversion of the manor-house at Eltham, just to the south-east of London, into the great moated and fortified palace of which he gave the reversion to Edward of Caernarvon and which then came to the crown on his death. Queen Isabella, not long after she took full possession of Eltham, had the moat-side wall buttressed and rebuilt, and there is little of Bek's work that is still recognizable at the palace today. Nevertheless, one at least of Bek's octagonal corner turrets has been revealed by excavations on the site, and there can be little doubt that both the scale and the actual form of the main moated enclosure at Eltham, although not its fifteenth-century outer court, are properly attributable to the bishop.[36] A fortified palace on this scale was characteristic of a man who, delighting in his wealth, conversed on equal terms with the kings, popes, and cardinals of his day. But it was also a reflection of the times. In the next generation Ralph of Shrewsbury, bishop of Bath and Wells (1329–63) and a successor of Robert Burnell, was to build himself a

100   Polygonal mural towers (right) at the bishop of St David's fortified manor-house at Llawhaden, with the gatehouse as rebuilt some decades later

moated and walled enclosure round his palace at Wells as a protection against his own citizens. It remains there still as one of the most remarkable witnesses to the strength of the divisions which, in the Church as elsewhere, rent fourteenth-century society.

101 The gatehouse and moat at Bishop Ralph of Shrewsbury's fortified episcopal palace at Wells

Chapter 6

Castles of the Hundred Years War

Edward III's claim to the French throne, repeated formally on 7 October 1337 as one of the opening salvoes of the Hundred Years War, was not, by the standards of his day, unreasonable. Charles IV's death in 1328, with no direct heir to succeed him, had brought the long-lasting Capetian dynasty to an end. And it had been the election of Charles's cousin, Philip of Valois, to the unexpectedly vacant throne that had deprived the young Edward of what he continued to regard as his rightful inheritance through his mother, Isabella of France, sister of the last Capetian king. Edward's deprivation was deeply felt. But the political complications, both on his own side of the water and in France, were formidable. His youth, his own succession problems, and the tutelage he endured under the evil regime of Isabella and Mortimer, all worked against him. It was almost ten years before Edward, provoked by Philip VI's intervention in Scotland and by his 'confiscation' of English-held Gascony, could revive the argument about the French succession, claiming quite correctly to have been Charles IV's nearest male heir—his nephew rather than (as was Philip) his cousin.

Of course, the real reason for the widening of the existing and continuous conflict with France was not the succession dispute on its own. However, the confrontation of two young and ambitious kings on this and on the other issues that divided them was to breathe new life into an old hostility, at the same time engaging the support of their aristocracies. The war with France, although not a popular war in the modern sense, was widely used on both sides of the Channel as the occasion for displays of national and chauvinistic sentiment. The English king's feelings about his 'most clear right', and the early spectacular victories of the war, opened the way in England for martial investment of an altogether new order on the part of both government and governed. Contemporaneously in France, the boom in castle-building of the later Middle Ages owed much of its drive to the English invasions, being deliberately fostered by the crown.[1]

One of the most obvious consequences of the renewal of the war, and in particular of the war at sea in which both sides were continually making themselves more expert, was the refurbishing of existing coastal defences and the building, more rarely, of new ones. Very early in the war, a French fleet in the summer and autumn of 1338 had terrorized the entire south coast of England, sacking Portsmouth and Southampton. And although the English naval victory at Sluys on 24 June 1340 temporarily lifted the threat, rumours of further raids became the common currency of the later, less successful decades of Edward III's reign, evoking a response in castle-building. It was in the 1360s and 1370s, under pressure from the king and with his help, that the town walls of Southampton were completed round their full circuit, closing the port's approaches from the sea. In the next reign, under Richard II, the

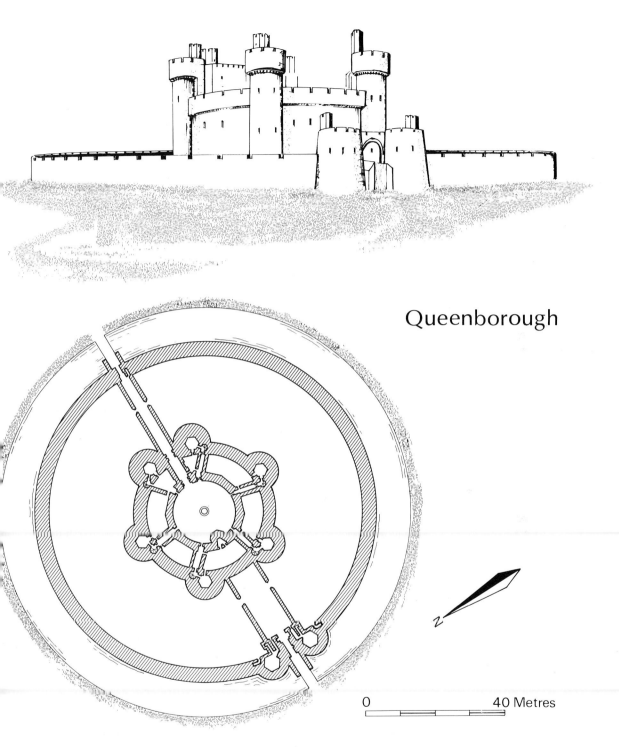

Queenborough

0   40 Metres

102 Edward III's coastal defence castle at Queenborough, demolished in the mid-seventeenth century
     but re-drawn here from a late-sixteenth-century plan and from a sketch of the castle made shortly
     before its demolition (*King's Works*, ii: 795 and plate 47B)

royal castle at Southampton was to be almost entirely rebuilt, with a great new tower on the former castle mound designed by the King's best architects.[2] Portsmouth, raided for a second time later in the war, was surveyed in 1386 with a view to fortification of the harbour, and a tower built there 'for the safe keeping of the king's ships', although not before the first great expansion of the English navy in the later years of Henry V.[3]

Earlier than either of these, repeated French raids (and the threat of more) had underlined the need for a more systematic defence of the Thames estuary, to be met in part by the building of a new castle at Queenborough, in the Isle of Sheppey (Kent), which, together with the town that was founded to support it, came to constitute a major investment on the part of the crown—the last new royal castle of medieval England and a building project conceived on a scale not seen since Edwardian Wales. Queenborough Castle has now wholly disappeared. However, a plan and a view of the fortress have survived from the seventeenth century, and these are enough to show us a building hard to parallel within its own century and much more closely resembling the artillery fortifications of Henry VIII, several reigns and almost two centuries later. Bellver, in Majorca, a castle built in 1309–14 to a similar circular plan, has sometimes been cited as a parallel, nor is it impossible that Edward III's Queenborough could have owed something of its form to that building.[4] Certainly, Edward had met the king of Majorca, with other kings and princes, at Amiens in the summer of 1329, not long after Bellver had been completed. Moreover, the Amiens homage had proved to be a particularly splendid and memorable occasion, and Edward III, still only sixteen at the time, had been at an especially impressionable age. Nevertheless, there is nothing else in England to compare with Queenborough, and Edward himself, only beginning on its construction in his later years, was very fond of the castle when completed.

Although uncompromisingly military in its rigidly geometric plan, the perfect circle of the great six-towered central 'rotunda' exactly matched by the line of the lower outer curtain, Queenborough was also comfortably fitted out with all the usual accommodation considered appropriate to a royal residence. Begun in the spring of 1361 and visited for the first time by Edward III two years later, the main residential accommodation in the rotunda at Queenborough was already receiving its finishing touches in 1365, after which Edward would stay there regularly. As at Bellver and at such earlier circular keeps as Restormel and Castel del Monte (above, pp. 29–32), the accommodation was disposed about an inner ward, with the castle well as the precisely central feature of the entire complex. It included the king's great hall and his chambers, a chapel, a kitchen, and a number of other ground-floor guardrooms and stores. Fireplaces and glazed windows added touches of luxury, making Queenborough a castle such as the king could well live in, while it clearly served him too as his own personal military toy.

Whitewashed, be-flagged, and with its many towers finished off at the top with timber domes, Queenborough must have stood out spectacularly on the flat shore of the estuary as a deterrent to any sea-borne invader. Itself the ultimate expression of the concentric plan as worked out during the Middle Ages, a nice additional touch at Queenborough was the siting of the main entrance to the inner and outer wards at the opposite points of the compass, reminiscent of such Edwardian castles as Criccieth (above, pp. 82–3). To achieve such an effect would have been one obvious virtue of concentricity when the castle was first laid out by Edward's designers.

103 The twin drum towers on the east front at Hadleigh, sited to overlook the Thames estuary in anticipation of a French attack

Another must surely have been the maximal use of the trebuchets, mangonels, and other engines with which Queenborough, we know, was equipped. Stone-throwing artillery, by Edward's time, had reached a high pitch of sophistication, being still very much more effective in these early years than the cannon that were beginning to attract general interest. Queenborough is a castle of the artillery age, but of an artillery as yet innocent of gunpowder.[5]

Not as precociously sophisticated as Queenborough, but nevertheless meeting many of the same needs, Edward's other major project on the Thames defences was at an existing royal castle, well placed on the high ground at Hadleigh (Essex), where the two great drum towers of the king's new east curtain on the edge of the bluff could dominate the marshes and estuary below. Hadleigh, on which work began in 1361 exactly contemporaneously with Queenborough, was similarly seen as an answer to the threat of further French raids on the coast such as had been felt as a danger through most of the reign. But it had another purpose also, just as Queenborough would have, as a comfortable residence for the ageing king, now in his late forties, within easy reach of London. Edward came to Hadleigh often, and would have taken the short boat trip across the estuary to Queenborough—the castle and town he had built from nothing and from which he continued to derive much satisfaction. At Hadleigh, the domestic buildings already on the site were put back into repair as one of the first stages in the rebuilding. However, the major effort was directed most particularly at the total reconstruction of the castle's east front, to present an impressive façade towards the sea. Here, a massive new curtain wall,

104 John Lord Cobham's gatehouse at Cooling, built in the 1380s and fashionably equipped with heavy machicolations in the contemporary French style

better built than at any other point in the castle, was equipped at the angles with impressive drum towers, being the first thing that any invader would have seen. Other new defensive work at Hadleigh included the rebuilding of the main gate on the north, with an elaborate projecting barbican and with a great half-round tower to one side. And there were major works, of course, on the king's new lodgings, beginning quite early in the programme, including Edward III's own great chamber, well heated and glazed, with a new chapel immediately adjoining it. Both of these buildings were battlemented, and they seem to have been sited alongside the south curtain wall, where they could have contributed by their bulk to the castle's impression of strength.[6] Hadleigh, unlike the very much more expensive contemporary project at Queenborough, was an improvisation, skilfully contrived to make the best use of an already strong site and to do so at comparatively low cost to the king. It must always have owed a good deal of its effect to the complementary works on the opposite shore of the estuary.

First impressions, in a warfare of raids, are obviously of particular importance. In both England and France, where the strategy of the raid was well developed, castle-builders in the later Middle Ages were to place special emphasis on great gatehouses and on lofty towers for the effect that these made, while pleasing their clients in another way by introducing every refinement in their lodgings. When that old soldier, diplomat, and servant of the crown, John Lord Cobham (d. 1408) built a castle in the 1380s 'in help of the cuntre' at Cooling (Kent), just up the Thames estuary from Queenborough, he equipped it most formidably with the handsome, strongly machicolated, double-towered gatehouse which has survived almost alone of its buildings. At the same period, and probably in response to the same raids on the coast, Roger Ashburnham was fortifying his manor-house at Scotney, near

105 The water defences and a surviving angle tower at Roger Ashburnham's fortified manor-house at Scotney

Lamberhurst, its four corner towers (of which one only has survived) again threateningly machicolated round the top. Behind Hythe, regularly menaced by French raids, John de Cobham's relative by marriage William Courtenay, archbishop of Canterbury (1381–96), re-fortified Saltwood with a proud new gatehouse, machicolated and formidably battlemented, which thrust forward boldly over the moat as a great residential tower. None of these castles would have been difficult to take. And Archbishop Courtenay's Saltwood, in particular, for all its clear impression of strength, was always more of a defendable palace than it could ever have counted as a fortress. Yet they made impressive use of the very latest defensive thinking, much of it learnt in the wars in France, and they would all have been capable of at least some resistance to the short-term menace of a raid.

At Scotney, the broad surrounding moat has survived virtually intact, and it is to this that the castle owes whatever impression of strength it retains. But at Cooling the moat, although present still in part, has largely gone, while at Saltwood the original water defences, once so important to the castle's protection, have been allowed to dry out altogether. In contrast, the exactly contemporary Bodiam, just over the county border in East Sussex and about midway between Scotney and the sea, has preserved both its water defences and the form of its buildings so remarkably untouched as to make it one of the most obvious text-book examples in England of the military architecture of the period.

On low-lying sites without other natural protection, water defences had long been relied upon as a security against mining and assault. In the thirteenth century, stone-throwing siege engines were being kept at a safe distance by the large irregular lakes of such castles as Leeds (Kent), Kenilworth (Warwickshire), and Caerphilly (Glamorgan). However, it had been in the fourteenth century in particular that the quadrangular fortress, with its great gatehouse tower and with its precisely tailored water-filled moat, first came into general use. And Bodiam belongs within a very broad class which included on the Continent such contemporary castles as Gudenau, in the Rhineland, and Sully-sur-Loire, in France, and which in England had been anticipated at Maxstoke (Warwickshire) and elsewhere. Certainly, when Sir Edward Dalyngrigge obtained Richard II's licence to crenellate Bodiam 'and to construct and make thereof a castle in defence of the adjacent countryside and for resistance against our enemies' he would have had many models to guide him, not least from overseas. As a young man, he had fought in France under the command of Sir Robert Knollys. Enriched by these campaigns and by a fortunate marriage to the Wardeux heiress who had brought him the estate at Bodiam, he had both the means and the professional expertise he needed to do the king's bidding, fortifying the River Rother (then navigable by sea-going ships as far as Bodiam Bridge) against any assault by the French.

Bodiam has been dismissed as a major fortress, and many of its characteristics are indeed those of a well-planned fortified manor-house.[7] Nevertheless, Sir Edward

106 Archbishop William Courtenay's great residential entrance tower at Saltwood, intended to deter French attacks

107 The late-fourteenth-century water defences at Sully-sur-Loire, in a style much imitated in England

Dalyngrigge's serious purpose at Bodiam is evident enough in the careful design of the castle's approaches and in the exceptional strength of its deeply machicolated gatehouses—the great twin-towered gatehouse at the centre of the northern front and the postern tower symmetrically placed on the south. Both gatehouses were accessible only by bridge or causeway, the complicated approaches of the main gate especially being a model of multiple defence. The now straight causeway across the water from the north took a right-angled turn, as originally designed, to join the outer bank of the moat on the west. A drawbridge protected the islet on which the turn was made, with a second drawbridge in front of the barbican tower on the next stage of the approach and a third cutting the final section of the causeway in front of the gatehouse itself. In the gatehouse there were gun-ports, among the earliest of their kind, with all the more traditional apparatus of defence—the three separate portcullises and three pairs of doors, and the murder holes concealed in the bosses of the vault.[8]

Another characteristic of both gatehouses at Bodiam, very typical of their date, is the prominent display of heraldry, high on each façade: the arms of Sir Robert Knollys, Dalyngrigge's former captain, above the south postern, with those of Wardeux, of Radynden (a related family), and of Sir Edward Dalyngrigge himself over the great gate on the north.[9] And it is very plain that Bodiam, although intended

108 *Above* A cannon in use at the siege of La Rochelle; French, 1400–1450

109 *Below* The north-east tower (centre) and east range at Bodiam, with the chapel window piercing the wall to the left of the tower, and with the great north gate to the right of it

certainly to play its part in the king's wars, had also its purpose in the celebration of Sir Edward's prowess and in the permanent commemoration of his line. Like many returned soldiers, of whom Sir John Fastolf in the next century is another obvious example (below, pp. 166–7), Dalyngrigge had determined to end his days in the state he must have felt he had won. Bodiam is not as extravagant as some of the magnate fortresses which were beginning to rise in the kingdom. Yet its accommodation is generous, as befitted a man of wealth, with great hall, great chamber, and chapel as the public rooms, and with many separate suites and lodgings in addition. The most elaborate of these suites, on the first floor of the east range, was reserved for Dalyngrigge himself. Its hall was the only apartment in the castle with a crenellated fireplace. From its chamber there was access to two smaller sleeping chambers, each with its garderobe, in the square tower in the middle of the east curtain. Another door, in the north-east corner of the chamber, opened into a private pew, or first-floor side-chapel, overlooking the altar and giving Dalyngrigge and his family independent access to the great chapel otherwise common to the garrison as a whole.[10]

110 Bodiam from the air, to show Sir Edward Dalyngrigge's private range (top), east of the great court, and the wide water-filled moat; originally, the approach to the castle was from the west, joining the octagonal islet at a right-angle in front of the main gate

This separate provision for the lord at Bodiam, it was once argued, could have been designed for his better security, reflecting his distrust even of the men in his own employ.[11] However, Dalyngrigge was an old man when he built his personal fortress, and it is very much more likely that what he sought to create there was the privacy due to his years. Certainly, the seclusion in some measure of the lord's apartments was the invariable characteristic of all castle architecture of the later Middle Ages, quite as true of the private lodgings of the Grand Master of the Order of Teutonic Knights at Marienburg (Poland) as it was of a much smaller castle like Bodiam.[12] After Sir Edward Dalyngrigge, the next war veteran to obtain a licence to crenellate, on 11 June 1386, was Sir Richard Abberbury, desiring to 'build anew and fortify' his manor-house at Donnington, in Berkshire, the long-term residence of the Abberbury family which had been there for almost a century. If the lord's comfort and his privacy had not been built into the earlier manor-house at Donnington, these were certainly given thought in its reconstruction.

Donnington, in more ways than one, is a typical product of the period. Sir Richard Abberbury had fought in France with the Black Prince, spending many years thereafter in the household of Richard II, the prince's son and heir, both before and after he became king. What he did in 1386 at Donnington was not to re-fortify the manor-house as a whole, which was already equipped with circular angle towers and square towers in the curtain very much in the style of Bodiam, but to furnish the building with an imposing gatehouse, for display as well as for defence. Donnington

111 Sir Richard Abberbury's residential gate-house at Donnington, very similar in style to the gatehouse at Saltwood and built in the 1380s

112 The early-fourteenth-century keep (centre) on the motte at Dudley is sometimes cited as the model
     for Nunney, although the true ancestry of Nunney is more likely to be found in France

is placed on high ground overlooking the main road from Winchester to Oxford, one
of the principal north-south thoroughfares of the kingdom. And Sir Richard's new
gatehouse, deliberately sited on the east side of the castle to face the road, would
undoubtedly have advertised its presence. In other ways, too, the details of the
building are very clearly intended to demonstrate the wealth and the importance of
its owner. Ornamental string courses separate each stage on the towers, rising
decoratively over the windows at first- and second-floor level above the great door.
The door itself is framed with handsome ornamental mouldings that would have
looked just as much at home in a church, while a fine vault, equally ecclesiastical in
inspiration, crowns the long entrance passage.

Donnington's gatehouse has clear affinities with the even grander and more
militarily purposeful double-towered entrance of Archbishop Courtenay's contemporary gatehouse at Saltwood. But it belongs also to the long line of such tower-
house gatehouses which begins with the residential gatehouses of Thomas of
Lancaster's Dunstanburgh and Gilbert de Clare's Tonbridge (above, pp. 96–8), and
which would end much later in remarkable showpieces like the first Lord Marney's
multi-storeyed gate tower at Layer Marney (Essex), a work of the 1520s. Both the first

Nunney

Anjony

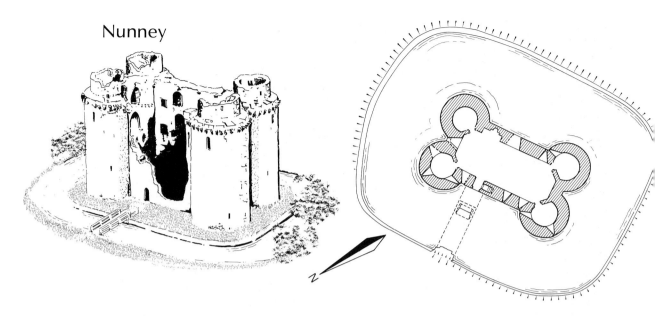

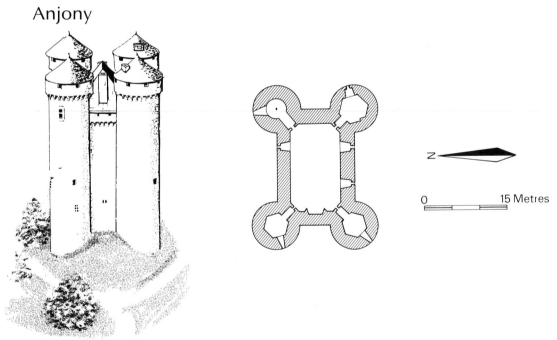

113 Nunney, in Somerset, and Anjony, in the Auvergne: two tower-houses of the Hundred Years War; the platform in the moat, on which Nunney now stands, is modern

and the second floors of the Donnington gatehouse are given over to comfortable apartments, each with a fine window, a fireplace, and a garderobe. They would have made a convenient addition to Sir Richard's existing quarters in the courtyard behind the gate, providing a good observation point, especially in the more lavish second-floor suite, for the old knight to watch the traffic on the king's highway below.[13]

Sir Richard's emphasis on the gatehouse, although made more obvious than usual by the comparatively small scale of the castle it fronted, was conventional enough in its period. Much less common was the solution of another returned soldier, Sir John de la Mare of Nunney, in Somerset, whose 'crenellation' of his manor-house, licensed rather earlier in 1373, had amounted to nothing less than a complete rebuilding in a style borrowed directly from France. Very little is known about Sir John's early military career. However, it has been suggested that one of the reasons for this lack of information may have been that he fought in the traditionally English-held territories in the province of Guyenne, in south-west France, collecting his profits in the lesser skirmishes which were then never subsequently recorded. If he did so, he would have seen castles like Anjony, in the neighbouring Auvergne, on which to model his own fortalice at Nunney, and this would seem, indeed, a more likely source than the early-fourteenth-century keep on the motte at Dudley (Staffordshire) which has sometimes been given as a parallel.[14] There is some dispute still about the date of Anjony; it may be as late as the mid-fifteenth century and one obvious difference from Nunney, besides its greater height, is the way that its four towers rise clear above the line of the curtain.[15] However, this very difference serves to emphasize the up-to-the-minute quality of Sir John's late-fourteenth-century design, for the continuous defensive line of Nunney's machicolated fighting gallery, encircling the entire upper floor of the castle, was one of the more important innovations of

114 One of the angle towers at Nunney, showing the corbels at the top that formerly
supported a covered fighting gallery in the
French style

contemporary castle architecture in France, to be seen in the long covered galleries of Vincennes, Pierrefonds, and Sully-sur-Loire, or in a different application (although the principle was the same) in the broad roof-top platforms of Tarascon and of the Bastille, in Paris.

Whatever the precise model of Sir John de la Mare's castle at Nunney, he followed the French tradition again in equipping his tower-house with the full apparatus of domestic living, bringing together in the same free-standing building the functions of both residence and fort. Inevitably, as such combinations have a way of becoming, neither function was an aid to the other. The main door at Nunney was ill-defended, relying too much on the moat and drawbridge and having little else besides these to protect it. In the interior, whereas the family apartments on the second and third floors were well-lit by large windows and were comfortable enough in consequence, the narrow firing-loops and only occasional small window on the lower two floors must have kept these levels gloomy and oppressive at all times. It was on the ground floor, in consequence, that the kitchen was sited, with servants' rooms and other domestic offices above it. Over these was the great hall, occupying most of the second floor, with additional chambers in the towers. Higher again, on the third and top floor of the building (although still below the line of the fighting gallery), there were the chambers of the lord and his immediate family, with garderobes in the north-east and south-east towers, and with a chapel in the tower to the south-west.[16]

115 Interior view of the tower-house at Nunney, with floor-lines at the back clearly distinguishing the ground- and first-floor service areas from the two residential levels above them

116 The east gate at Farleigh Hungerford, built by Walter Lord Hungerford in the 1420s as the main
entrance to the great outer court with which he had extended his father's fortified manor-house

Beyond the moat at Nunney there was a curtain wall on three sides of the castle, perhaps originally complete across the fourth. And there may have been an outer bailey and other buildings to supplement the one great tower that has survived. Nevertheless, the form of the castle, in an English context, was clearly experimental, nor was it to be taken up by any imitators. When, later in the same decade, Sir John de la Mare's relative and near neighbour, Sir Thomas de Hungerford, began the fortification of the manor-house he had recently bought as a family seat at Farleigh, near Bradford on Avon, he chose to do so on a very much more conventional plan. Sir Thomas, so far as we know, was no soldier. He had sat many times as a member of Parliament, first for Wiltshire, his native county, and then (after he moved there) for Somerset; had become speaker of the Commons in 1377 with the help of John of Gaunt, his patron; and was to serve on many local commissions with Sir John de la Mare and with others among his neighbours and fellow landowners. Certainly rich enough to build what he wanted and well acquainted with what his kinsman was doing at Nunney, he opted rather for a traditional four-square layout, with drum towers at the corners and with a gatehouse placed conventionally in the middle of the south curtain wall, just where he would have seen it in the fortified manor-houses of the majority of his associates and friends.

Such military qualities as Farleigh possesses and which are owed to the strong barbican before Sir Thomas's gatehouse, to the water defences on the western side of the castle, and to the great outer bailey to the south, are the contribution rather of Sir Thomas's son and heir, Walter Lord Hungerford (d. 1449), who served in Parliament as his father had done but who had also made a career for himself as a soldier. Sir Walter was raised to the peerage in 1426, and this alone would have been reason for an enlargement of the fortified manor-house he had inherited. However, by the time he came to rebuild Farleigh Hungerford in the 1420s, he had fought many campaigns with the king's army in France: he had been at Agincourt (1415) and at the siege of Rouen (1418) with Henry V, and had fought at sea as an admiral of the fleet under the command of John, duke of Bedford. What he now set in motion at Farleigh was the conversion of his father's fortified manor-house into a full-blown castle and into a residence fully appropriate for a baron. To do this, he needed to enclose the existing parish church which stood just to the south-east of his father's gatehouse and which he now converted into the castle chapel, retaining the original dedication to St Leonard. As part of the same programme, the parish church was to be rebuilt entirely on its present site away in the village.[17]

Two fortunate marriages and the profits of royal service had enabled Lord Hungerford to improve his property even to the point of moving a church. And what could be done locally by a peer of longer standing, similarly wealthy and also returned from the wars, is best seen at Wardour (Wiltshire), built for John, fifth Lord Lovel, at the turn of the fourteenth and fifteenth centuries following the licence to crenellate he had obtained in 1393. Wardour, now known as 'Old Wardour' since the building near by of an eighteenth-century mansion with the same name, is certainly the most remarkable of this group of Hundred Years War castles, again displaying, as Nunney had done, the very clear influence of France. A precisely planned hexagonal tower-house, built around a central courtyard and well, Wardour may have been modelled on another late-fourteenth-century hexagonal castle at Concressault, in Berri, where the reigning duke, Jean de Berri, was himself a builder of extraordinary genius and invention. But great tower-houses of this kind had come into general fashion, especially in France, by the late fourteenth century. And it is perhaps better to look for the inspiration of Wardour in a whole class of such buildings, which was to include the slightly earlier octagonal tower keep of the Breton castle at Largoët (Elven), with the extraordinary pile, also of the late fourteenth century, at Septmonts in Aisne (north-east of Paris), and with Rambures in Picardy, a work of the next generation. In England, the nearest parallel is the keep at Warkworth, in Northumberland, built for Henry (d. 1408), the first Percy earl, and again thought to have been French in its inspiration (below, pp. 131–2).

Lord Lovel's tower was extensively modernized in the late sixteenth century, so that many of its details now display a pronounced northern Renaissance character. Nevertheless, the planning of the whole is clearly late-fourteenth-century, showing a unity that could only have been achieved in a single-period building, with a sophistication of design—one set of apartments intermeshing with another—still most unusual at the time. Although more of a miniature palace than a castle, Lord

117 John Lord Lovel's hexagonal tower-house at Wardour, primarily residential but also equipped originally with turrets at the angles and with other defensive devices

Lovel's tower was defended at its entrance by a portcullis and by machicolations over the door; there were projecting turrets at each of the four angles of the building; and the ground floor (as at Nunney) was lit only by loops. Higher up, at first-floor level, the character of the building changes entirely. A pair of tall windows on the courtyard side of Lord Lovel's first-floor hall is matched, without thought of protection against assault, in the outer wall over the main door. There was a grand stair from the courtyard to the hall, entering its east end next to the service rooms and kitchen; at the other end of the hall were the private apartments of Lovel himself, with his chapel and great chamber, and with a newel stair in the north tower to connect these with another family suite just above. Guest suites and the lodgings of the various household officers would have taken up the four storeys to the south and west of the hexagon, largely destroyed in the Civil War sieges of Wardour in 1643–4 [18]

Wardour, like Nunney in the adjoining county, is a true castle of the Hundred Years War, marked out by its 'Frenchness' as the work of a returned soldier who had probably financed it largely out of the ransoms and other profits of the war. Yet it is also, in its ostentation and in the quality of the accommodation it offers, a castle of chivalry—a fitting vehicle for the display of that hospitality and largesse which had come to be expected of the late-medieval nobleman, whether in France or in England. These certainly, rather than defence, were what brought about that 'first great flowering of English domestic architecture' which one informed commentator has seen as a characteristic of the period.[19] How they were reflected in individual buildings will be the theme of the following chapters.

Chapter 7

Castles of Chivalry
I: Before 1400

The 'calamitous' century that opened with economic disaster and civil disorders, that saw the onset of endemic plague with the Black Death of 1348–9, and that witnessed some of the worst excesses of a more or less continuous foreign war, brought personal tragedy to many. Particularly at risk, of course, were those who were already very poor. They had no reserves if the harvest failed, little resistance to disease, and no power to drive off the king's tax-collector. Even among the magnates, although for very different reasons, there were failures. The de Lacy earls of Lincoln and the Valence earls of Pembroke each reached the end of the line early in the century with Henry de Lacy (d. 1311) and Aymer de Valence (d. 1324) respectively. William de Clinton's newly re-created Huntingdon earldom died with him in 1354. Roger Bigod (d. 1306) was the last of his name to hold the earldom of Norfolk, and John of Gaunt's mighty Lancaster inheritance came to him by a genetic accident through his wife Blanche, daughter of Henry of Grosmont (d. 1361) and a descendant of the first earl, Edmund Crouchback, brother of Edward I.[1]

But to see the century only as a series of disasters would be to ignore much that, at least in the magnate class, pointed in a very different direction. It was precisely the troubles on the northern frontier with Scotland that brought the Nevilles and the Percies into prominence. In the Welsh Marches, lordship had rarely been as profitable as it came to be in the later fourteenth century, well after the merely temporary set-back of the Black Death.[2] Sir Edward Dalyngrigge and Sir John de la Mare were not the only English warriors to bring back fortunes from their French campaigns. The earl of Derby (Henry of Grosmont, later earl and duke of Lancaster in turn) and the fitz Alan earls of Arundel profited there as well.

What this could mean in terms of building is still visible all over the country. One of the better purposes to which Henry of Grosmont applied his war gains was the further endowment and extension on a magnificent scale of his father's new hospital near the castle at Leicester.[3] But he spent lavishly also on the rebuilding of the palace he had inherited at the Savoy, in London, paid for out of the profits of his 1345 campaign, and was well known for the state that he kept there. The fitz Alans, similarly, were to turn their great wealth to both pious and lay purposes at Arundel. The founders of a collegiate hospital and chantry at Arundel, parts of which still remain, they were also the rebuilders of the castle there, although practically nothing of their work is visible now through two successive nineteenth-century reconstructions.

Richard fitz Alan was a man of exceptional wealth, a money-lender on a grand scale to many of his contemporaries including the king, and the possessor at his death of some ninety thousand marks in hard cash, almost half of which was stored in the 'high tower' (the keep) at Arundel.[4] Much of it had come to him by one of those dynastic mishaps characteristic of the century, when the failure of the ancient Warenne line with John de Warenne (d. 1347) brought him the earldom of Surrey through his mother. But he had also derived much profit from his offices and estates in Wales, where his lordship of Chirk was giving him higher receipts in the 1360s and 1370s than it had done even before the Black Death.[5] In addition, he had been one of the royal commanders in Scotland in 1337–8, had fought alongside Edward III at sea at Sluys in 1340 and on land at Crecy in 1346, and continued to serve the king, whether as diplomat or soldier, at almost every stage of the French war. Arundel was beyond question an able financier, a quality he shared both with his father Edmund and his son Richard fitz Alan the younger. Under their regime, the family estates prospered and grew. But like all their associates in the late-medieval peerage, where the fitz Alans stood to gain most was by a fortunate marriage alliance or by a successful commission for the king. And in these their experience was not untypical.

One family that rose fast and far in the fourteenth century, although it never achieved the national importance of the fitz Alans, was the Courtenays of Devon, beginning with Hugh de Courtenay (d. 1340) whose accumulation of manors, the result of two major inheritances in the 1290s, eventually brought him the earldom of Devon just five years before he died. Earl Hugh's policy, designed to broaden the family interest in the region, was to marry his children into the more important local dynastic lines; his successors found husbands and brides for their offspring among the greater aristocracy of the realm; and the Courtenays climbed high in consequence. The family produced few notable soldiers. It took no prominent part in the politics of the court. Compared with others of their rank and expectations, the Courtenay earls of Devon were never rich. Nevertheless, they quickly attracted to themselves a powerful affinity, becoming the major voice in the county. There were 135 men and women in Earl Edward's retinue in 1384–5, as recorded in the earl's livery roll of that year. Included among these were eight knights and forty-one esquires. At Tiverton Castle, Edward de Courtenay's major seat and the administrative centre of his earldom, the total of household officials and domestic servants had risen to sixty-one persons or more.[6]

118 The gatehouse, much altered in the sixteenth century, of the Courtenay fortress at Bickleigh, of which it is the only important survival

119 The Courtenay castle at Powderham: late medieval but with many eighteenth- and nineteenth-century additions

Enough still remains at Tiverton to show that it was once a powerful fortress, quadrangular in plan with towers at the angles and with a great gatehouse in the surviving east curtain. However, at Bickleigh, another important Courtenay castle, little survives except the handsome (but much altered) fifteenth-century gatehouse. And Powderham, of course, although luckier in its survivals, has been tampered with regularly since the sixteenth century and was not in any event, after the fourteenth century, a castle of the main family line. There are many better models of what such a dynasty required in the less favoured regions of the North, where families like the Percies and the Nevilles, in direct competition with each other, accumulated great retinues for the defence of the Marches, and then had to build fortress-palaces to accommodate them. Sadly, even in the North those talented prophets of Victorian Gothic, William Burn (at Raby) and Anthony Salvin (at Alnwick and Warkworth), obscured as much as they illumined in the buildings they so modified and extended. But whereas at Arundel, by one chance or another, practically nothing has escaped the attention of the restorers, and at Tiverton the medieval fortifications were allowed to decay when a sixteenth-century mansion was built within part of them, each of the great northern fortresses has preserved individual features of importance at least sufficiently intact to serve as a guide to the taste of the period. They belong in a class of their own.

Alnwick, in Northumberland, was bought by Henry Percy in 1309–10, almost a generation before his son, another Henry, acquired Warkworth as parcel of the Clavering estates, all of them again in the same county. Both were elements in a rapid expansion which carried the Percy interest north from its earlier bases in Yorkshire and West Sussex into Northumberland and eventually Cumberland as well. The Cumberland estates came to Henry, the first Percy earl, on his marriage in 1384 to the Lucy heiress, Countess Maud, a recent and available widow. But acquisition of lands by marriage and inheritance was not the most characteristic pattern in the Percy rise to prominence, at least in its earlier stages. And it was as mercenaries chiefly, obtaining a good price for their services from the crown, that they fought their way into full possession of the Northumbrian earldom, vacant since the mid-1190s.[7]

Not surprisingly, the building works at Alnwick and at Warkworth which accompanied this progress reflect both the military competence of the men who commissioned them and the demands of a status which, even before the acquisition of the title in 1377, was forever accelerating upwards. At Alnwick, where the systematic modernization of the fortifications began immediately after Henry Percy's purchase of the castle, the main building programme had already been completed before the death of his son and successor in 1352. The elder Henry had found the castle as a shell keep standing approximately centrally in an irregular walled enclosure which it divided into an outer bailey towards the town on the west, with an inner bailey sheltering behind it on the east. His first action was to fortify the keep with a cluster of no fewer than seven semi-circular towers, one of them attached to his new great hall to the east of the enclosure, next to the square-towered gatehouse on the south. Several of the interval towers in the re-fortified outer curtain wall were also his work, as was the middle gateway between the two baileys which it separated by another formidable line of defence.

120 Alnwick: built for the Percies in the first half of the fourteenth century with an unusual multi-towered keep (centre), but subject to much rebuilding in later generations including a campaign of works directed by the Victorian architect, Anthony Salvin

Henry, first Baron Percy of Alnwick, died in 1315, the year after Edward II's defeat at Bannockburn (at which Percy himself had been present) had opened the North of England to the Scots. His son, the second baron, was to spend most of his life, with only a brief intermission in the wars in France, fighting the Scots, and it was this continuous experience of warfare in the North that both confirmed the Percy family in its northern Marcher role and gave Henry himself the expertise to complete his father's programme at Alnwick. Concentrating especially on the castle's gateways, these being its most vulnerable points, the second Baron Percy extended the gatehouse of the already heavily fortified keep, adding twin polygonal towers to its outer front and increasing the length of the entrance passage. But his more important work was on the town approaches to the outer (western) bailey, which he rebuilt with a new gatehouse flanked by polygonal towers and with an especially formidable double-towered barbican considered to be one of the finest of its period.[8]

It had been Henry again, the second baron, whose promise of a lifetime of military service with the king, bringing a small army of his own to the wars, had been rewarded with the grant in reversion of Warkworth. But although both he and his son, the third Baron Percy (d. 1368), were frequently in residence at Warkworth, their re-modelling of the castle would seem especially to have been directed towards the improvement of the fortifications in the great south bailey, with some limited rebuilding of the accommodation. And it was left to Henry, the fourth baron, raised in 1377 to the newly re-created earldom of Northumberland, to give Warkworth its major innovatory feature, its extraordinary tower-house, or keep.

121 Stone soldier-figures, restored but probably authentically medieval in form, on the barbican at Alnwick

122 Warkworth from the air, with Earl Henry's tower-house (top centre) at the north end of the bailey;
in the bailey itself, the foundations are those of a collegiate church (centre), probably never
completed, and of the great hall and other associated domestic buildings (left)

Henry, the first Percy earl of Northumberland, was one of the wealthiest and most powerful magnates of his day. Like his father, grandfather, and great-grandfather before him, he was to spend much of his time fighting the Scots in the North. However, both he and his grandson, the second earl, who completed the work on the keep at Warkworth, took a large part also in the wars in France, and much of the character of the finished building must certainly be attributed to this experience. Anthony Salvin's mid-nineteenth-century restorations on the keep at Warkworth have not helped it look especially authentic. Nevertheless quite enough remains untouched by Salvin to show the tower to have been a building of exceptionally sophisticated design, parallels for which are easier to find in such a monument of Valois France as Louis d'Orléans' Pierrefonds, where work began in the 1390s, than anywhere closer to home. Like other tower-houses, including the rather earlier Largoët-en-Elven and the English examples at Nunney and Wardour, the latter being more nearly contemporary (above, pp. 124–5), the essential quality required of the Percy keep at Warkworth was that it should include within the same building the whole range of domestic accommodation expected of a nobleman's household.[9] Accordingly the ground floor, protected at the entrance by a portcullis and a pitfall hidden just behind it, was given over to guardrooms and stores, lit only by the light-well, or lantern, which rose centrally through the full height of the building, and by narrow firing-loops in the outer walls. Above this, the earl's personal quarters were fully equipped with their kitchen and service rooms, great hall, chamber, additional

123 A Buckler drawing, now in the British Museum, of the former Neville fortress at Raby before its nineteenth-century reconstruction

bedchambers and ante-rooms, and chapel—all of these duplicating the existing provision in the bailey to the south of the keep. Obviously, the intermeshing of accommodation of this variety within a single building required sophisticated planning. At Warkworth, the hall, the kitchen, and the east end of the chapel rose through two storeys; elsewhere, additional suites of chambers, served by stairs of their own, were fitted in over the great chamber and north tower, over the service rooms and first-floor ante-room in the south tower, and over the west end of the chapel. Other small rooms were found space above, with three further chambers in the prominent look-out tower which put a finishing touch to the building.[10]

Earl Henry's keep at Warkworth was an obvious extravagance: a celebration of the Percy name, which it commemorated with an ostentatious display of heraldry, and of the dynasty's powerful role in the North. And one of the reasons why it took this form was very clearly the rivalry of the Nevilles. Ralph Neville, sixth Baron Neville of Raby, was created first earl of Westmorland on 29 September 1397. Within a few years, he was in violent dispute with his cousin, the first Percy earl, then in rebellion against the Lancastrian usurper, Henry IV. It set the seal on an opposition between the families which had been growing, in any event, over the past century and which was surely inevitable, given the competing interests of both in the region.

Already two generations before, in the fourth baron's time, Ralph Neville (d. 1367) had been appointed in 1334 to the joint wardenship of the Marches, sharing that office with Henry Percy, second Baron Percy of Alnwick. And it was under Ralph Neville in particular, and then under his son John, that the Neville family interest built up in the North, centred on the original Raby barony in County Durham. Certainly Raby Castle, transformed during the course of the fourteenth century, mirrors the dynasty's ascent. Its Neville Gateway, built by John (d. 1388) and deeply machicolated in the French manner which he must have learnt during his long service overseas, became the vehicle also, just as the keep at Warkworth would do, for a display of the family's heraldry—the cross of St George in the centre (to signify the coveted Garter knighthood conferred on John Neville in 1369), with the saltire (a St Andrew's cross) of the Nevilles to the left, and the Latimer cross (emblem of his second wife, Elizabeth, the Latimer heiress) to the right. In other ways, too, Raby Castle was more spectacular than it was easily defendable. To be sure, it had its moat and its outer walled enclosure, giving it the essential elements of a systematic concentric defence. However, the massing of the towers behind these outer defensive rings has nothing of the carefully planned regularity of the true Edwardian concentric castle, being self-consciously theatrical in effect. The two stone soldier-figures now on the battlements of the outer gatehouse, have been moved from similar positions elsewhere in the castle. But they are authentically late-fourteenth-century in date, belonging to a class of such figures found also contemporaneously at other northern castles like Alnwick and Hylton (County Durham). With the corner turrets, the heraldry, and the exaggerated crenellations that everywhere characterized the building, they would have contributed to the ostentation of the complex as a whole and to its purpose as a monument of chivalry.[11]

124   The Neville gate at Middleham, corbelled at the top to hold a projecting fighting gallery with a diagonal turret on the corner

Raby continued in use as the principal Neville residence until its forfeiture by Charles Neville, the sixth earl, after the rebellion of 1569. Bought by Sir Harry Vane in the seventeenth century, it entered another era of particular prominence when the Vanes became dukes of Cleveland from 1832, hiring William Burn in the 1840s to reconstruct the family castle in a manner appropriate to their rank. Through all this, little of the medieval accommodation at Raby, with the exception of the remarkable late-fourteenth-century vaulted kitchen, has remained untouched by the modernizers. For the authentic feel of the late fourteenth century in the North, we would do better to look elsewhere—to Middleham and Sheriff Hutton, both Neville fortresses, to Lumley, and most particularly to the castle at Bolton, by far the best preserved of the four.

Middleham had first come to the Nevilles in the late thirteenth century, before the family's climb to power in the North, and they never did a great deal with it. Its major defensive feature remained the great keep, modified certainly but not greatly changed since its twelfth-century construction, and still the lord's personal residence in the castle (above, p. 41). What the Nevilles were to do, characteristically, was to strengthen the defences of the existing outer circuit, adding new towers and rebuilding the gatehouse in a more impressive and up-to-date style. If, that is, the essential elements of Middleham's defences were kept unaltered, the outward appearance of this Yorkshire fortress was very largely transformed at this period. Most impressively, the three-storeyed gatehouse was finished off at the top with diagonal corner turrets and with a crenellated parapet carried forward on corbels on

125 *Left* Turreted diagonal crenellations, restored but authentic in style, at Lumley Castle, a building of the late fourteenth century

126 *Opposite* The castles built for Louis d'Orléans at La Ferté-Milon and Pierrefonds. La Ferté-Milon, left unfinished on the duke's murder in 1407, was subsequently demolished in the late sixteenth century, leaving only the entrance façade; Pierrefonds was rebuilt for Napoleon III under the direction of Viollet-le-Duc

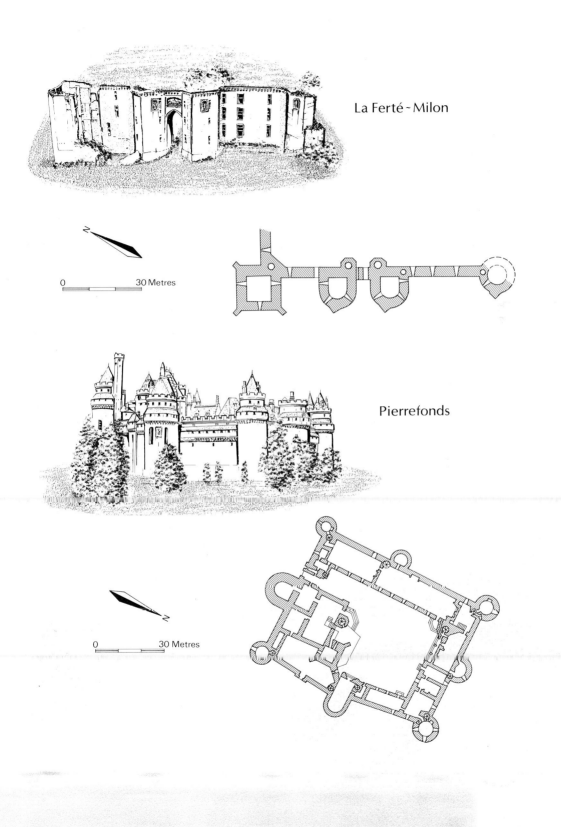

La Ferté-Milon

Pierrefonds

the exposed north and east sides. Stone figures, as at Raby, stood sentinel on the parapet, while the use of corner turrets recalls the more extravagant diagonal crenellations of Lumley (Co. Durham), like them deriving very probably from France.[12]

Much of Lumley is now disguised by later alterations. However, its unusual crenellations, although restored, are original work of the last years of the fourteenth century, adding that touch of the spectacular to the fortifications which was to be everywhere recognizably the mark of the period, in England just as in France. Lumley was the creation of Ralph, first Baron Lumley (d. 1400), who obtained a licence to crenellate his manor-house in 1392, and who must have been influenced, as were the Nevilles at Sheriff Hutton (Yorkshire), by Richard le Scrope's great fortress of almost identical plan which was then rising at Bolton, in Wensleydale. Each of these castles is built round a quadrangle, with great squared-off towers at the corners connected by ranges of buildings. Together, they became a model for the North.

Significantly, what this plan allows is the provision of comfortable domestic accommodation, convenient and well-lit, without any of the awkward corners and indivisible circular chambers which the requirements of defence had forced on earlier military architects. Of course, had defence been the only purpose of these buildings, such constraints would still have had to be observed. But the increasing style and magnificence of a magnate's life had brought about, understandably, an over-riding preference for buildings that could easily be lived in. In the great contemporary castles of France, so influential in England, of which Louis d'Orléans' Pierrefonds and La Ferté-Milon are among the more obvious examples, round and multangular towers of many kinds were still in use, even if largely for their visual effect. But they were linked, usually, by rectangular ranges, while the abandonment everywhere of the less convenient circular plan was to become characteristic of late-medieval military architecture.[13]

Sheriff Hutton, licensed in 1382 at the petition of John Neville but probably built

127   The four great towers and other fragmentary remains of the castle at Sheriff Hutton, built for Ralph Neville, first earl of Westmorland

principally by Ralph, the first Neville earl, has lost most of its accommodation, its curtain walls are gone, and even its towers are largely collapsed. However, there are many traces still in what is left of the buildings of good windows, fireplaces, and garderobes. The scale is impressive, and it is obvious that Sheriff Hutton, on the analogy of Bolton which it resembles in so many ways, was a fortified palace of considerable luxury fully appropriate to the status of the new earl.

Indeed, there is much in the history of Bolton itself which reveals the importance contemporaries placed on the trappings of chivalry and in particular on the castle as its symbol. Richard le Scrope, first Baron Scrope of Bolton (d. 1403), had served both the king and John of Gaunt, duke of Lancaster, for many years and in many capacities before retiring to the North in the early 1380s to devote himself to the defence of the northern Marches, to pious works, and to the completion of his castle at Bolton. He had fought in France and in Spain, seeing service in almost every major campaign through the middle and later years of the century, and he had taken his part also in the government of the realm, being Treasurer of England from 1371 to 1375 and Chancellor twice, in 1378–80 and again in 1381–2. During these years, he had amassed great wealth. But he had started life as the third son of a lawyer, Sir Henry le Scrope, chief justice of the king's bench, and misgivings about his gentility as the son of a 'man of law' remained with him for the rest of his time. Certainly these were aired especially publicly during the long and celebrated dispute with Sir Robert Grosvenor, lasting a full five years from 1385, when Richard le Scrope, on campaign with Sir Robert in Scotland, challenged his right to bear arms (azure, a bend or) identical with his own. And these, of course, were precisely the years when Baron Scrope, first promoted to that dignity in 1371 just before taking up office as Treasurer, was most active in the building of Bolton. When Richard le Scrope, 'Lord of Bolton', drew up his will in 1400, his many carefully specified individual bequests included much silver plate bearing his arms, with bed-hangings embroidered with the same.[14] But it had been for Bolton itself and for the right of his heirs to inherit his estates that the old man had pleaded 'humbly and in tears' before Henry IV at the formal attainder of his eldest son, the late earl of Wiltshire, executed in the summer of 1399 for alleged crimes under Richard II. And the castle at Bolton, just completed only a year or two before, was undoubtedly Richard le Scrope's richest prize.

A licence to crenellate Bolton had been granted in July 1379. However, work had begun there certainly in the previous year, for a contract for the building of the kitchen tower (now collapsed) and an adjoining range is dated 14 September 1378, and the clear implication of the wording of the document is that these were not the first buildings to be erected.[15] In 1375, Richard le Scrope, already an experienced soldier, had taken up the commission of joint warden of the west Marches against Scotland, and it was to be some years yet before he abandoned the active military life. Nevertheless Bolton, like Bodiam in the following decade and like many of its contemporary equivalents in France, was at least as much a palace as a fortress. Its carefully squared-off plan, with great oblong towers at the angles and with similar (but much smaller) turrets projecting from the centre of the north and south ranges, was ideally suited for the provision of comfortable halls and chambers on the first and second floors of the four courtyard ranges and in the two additional storeys of each tower. The ground floor, lit only by loops, was given over very largely to guard-rooms, stables, and stores. However, there were some lodgings even at this low level, while the entire upper floors were similarly planned as a whole elaborate series of

128 Richard le Scrope's four-square fortress-palace at Bolton, showing the three surviving corner towers and the accommodation ranged round an open court at the centre

additional lodgings and separate suites, carefully and even luxuriously appointed to accommodate Richard le Scrope, his family, guests, and household.

On one recent analysis, there were twelve individual lodgings at Bolton and no fewer than eight self-contained household suites, all contained within the walls of the one great building.[16] And while this was certainly no larger than would have been expected contemporaneously of a baron of Richard le Scrope's acknowledged standing and great wealth, what distinguished Bolton, in a single-period building, was the sophistication of the planning required of its architect to meet each one of these many different needs. Nor was defence totally lost in the process. Bolton is not fortified as an Edwardian military engineer would have wished it. There is no multiplication of defensive lines, and the gate-passage, although secured by a portcullis at each end, has nothing of the elaboration of the Edwardian approaches to castles like Goodrich or Caernarvon. Yet any unwelcome intruder, if he had fought his way into the central court at Bolton, would have found himself worse off than before. Firing-loops in the inner walls of the ground-floor rooms commanded every angle of the courtyard. The doors, placed (with one exception) inconspicuously in the corners, were defendable from above by diagonal machicolations in the towers. The upper storeys were accessible only by way of narrow spiral stairs.[17]

129 Four scenes, including castle interiors, from an illuminated manuscript life of Alexander; English, *circa* 1400

One very good reason for the defence of Bolton was the quality of the plate and other furnishings it housed. Richard le Scrope's will, in 1400, was to list many of the finer of these, and it becomes clear, whether from this or from the numerous equivalent wills and inventories of the period, that costly though a building like Bolton might have been, it was hardly more so than its contents. Richard fitz Alan, earl of Arundel, was a greater figure in the land even than Baron Scrope, and the unhappy chance of his execution in 1397, followed by the forfeiture of his goods and their subsequent listing for the crown, has preserved a series of lists and inventories which, taken with his own will of 1393, tells us much of the taste of the period. The earl's armour included gauntlets of both London and Flemish work; he had a basinet (a steel headpiece) fashioned in Milan, decorated with silver inlay on the visor and collar; there was chain mail from Lombardy and from Westphalia, suits of plate armour partly gilt, and sets of daggers, enamelled on the mounts and with hilts of beryl and of ivory, one of which (like the tournament saddles) was 'garnished' with the earl's coat of arms. These arms again—the arms of Warenne and of Arundel—were to reappear on the tapestries and bed-hangings from the earl's apartments at Arundel Castle and elsewhere:

> Item a bed of striped bawdekyn, with borders of green, with eagles embroidered therein carrying the arms of Warenne and Arundel, with 10 rugs of blue and white, with borders of green, with blue eagles carrying the said arms, of tapestry work, with 6 cushions of bawdekyn, striped and with borders as above, with a cross-cloth and 3 curtains of the same set.
> Item a bed of bawdekyn of blue colour with red work, with a half-selour embroidered with 3 golden lions and the arms of Warenne and Arundel, with 3 curtains of blue tartarin, with 10 blue rugs of tapestry work marked with the arms of Warenne and Arundel . . . etc.

One set of hangings, bequeathed in 1393 to his second wife Philippa Mortimer, carried the arms of three of the earl's sons-in-law in addition to his own—those of Thomas Mowbray, earl of Nottingham, second husband of Elizabeth, of John, Lord Charlton of Powys, married to Alice, and of Joan's husband, William, Lord Bergavenny. To his wife again, Arundel left a pair of candlesticks, 'for use at supper in winter', embattled at the rims, with pendants bearing his arms. There were silks and satins, fine linens and ermine. A coverlet and a tester (bed canopy), listed in 1397, were 'marked with a castle on each piece'.[18]

Much of the domestic splendour of the period has been captured for all time in such contemporary masterpieces of the illuminator's art as the Limbourg brothers' *Les Très Riches Heures du duc de Berri*, among the miniatures of which there is a representation—the best we have—of Jean de Berri's fantastical castle at Mehun-sur-Yèvre.[19] But something of the same quality can still be seen in the surviving architectural details of an important contemporary building like John of Gaunt's impressive hall at Kenilworth (Warwickshire)—in the expensive panelling of the stonework, in the window seats, and in the lavish mouldings of the doors, the windows, and the fireplaces of an apartment built for a magnate who for long claimed the throne of Castile.

It was John of Gaunt, indeed, who first transformed Kenilworth from the great fighting castle of Simon de Montfort and of the baronial rebellion into a fortress-

130 A view of Kenilworth from the mere to the south, with (from the left) Saintlowe Tower, Gaunt's Tower, Leicester's Building, and the keep

palace remote from the austerities of the past. Rebuilding the greater part of the inner court and leaving only the twelfth-century keep untouched, he equipped Kenilworth with an entire range of state apartments, centred on the magnificent first-floor hall over its finely vaulted undercroft, but including many chambers in addition, the best of them (to the south of the hall) being for the duke's personal use. The great windows

131 Three hall windows at Kenilworth, showing the exceptionally high quality of the stonework in John of Gaunt's additions to the castle

132 Edward III's great fortress of chivalry at Windsor from the air, with the lower ward and Henry VII's St George's Chapel (left), the Great Tower (centre), and the upper ward (right), the scene of the bulk of Edward III's expenditure

of the hall and of the other apartments looked out as openly over the surrounding countryside as they did over the courtyard within, and it is plain that defence was no longer the first consideration of the architect of Lancaster's Kenilworth. Nevertheless three towers—the Strong Tower, the Saintlowe Tower, and Gaunt's Tower—were built as an integral part of the new works.[20] They may indeed have given an impression of strength to the building, but their purpose more particularly was to underline its status as a castle of chivalry and as a favoured residence of the realm's greatest magnate, next only to the king in the patronage he could deploy and in the men he could attract to attend him.

At the more domestic level of the fortified manor-house—at Nunney, for example, and even at Bodiam—the common hall had lost a good deal of its importance as more emphasis was placed on the private apartments of the lord and on the separate lodgings of the more important members of his household. However, the parade of chivalry that had become so much a part of the public life of the late-medieval nobleman was enough to ensure the hall's survival in all greater buildings, archaic though it might seem in private. One of the grandest medieval halls to survive intact was built for Edward IV at his palace at Eltham and was finished as late as 1480.[21] And there can be no doubt that Edward III's St George's Hall, begun back in the 1360s, was as much the focal point of the king's new palace at Windsor as was the hall at Kenilworth, two decades later, at the centre of John of Gaunt's state apartments.

133 Two folios from the Powell Roll of Arms (1345–51), recording the heraldry of Edward III's nobility, including Sir Henry Scroup (top left)

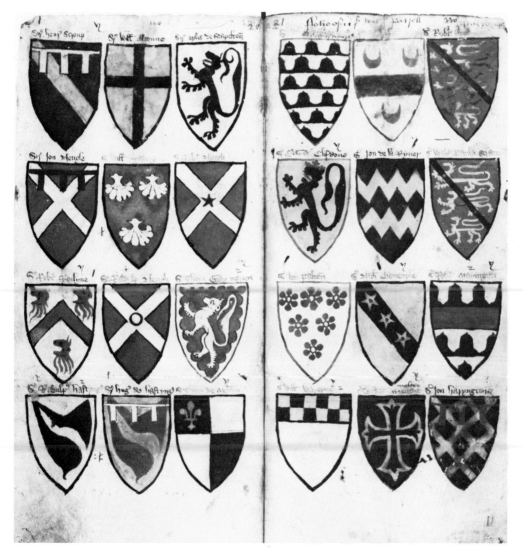

Edward III's rebuilding of Windsor was, without question, the most expensive single programme of royal works ever undertaken in medieval England. Yet it had little or nothing to do with the defence of the castle, being directed rather, almost exclusively, towards the transformation of Edward's birthplace into a palace for his dynasty and into a fitting headquarters for his own Order of the Garter, founded in 1348 as one of the earliest and most envied of the late-medieval orders of chivalry. Edward's Windsor, it has been well said, 'expressed a concept of kingship as surely as Versailles.'[22] And of course it had its equivalent in the similar transformation, undertaken contemporaneously by the first Valois kings, of a former royal hunting-box at Vincennes. It was the Valois John II, shortly after his accession, who founded in 1351 the rival Order of the Star. Both in England and in France, the encouragement of the nobility and the bolstering of its self-pride were considered to rank among the more important of the obligations of kingship.

At Windsor in the 1340s, an earlier project for a resurrected Order of the Round Table had failed to win general acceptance. A 'house which should be called the Round Table' was erected in 1344 at considerable expense, but nothing thereafter was heard of it. Very probably, it was this first failure that persuaded Edward III to invest as much as he did in the collegiate Chapel of St George which, with all the necessary associated buildings, occupied his attention in the 1350s. This was costly work, rushed through in the comparatively short period 1350–57 and totalling almost £6,500 in the money of the time. However, it was to be far outshone by the next major works on the new royal apartments in the upper bailey at Windsor, scarcely finished before the king's death. Returning to the theme of Edward's chivalry again, these included the new Hall of St George. But significant too were the numerous private chambers assigned to the two royal households, the king's and the

134   Karlstein Castle, Bohemia; built in 1348–67 for the Emperor Charles IV near his capital at Prague, just as the French and the English kings were engaged in similar projects at Vincennes and Windsor; note the reappearance at Karlstein of the tower-house tradition, already gaining popularity in the West

135 A fortress of chivalry of the late fourteenth century: Louis of Anjou's Saumur

queen's, while other major elements of the final works to be completed at Windsor during Edward's reign were the long ranges of individual lodgings to the south and east of the upper bailey, built against the existing curtain wall on those quarters.[23]

Windsor, characteristically for its age, brought together the public functions of a fortress of chivalry—the great common hall and kitchens, the chapel, and the many individual lodgings of the retinue—with the provision of comforts and even privacy to an unprecedented degree for the king and for the members of his family. In just the same way, the Valois dynasty's Vincennes was equipped with its huge public court, while the king's personal quarters in the castle, completed by Charles V (d. 1380), were separately disposed in a six-storeyed tower-house to one side of the perimeter, cut off from the remainder by its own moat.[24] At neither palace was money spared to make each a model of sumptuous living, an occasion for display and an opportunity for extravagance where this might serve some political purpose in establishing the dignity of the king. It was at Vincennes that Charles V kept his personal library, with some of the best of his collection of tapestries, and with other works of art on display. Edward III had his great mechanical clock at Windsor, set up on the keep in the early 1350s and one of the first of its kind.

When labour was short immediately following the Black Death and when others were doing their best to hold on to whatever skilled workers they could attract, Edward nevertheless brought to Windsor 'almost all the masons and carpenters throughout the whole of England . . . so that hardly anyone could have any good mason or carpenter, except in secret, on account of the king's prohibition.'[25] It was not always easy to keep them there, for wages were going up despite the Statute of Labourers of 1351 and all other similar efforts to control them. In 1362, 'for excessive gain . . . almost all the masons and craftsmen hired for the king's works in his castles of Windsor, Hadleigh and Sheppey [Queenborough] and in other manors and places

136 The fourteenth-century east front at Warwick, with the great gatehouse (centre), Caesar's Tower (left), and Guy's Tower (right)

have secretly withdrawn, and are retained with religious persons and other masters, clerks and laymen, to the king's hurt and the hindrance of his works, whereat he is moved to anger'. Yet the king himself was breaking the statute, paying his workmen above the rates it laid down.[26] Even he could not have triumphed over his competitors in the diminished labour market if he had relied on impressment alone.

One of those certainly in competition with Edward III at this time would have been his old associate and companion-at-arms, Thomas Beauchamp (d. 1369), earl of Warwick. Earl Thomas was a hero of Crecy and of Poitiers. He had been one of the founding members of the Order of the Garter, sharing with the king many of the preoccupations, not least with building, brought on by their joint experience in France. Accordingly Warwick Castle, as transformed by the earl and his son, has many resemblances in detail to the king's works at Windsor while also being very French overall.

It was the east front at Warwick, facing the town, that was given particular attention. And it is here, in the lofty central gatehouse and in the two great corner towers (Caesar's Tower, to the south of the gatehouse, and Guy's Tower, to the north), that the French inspiration is most obvious. Both earls fought in France, the second Thomas Beauchamp (d. 1401) with rather less success than his father, and each in turn was responsible for one of the towers—Caesar's Tower trilobed in plan with a distinctive double parapet paralleled at Vincennes, Guy's Tower twelve-sided but very close in style to the octagonal tower-house at the Breton Largoët-en-Elven.

Neither parallel, of course, is exact. However, they underline the presence in both countries, perhaps at this time more than at any other, of a common building tradition which in art, understandably, has come to be labelled 'International Gothic'. Of this, the most distinguished example in castle architecture was Jean de Berri's Gothic masterpiece Mehun-sur-Yèvre, now unfortunately largely demolished. But other works of that same royal duke, brother of Charles V, have survived better in the ornate Tour Maubergeon and rebuilt great hall at Poitiers, and again the parallels with Warwick are obvious. At Warwick—as at Poitiers, at Kenilworth, and at Windsor—the rebuilding of the hall on a more magnificent scale was an important component of the fourteenth-century re-modelling of the castle. At all of them again, the lofty towers that were the mark of the period, while never without some defensive purpose, were still more obviously both decorative and residential.

Caesar's Tower and Guy's Tower, strategically sited at vulnerable corners of the defensive circuit at Warwick, each have their guardrooms on the uppermost tier, approached by a separate stair. They sit astride the curtain wall, and their entrances are at wall-walk level. But integral though they might be to the defensive system of the castle, their more usual function was to house important members of the earls of Warwick's retinues, each of whom might have had his apartment on a separate floor of one of the towers. Thus Caesar's Tower, on its second, third, and fourth storeys, had a single vaulted chamber across the centre of the building, with small adjoining chambers in the thickness of the wall, one of them a bedchamber or closet, the other a

137 Warwick Castle from the air, to show the principal apartments on the south of the courtyard (centre) and the strongly fortified east front (right)

lavatory. And Guy's Tower, on the four storeys below the guardroom, is equipped almost identically. In both cases, another intra-mural stair serves the residential apartments.[27]

Residential and defensive though each might be, the names that were chosen for these two great towers indicated their third essential purpose. Guy of Warwick was a hero of romance, a slayer of dragons, and a knight 'of grete renowne' from whom the Beauchamp earls of Warwick claimed direct lineal descent. If they chose to give his name to one of the finer of their towers, it was to do honour to themselves as much as

138   Tournament scenes; Flemish, 1450–75

139 The north front of the tower-house at Warkworth, with a great Percy lion sculptured in relief on the centre bay

to their fictional ancestor. Similarly Caesar, as a hero of Antiquity, was to be given a tower of his own again at Louis d'Orléans' Pierrefonds, where he would share the honour with Hector and Alexander, with Charlemagne and Godfrey of Bouillon ('Defender of the Holy Sepulchre'), among others. At Pierrefonds, too, there was a Hall of Heroines, while the continued popularity of the Arthurian legends, especially attractive to late-medieval devotees of chivalry on both sides of the Channel, was celebrated by Louis d'Orléans (just as Edward III had tried to do at Windsor) with a Hall of the Knights of the Round Table.

High on the walls of Pierrefonds, as they are again on Louis d'Orléans' other great fortress-palace at La Ferté-Milon, are splendid sculptured panels, both heraldic and religious in theme. They recall the arrogant heraldry of the Percy lions at Warkworth (Northumberland), one of which stares out over the surrounding country from the northern bay of the keep, in the general direction of Scotland. Each of the fourteenth-century Percy lords of Warkworth had spent his life in border warfare, performing an essential service for a king whose preoccupations, generally, were elsewhere. But they had grown, in the course of time, over-mighty. Such servants, as the Percies themselves were to demonstrate very early in the next century, might be dangerous. If the crown continued to license castle-building on this scale through the fifteenth century as well, it was certainly not because the perils of such a policy had gone unappreciated. Rather, the forces that the king himself had been at least partly responsible for unleashing, were now beyond his powers to control.

Chapter 8

Castles of Chivalry
II: The Fifteenth Century

The troubles that had haunted the fourteenth century refused to go away in the fifteenth. Indeed for many—and this time especially among the landowning classes—they continued to grow even worse. The last 'Indian summer' of prosperity on the estates had come to an end already by the mid-1370s. A succession of good harvests, beginning in 1375, brought down prices to where they had been a full century before, and meanwhile wages continued to climb.[1] By the end of the century, all but the most conservative of landowners had abandoned direct farming on the great majority of their estates in favour of a policy of leasing. And few did well financially out of the change.

There were, of course, those who like the Greys of Ruthin continued to draw profits from their estates. The Greys did it by careful management, by judicious marriages, and most of all by an untroubled succession of male heirs.[2] The Duchy of Cornwall too, in the precociously prosperous south-west, witnessed rising rent rolls and an active land market through the whole of the later Middle Ages.[3] However, the general experience was rather different. Without some other source of profit or good fortune, it became very difficult in the fifteenth century for even the ablest and most engaged of land managers to obtain a satisfactory return on a great estate. On the Talbot estates at Whitchurch, in northern Shropshire, it seemed to matter little how well administered they were; the economic trend through the fifteenth century was towards a descent of rents, and nothing the individual Talbot lord might do could check, much less arrest altogether, the fall.[4]

At Whitchurch, the steepest descent in receipts had occurred in the last two decades of the fourteenth century, continuing in the first decades of the fifteenth. And if part of the trouble, as always, was that individual tenants could not afford to pay their rents, it was also true that the Talbot tenantry, along with many others, was increasingly resentful of the obligations imposed on it and reluctant to meet them in full.[5] That final generation of landowning prosperity following the Black Death had not been won without cost. To maintain their revenues in the face of a still shrinking labour market, manorial lords everywhere attempted to reassert their rights, claiming dues and services from their tenants which had been given less emphasis in better days, and even in some cases hiking up rents.[6] Accustomed to cheap labour as the chief support of a life-style now expected of every nobleman in the West, justices who were also manorial lords enforced as best they could the provisions of the ill-fated Statute of Labourers (1351). Inevitably, discontent mounted in the countryside, and long before the outbreak of the Peasants' Revolt in 1381, there were fears of a French-style *Jacquerie* (1358) in England.

One of those who drew upon themselves in 1381 the particular fury of the peasants was John of Gaunt, duke of Lancaster (d. 1399), whose blatant extravagance at

Kenilworth and elsewhere must have seemed especially obnoxious in the light of his lamentable failures as a soldier. In 1388, it was the auditors of Lancaster's estates who drew up a report on the declining revenues they encountered, which remains one of the clearest contemporary statements of the similar difficulties then being experienced everywhere by landowners. The rebels in 1381 had burnt many of John of Gaunt's rentals and other estate records when they sacked his London palace at the Savoy. In many manors, shortly afterwards to be leased, direct farming was being carried out at a loss. In others, the traditional manorial officials—the bailiffs and reeves—were neglecting their tasks or refusing outright to perform them. The business of the manorial courts, likewise neglected, was far less profitable than it had been in the past. Tenants everywhere were hard to find; labour was expensive and daily increasing in cost; the profits of the manorial mill, even if a miller could be found for it, were low, as were those of the duke's fisheries and woodland enterprises, with declining pasturage in his forests.[7]

Where, in the past, the initiative had usually remained with the lord, it was his tenants increasingly, after 1381, who took the lead in changes on the estates. Certainly, the self-confidence of the gentry had been shaken. Unfree tenure, now widely recognized as invidious, pricked their consciences, so that they might be moved, as Sir John Constable was in 1407 on the occasion of the drawing up of his will, to return goods unjustly withheld from the sons of deceased villeins—'And if I have swindled anyone in either movable or immovable goods, or harmed his body, or kept back the wages of any servant unjustly, I wish that my executors satisfy them faithfully and immediately'.[8] But Sir John came from East Yorkshire where villeinage had lasted longer than it had further south, and there were many rural communities in southern and Midlands England which, having already disposed of the burdens of serfdom, were making good progress in other directions as well. Lighthorne, for example, was a Warwickshire village wholly owned by the Beauchamp earls of Warwick whose great castle (above, pp. 146–8) was only a few miles away. Yet by the 1390s, shortly before the first leasing of the earl's demesne at Lighthorne, his tenants were exempt from the labour services that were now in any event impossible to enforce. Meanwhile rents also were continuously declining, so that by the 1430s, when they stabilized again, they had lost almost a third of their original pre-plague value, with many holdings still vacant because of the shortage of tenants.[9]

We do not know how militant the earl's tenants at Lighthorne might have had to be to secure such reductions in their burdens. However, well-organized and frequently successful rent strikes were certainly not uncommon from the late fourteenth century, while one of the problems that haunted landownership in late-medieval England was the impossibility of recovering arrears.[10] Of course, if this were true of the old-established manorial estates of central England, it was still more likely to be the case in the more overtly hostile society of Wales. The difficulties should not be over-stated. Improved record-keeping had created long memories in the exchequer, and an efficient system of revenue-collection, such as had developed on the Lancaster estates, might be relied upon to gather in, over the course of time, almost the last penny that was due.[11] Nevertheless even the Lancaster estates, neglected and mismanaged under Henry VI, were in serious difficulties before the mid-fifteenth century. And where, as was particularly the case in Wales, an unusually high proportion of the lord's revenues came not from rents (reasonably acceptable) but from fines and subsidies arbitrarily imposed and deeply resented by the tenantry, prompt payment was understandably rare. A full decade before Glyn Dŵr's rebellion of 1403, there were signs of severe strain on many Marcher estates which, in happier times, had sent cartloads of gold back to England. This was true, for example, of the Arundel estates in Chirk, once a rich source of revenue for the fitz Alans, as it was again in the Caus and Newport lordships, formerly yielding fully a third of the Staffords' landed income and now, within the decade, dropping to less than a quarter.[12] On the Mortimer lordships at Denbigh and Usk, it was Glyn Dŵr's rebellion itself which was followed by a permanent reduction in receipts.[13]

Indeed, if landed income had been all that the magnate relied upon to preserve the life-style expected of his rank, many of the great families of fifteenth-century England would have foundered much quicker than they did. It has been said of the Percies, for one, that 'had the number of manors in the possession of the Earls not increased, the Percy estates would by 1461 have lost about a quarter of their value in 1416' (when restored to the second earl after his father's attainder and death).[14] But the salvation of the Percies lay first in the profits of their hereditary wardenship of the East Marches against Scotland and second in the financial rewards of their marriages. This combination of profitable royal service and astute dynastic marriage alliances was to serve many of their contemporaries equally well, being the principal explanation of the continued building works in which a proportion were still able to indulge.

Another related cause of the accumulation of great fortunes in fifteenth-century England, when economic conditions might otherwise have seemed to be against it, was the steady reduction in number (usually by natural causes) of the ancient nobility, and the failure of the crown to replace it. Thus the Stafford fortune, gathered together mainly by the first and third dukes of Buckingham, Duke Humphrey (d. 1460) and Duke Edward (d. 1521), owed its true beginning to Humphrey Stafford's inheritance from his mother the Dowager Countess Anne in 1438, immediately quadrupling his income and bringing him a galaxy of new titles.[15] In 1444, when created duke, he was already able to style himself 'the Right Mighty Prince Humphrey Earl of Buckingham, Hereford, Stafford, Northampton and Perche, Lord of Brecknock and Holderness'.[16] Nor was this the end of Duke Humphrey's accumulations, for his service in the French wars and other duties for the king continued to bring him new estates.

Having profited himself so much from the accidents of inheritance, it is understandable that Duke Humphrey should have taken great care to marry off his many children into some of the greatest families in the land. His eldest son, Humphrey Stafford, who pre-deceased him, married Margaret Beaufort, daughter of Edmund, duke of Somerset; his grandson Henry, the second duke, married a Wydeville; Edward, the third duke, took Eleanor Percy as his wife.[17] And just the same pattern was observable too in the other rising families of the day. It was Ralph Neville (d. 1425), the first earl of Westmorland and builder of the castle at Sheriff Hutton (above, pp. 136–7), whose twenty-two children by his own two marriages—one to a Stafford, the second to a daughter of John of Gaunt—contrived between them 'an almost interminable series of matrimonial triumphs'.[18] The Nevilles had done well enough in the fourteenth century; in the fifteenth, they were to do still better, establishing a family interest which by the 1450s was one of the strongest in the land.

Richard Neville (d. 1471), earl of Warwick, had come into the great Beauchamp inheritance as the result of an earlier alliance between two children of Earl Ralph and two of Richard, the fifth Beauchamp earl. It was Warwick who both raised and unseated kings in his day, earning himself the sobriquet 'Kingmaker'.

Warwick's first success was the elevation to the crown of Edward, earl of March and son of Richard of York, and it was Warwick who temporarily un-made Edward IV again in the crisis of 1469–71. But during these years another family, the Wydevilles, had begun to make its way under the patronage of Elizabeth Wydeville, Edward's queen, earning Warwick's bitter enmity as it did so. Opinions still differ as to the malignity of the Wydeville influence in the 1460s, nor is it entirely clear how much the family gained directly from the crown. Nevertheless, what is certain is that during the three years following Elizabeth Wydeville's secret marriage to the king on 1 May 1464, the Wydevilles both arranged and completed no fewer than seven advantageous marriages, bringing them into alliance with great families like the Arundels, the Staffords, and the Greys of Ruthin, and that this could not have been done in any other circumstances or without the wholehearted support of the king.[19] What the Wydevilles, through closet politics, had managed to build up in just three years, others were to spend generations in achieving. Yet the principles were exactly the same. Where estate revenues were in a condition of zero or even negative growth, the two remaining methods of advance open to the nobility of fifteenth-century England were royal service and the bringing together of financial interests by marriage. Nothing else—and certainly not efficiency in estate management—could bring rewards on a comparable scale.

The Nevilles and the Wydevilles are the classic examples of family advance by marriage. However, their interests in each case were widely diffused through the whole kinship, and it was the individual new fortunes of the middle decades of the century that were more likely to result in great buildings. William, Lord Herbert, created earl of Pembroke in 1468, was the assembler of one of these fortunes; William, Baron Hastings, of another. Both were military men, active in the service of Edward IV and essential props of the Yorkist cause, for which support they were richly rewarded. And both left a memorial in major new fortresses—the one at Raglan, the other at Kirby Muxloe and at Ashby de la Zouch.

The sudden ascent of the Herbert family had begun with William ap Thomas, who had fought with Henry V in France and who acquired Raglan by right of his first wife Elizabeth, financing its rebuilding from the profits of that marriage, of a second marriage to Gladys, widow of another war veteran, Sir Roger Vaughan, and of service to Richard of York in his lordships of Usk and Caerleon. But Sir William's contribution to the present fabric of Raglan, according to the most recent analysis of the castle's building history, is unlikely to have extended to more than the hall, the south gate, and the curtain wall enclosing the court on that quarter. And it was his son and heir, William Herbert, whose well-timed support of Edward at the battle of Mortimer's Cross in 1461 and subsequent spectacular rise as one of the young king's most reliable supporters, brought him the rewards he needed for a major reconstruction of the castle on an entirely new scale, both to protect the Yorkist interest in an unruly South Wales and to celebrate the rank he had won by his own recent endeavours.

Raglan, as one might expect, brings together these two purposes equally in its

140 *Above* Raglan Castle from the air, to show William Herbert's impressive tower-house (right), isolated from the rest of the castle by its moat

141 *Opposite* The gatehouse and Closet Tower at Raglan, reflected in the moat of William Herbert's keep

planning. Herbert had been a soldier all his adult life. Knighted by Henry VI in 1449, he had served immediately afterwards in the wars in France, subsequently upholding the Yorkist cause in continual campaigns in Wales both before and after the accession of his great patron Edward IV. What he built at Raglan was a castle in the contemporary French manner, its isolated tower-house and multangular mural towers being familiar enough in a continental setting but undoubtedly exotic in the context of Wales.

Raglan's novelty is unequal. The castle's gun-ports, for example, were clearly more decorative than they could ever have been effective, having only a restricted field of fire. Nevertheless, their use throughout the castle is one of the better indications of the new thinking that was being applied there, while such characteristics of the keep as the double drawbridge, rising flat against the face of the tower, are certainly entirely up to date. Raglan, unequivocally, is a fortress. It employs all the defensive devices of the latest castles of its day, from the strong residential tower keep, isolated within its water-filled moat, to the great gatehouse, hexagonal corner-towers, and many gun-ports. Sieges were not uncommon in Herbert's experience. He had himself taken Carmarthen in 1456, and towards the end of his life, with Raglan almost built, he was to reduce Harlech in 1468, capturing Jasper Tudor and his nephew Prince Henry (later Henry VII), and securing this last Lancastrian stronghold for the crown. Raglan was a castle of the Wars of the Roses at least as much as Bodiam and Cooling, Saltwood and Scotney, were castles of the Hundred Years War (above, pp. 112–18).

However, like these again, defence was far from being the sole purpose of Raglan's grandiose and extravagant rebuilding. William Herbert's fortune, after Mortimer's Cross, had come to him very rapidly. A privy councillor from Edward IV's accession, he was immediately granted a number of important offices, including those of chief justice and chamberlain of South Wales. On 4 November 1461 he was created Baron Herbert, was made a knight of the Garter the next year, and in 1468, following the siege of Harlech, was granted the earldom of Pembroke, having already received the castle and lordship of Pembroke on his earlier elevation to the peerage. Herbert's eldest son married a Wydeville, sister of the queen, and he took his reward from the king for the match.[20] His other children, similarly deployed, brought him alliances with the Percies of Northumberland, with the Greys of Ruthin, lately created earls of Kent, and with many more. For a man who had risen so far and so fast, the fortified manor-house of a Welsh country knight, even one as wealthy as his father had been, could no longer be regarded as adequate.

Raglan, as re-modelled for the new Baron Herbert after 1461, had two courtyards, the northern of which—entered by the great gatehouse and surrounded by service rooms and lodgings—was an addition to William ap Thomas's original plan. The great hall was rebuilt, as were its offices and adjoining chambers, and a chapel was constructed along its south side. New private apartments, decorated externally with Herbert heraldry, linked the east end of the hall with a fine six-windowed chamber, or gallery, built at first-floor level across the great gate and entrance passage. A handsome and well-equipped kitchen occupied the north-west angle tower, with a large cellar, lit by gun-ports and used as a wet larder, below it. Towards the south,

142 Provision for artillery at Raglan, showing in the circular gun-ports at the base of the gatehouse walls; note also the French-style machicolations on the wall heads, and the sculptured panels adjoining the windows of the domestic block to the left

William ap Thomas's gate-passage was blocked and the gatehouse itself became a unit in the lodgings which lined the inner courtyard on all sides. On the former castle mound, east of William ap Thomas's re-modelled hall, Herbert made his most original contribution to the castle defences in the magnificent residential tower keep which came subsequently to be known as the Yellow Tower of Gwent. With a kitchen on the ground floor, a hall on the first floor, and bedchambers on the floors above, it was clearly designed, as were many similar French tower-houses of the period, as an entirely self-contained residence for the lord—both a last retreat, if such were ever needed, and an important strengthening of the approaches to the gatehouse, which it adjoined and effectively commanded.[21]

The tower keep tradition was not new. At William Herbert's own castle at Pembroke, the ancient cylinder keep built by William Marshal in *circa* 1200 would still have been the strongpoint of the fortress. And of course there are even better parallels closer to Herbert's day in the great tower-houses of the Beauchamp earls of Warwick—Guy's Tower and Caesar's Tower at Warwick itself, as well as the more nearly contemporary Octagon Tower built by Richard (d. 1439), the fifth Beauchamp earl, at Cardiff Castle, with which Herbert would certainly have been familiar. Indeed, there is no need to invoke, as was recently done, the Wars of the Roses as the explanation for the revival of such keep-building in England.[22] When William Lord Hastings built another splendid example of the form at Ashby de la Zouch (Leicestershire), following the licence of 1474, the civil war was over and the Yorkists were securely in control. Laying out a second castle, six years later, at the old family seat at Kirby Muxloe in the same county, he chose for it rather a symmetrical plan in which, though the building was never completed, a tower-house would appear to have had no place.

Lord Hastings's circumstances were very similar to those of William Herbert. His father likewise had been a retainer of Richard of York. Raised to the peerage in the same year as Herbert, Hastings also was to be admitted in 1462 to the Order of the Garter, while the many lands and other profits with which his services to Edward IV were rewarded included the grant of Ashby de la Zouch, a forfeited Lancastrian estate. A successful soldier and a well-respected diplomat, he travelled widely in France, one of his more notable achievements being the negotiation, at Edward's side, of the treaty of Picquigny in 1475 by which the Hundred Years War was finally brought to an end. At Ashby, which became thereafter the family's main residence, many of these influences are reflected in a lavish rebuilding, the central feature of which was Hastings's great tower on the southern side of the courtyard. Hastings had found a hall and chamber block already at Ashby, with service rooms and a fine vaulted kitchen, all of them comparatively recently rebuilt. Preserving these, he added the accommodation that would raise this comfortable but unfortified and relatively modest country manor-house into a fortress-palace more appropriate to the rank of a close friend and counsellor of the king.

Ashby was never very systematically defended. With the town close behind it on the north, its defensive front, facing the open country to the south, must always have been very largely for show. However, there is no doubt that the Hastings Tower, at the centre of this façade, was intended to do duty as a strongpoint. Very solidly built, with walls almost three metres thick at the base, its only access to the court was by way of a narrow door, guarded by an individual portcullis. The tower had its own

143 The Hastings Tower (right), built in the 1470s for William Lord Hastings at Ashby de la Zouch, and the principal strongpoint of his manor-house

well; there were no windows at ground-floor level; the top of the building was a fighting platform, prominently machicolated in the French manner; and there were projecting semi-octagonal turrets at the angles. Obviously, too, the Hastings Tower had been fully equipped as an independent residence for the lord, in very much the style that Hastings himself would have observed in the French castles he visited, or in the tower-houses, also known to him as he travelled in the service of the king, characteristic of contemporary Scotland. The ground floor, as was common in buildings of this type, was given over entirely to store-rooms. Above this, there was a large kitchen, with a sink, a well-head, a great fireplace, and an oven, and with the machinery for raising the portcullis. There was a comfortable hall, with adjoining private chapel, on the third storey of the tower; above this again, Hastings's personal chamber had an imposing square-headed fireplace ornamented with the family heraldry, while other bedchambers, each with its privy, were situated in the seven-storey annexe built against the main tower on the east.

William Hastings was chamberlain of England, a peer of the realm, and a knight of the Garter; he was married to a Neville; his daughter, Anne, married a Talbot earl of Shrewsbury; Edward IV had made him rich on the profits of expropriated Lancastrian estates; after Picquigny, he was a pensioner of the king of France. Ostentatiously, the expensive panelled tracery, the fine window mouldings, and the insistent heraldry of the great tower at Ashby made these points for him, while the other buildings with which he re-equipped the manor-house again supported the new status he had won. Round the south courtyard, but now largely lost, were the

144 Borthwick, Midlothian: built in the 1430s and one of the more remarkable examples of the tower-houses Lord Hastings would undoubtedly have seen while conducting diplomatic missions in Scotland

lodgings of the men in his retinue. Of particular magnificence was that characteristic showpiece of a building of this date—the great chapel in the north-east corner of the court. More than a mere reminder of the piety of Lord Hastings, it was a very potent demonstration of his wealth.[23]

Nor was Ashby, of course, the only witness to Hastings's magnificence. In the last years of his life, before his summary execution in June 1483 brought work there effectively to an end, he began the construction of an entirely new fortress at Kirby Muxloe, originally preserving the old family manor-house within the enclosure but probably intending to replace it altogether when the rest of the new building was complete. Kirby Muxloe is an important building in several respects. Its plan is almost precisely symmetrical; it was built in brick, a newly fashionable material, while some at least of the bricklayers employed there had learnt their trade originally in Flanders; and it made full use of artillery defences as then still imperfectly understood. Fortunately, too, the building accounts of the entire operation at Kirby Muxloe have been preserved intact, from its beginning in the last week of October 1480 (when Ashby presumably was nearing completion) to the final minor works of preservation on the fabric ordered by Lady Katherine, widow of Lord Hastings, during the eighteen months following her husband's death.

Kirby Muxloe stands as William Hastings left it, his death a stepping-stone in Richard of Gloucester's ascent to the throne. Work had started with the clearance of the site and the digging of the moat. Carts were made and draught-oxen bought during the winter of 1480–81, and by the early spring of 1481, with quantities of

145   Kirby Muxloe Castle from the air, to show the water defences, the symmetrical plan of Lord Hastings's fortress, and the foundations within the courtyard of the earlier manor-house on the site

146 The west tower and gatehouse at Kirby Muxloe, with gun-ports at the base of the walls; the gatehouse, in common with the bulk of the rest of the castle, was left unfinished on the execution of Lord Hastings in 1483

stone and of bricks already delivered, the first foundations were being laid. At the beginning of May, the master mason, John Couper of Tattershall, was on site. He had learnt his trade at Ralph Lord Cromwell's great castle palace at his Lincolnshire home (below, pp. 167–72), and had clearly been hired for the skills he could bring to Hastings's very similar project at Kirby Muxloe, where stone and brick, used together as at Tattershall, were still exceptional in a building of this quality. John Hornne, the master bricklayer, joined the workforce at much the same time, as did the master carpenter, John Doyle. Under them, teams of masons, bricklayers, carpenters, and general labourers worked through the long summer season, from early May until late October, laying out the buildings as we see them now and making a start on the gatehouse.

During the winter, the unfinished walls were covered with straw to protect them against frost, and only the masons, in their newly built shed, could be kept continuously employed. However, early in March 1482 foundations were again being dug, and the bricklayers were back in action by April. With the whole building force employed through the summer, the project had advanced sufficiently by the autumn of 1482 for there to be work to be done under cover during the winter as well. It must have been then and in the spring of 1483 that the west tower was finished and that the gatehouse neared completion, with corbel stones being ordered

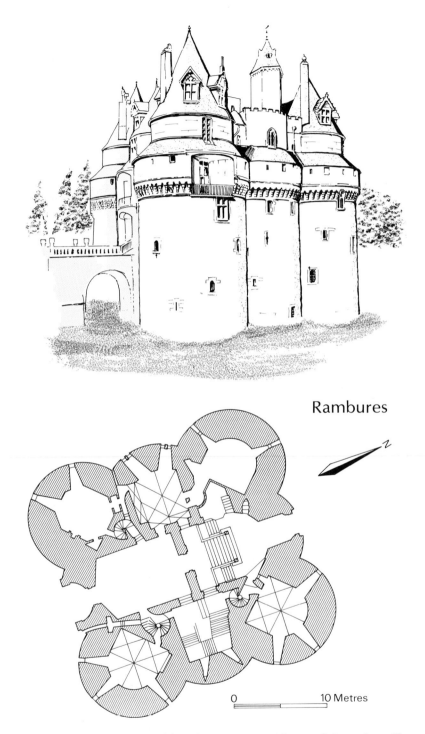

Rambures

147 Rambures, Picardy: a mid-fifteenth-century tower-house of the early artillery age, incorporating gun-ports and possibly a source for similar experimental buildings in England; like Kirby Muxloe, which it may have influenced, Rambures was built of brick with some of the finer detailing in stone

in April 1483 to carry the machicolations intended to protect the main gate. But that was as far as they got. Edward IV died on 9 April 1483. Before his son Edward V's deposition on 25 June and Richard III's accession the next day, William Lord Hastings was already dead, and the work at Kirby Muxloe, caught up in the national tragedy, had faltered and was coming to an end. What continued to be done after Hastings's execution was little more than the consolidation of the existing fabric and its protection, if necessary by roofing, against the weather. No bricklayers were employed at Kirby Muxloe after the end of the summer of 1483, and although work on the castle was not to finish altogether for another year at least, its scale had been very much reduced, trailing off to nothing by 6 December 1484 when the final accounts were drawn up.[24]

Quite enough, however, had already been achieved to show that Kirby Muxloe, had it ever been completed, would have been one of the most advanced fortified manor-houses of its time. Even more so than Raglan, it was designed as an artillery fortress in which the hand-gun at least, if nothing much larger, would be expected to

148 The gatehouse at Carisbrooke Castle, on the Isle of Wight, rebuilt in the early 1380s under the direction of the royal architect, Henry Yevele, and supplied at that time with gun-ports in the upper stages of the towers; notice the sighting-slits above the circular gun openings, repeated at Kirby Muxloe but not to be found at William Herbert's castle at Raglan

play an important role in the defence. Like Rambures, in Picardy, finished only a few years earlier and quite possibly known to Lord Hastings, gun-ports were included in the brickwork at Kirby Muxloe in a manner that was both practical and decorative.[25] Yet, with their restricted circular openings, they had scarcely advanced in form over those designed a century before for such castles as Cooling, Bodiam, and Carisbrooke. Nor is it clear, even at this date, that their uses were fully understood. Gun-ports in the surviving west tower at Kirby Muxloe directly faced the west turret and garderobe chamber of the great gatehouse, only a few metres away. From these, like the others in the castle, the only field commanded by the gun-port was the one directly in front of the opening itself. Any gun discharged from an opening so placed would have done more damage to the castle itself than to the enemy against whom it was directed, while even the guns that were more happily sited would have had to be as numerous as Hastings's gun-ports allowed to compensate for their individually narrow fields of fire. Within a very few decades, startling advances in military engineering would completely outdate such a castle as Lord Hastings, experienced soldier though he was, had envisaged at Kirby Muxloe in the early 1480s. Yet for his time, plainly enough, Hastings was right up with the fashion, both in his use of artillery and in the fine decorative brickwork and stylish octagonal turrets of the gatehouse he did not live to complete.[26]

In the meantime, of course, earlier castles had set the fashion that Hastings was to adopt and improve. Tattershall (Lincolnshire) was his most obvious model, and it was from there that he recruited his master mason, already skilled in that particular combination of brickwork and stone so much admired in his day. But there had been other brick castles, each of them the work of a returned soldier, rising in England in the 1440s. There was Sir John Fastolf's Caister (Norfolk), Sir Roger Fiennes's Herstmonceux (Sussex), and Sir Andrew Ogard's Rye (Hertfordshire). In the 1460s, another old soldier, John Lord Wenlock, a companion-at-arms of Hastings at the siege of Dunstanburgh (1462) and other campaigns, was to use some of the profits of his war service in making a start on the reconstruction of his manor-house at Someries (Bedfordshire), of which the handsome brick-built gatehouse still survives.[27] During the next decade, Bishop Thomas Rotherham of Lincoln, a client of the Wydevilles who had been with William Hastings at the negotiations at Picquigny (1475) and who similarly became a pensioner of France, engaged in the building of a great tower-house at Buckden (Huntingdonshire) for which the model, once again, seems to have been Tattershall.[28]

Between them, castles of this style created a tradition that was to last late into the sixteenth century, or as long as the castle itself would survive in more than the merest name. In general, that is to say, they were regularly planned, being designed as symmetrically as the site would allow around a central courtyard. At most, great emphasis was placed on the strength of the gatehouse which might frequently be used as the vehicle for conspicuously extravagant display. Many featured polygonal towers, their showy battlements and lavish machicolation echoing the fashions then current in France. They moved with the times in the provision of gun-ports, and almost all had a water-filled moat.

None of these castles would have passed the test of Edward I's military engineers. All too obviously, they sacrificed strength for comfort, military rigour for the striking visual effect. Nevertheless, it is worth remembering that almost all of them

149 John Lord Cobham's fortified manor-house at Hever, restored by Viscount Astor in 1903–7 but still retaining many original characteristics, including the water-filled moat and boldly machicolated gatehouse

were the work of veterans of the French wars. And it is certainly the case that the violence endemic in the fourteenth century had shown no signs of slackening in the fifteenth. Ralph Lord Cromwell, treasurer of England through the decade 1433–43, had at least one enemy, William Tailboys, a Lincolnshire squire, who would have done him severe violence if he could.[29] It was against the like of Tailboys that Cromwell fortified his two houses—at Tattershall, in Tailboys's own county, and at the manor of South Wingfield, in Derbyshire. Similarly, Sir John Fastolf's Caister, after his death, was to be besieged and taken from its Paston defenders who, by an earlier sleight of hand, had come into the Fastolf inheritance. When a band of heavily armed marauders 'covered with long beards and painted on their faces with black charcoal, calling themselves servants of the queen of the fairies [*servientes Regine del Faire*], intending that their names should not be known', broke into the duke of Buckingham's park at Penshurst (Kent) in 1451, they would not have constituted the sort of armed force which a well-prepared man need have feared.[30] Yet it was just this kind of casual violence, least controlled in the troubled middle decades of the century, that persuaded the rich, as it had done before (above, pp. 100–103), of the paramount need for defence. Both Tattershall and Caister were palaces, expensively built and appropriately furnished to suit the tastes, in their declining years, of men of unusual wealth. But they were very much fortresses as well.

Fastolf (of Caister) and Cromwell (of Tattershall) were old associates. They had campaigned together under Henry V, and had both been present at Agincourt (1415). Later, they had each accumulated a considerable fortune in the service of the king, by inheritance, and in private business ventures, including the purchase of land. For both, the visible symbols of worldly success were important. With other former

150 Wingfield: built during the last two decades of the fourteenth century for Michael de la Pole (d. 1415), earl of Suffolk, as a moated manor-house with an imposing three-storeyed gatehouse and polygonal angle towers; the domestic range (left) is of mid-sixteenth-century date

companions-at-arms, including Fiennes (of Herstmonceux) and Ogard (of Rye), they built themselves new castles as badges of achievement, taking their model from such newly completed fortified manor-houses as John Lord Cobham's Hever, in Kent, and Michael de la Pole's Wingfield, in Suffolk, but placing upon them a stamp of their own which reflected their personal experience in the wars.

Sir John Fastolf spent heavily on Caister. He was born there in *circa* 1378 at the manor-house which had been in his family's possession since 1363, and it was at Caister that he died in 1459 in the castle he had totally reconstructed. On a coastal site, Caister was exposed to attack from the sea—an attack that actually materialized in 1458 when the French were at its gates with 'many gonnes'. Accordingly, defence was especially important even at the beginning of the building campaign in 1432, becoming much more so from 1435 when Burgundy's abandonment of its long-standing English alliance opened the coast of Norfolk to a sea-borne attack from Flanders, at this period controlled by the Burgundian dukes. Certainly Fastolf, almost immediately after Burgundy's defection, was to order alterations at Caister to improve its defensibility, sending to London for a further stock of arms. And one of the measures required by the crisis was an increase in the fire-power of the great south-west artillery tower at Caister, at that time the principal defence of the castle on that quarter, and still its most impressive survival.[31]

Fastolf's tower at Caister was of five storeys, prominently machicolated at its top in the French manner and lavishly equipped with gun-ports. It was residential as well as military in purpose, having well-lit lodgings supplied with fireplaces and garderobes of their own, and constituting an important element in the accommodation of the castle, which was otherwise arranged, conventionally enough, round the four sides of the great inner courtyard. On the far side of the courtyard, the east range was pierced by the main gate-passage, leading by way of a gatehouse and drawbridge to a large rectangular barbican, or forecourt, walled on three sides and entered by another gate on the north. A water-filled moat surrounded the inner court, and was continued round the eastern forecourt as well. Another smaller forecourt, not moated, protected a second gate on the west, under the shadow of the great tower.[32]

Little survives at Caister apart from the tower and the outer walls of the ranges on either side. However, these are enough to give some impression still of a building expensively machicolated round the whole circuit of its walls: a 'ryche juelle', in the assessment of William Worcestre who knew it well, and a project that by its completion in the later 1440s had certainly cost almost twice as much as Sir Roger Fiennes's great castle at Herstmonceux, now so much the more impressive of the two. Both castles relied heavily on the water defences that were a common characteristic of military buildings throughout late-medieval Europe, and it is this that has provoked some over-ingenious identification of Caister with the *wasserburgen* of the contemporary Rhineland, which Sir John Fastolf, so much more familiar with the traditions of France, is unlikely to have used as a model.[33] At Herstmonceux, the multangular towers and the great turreted and machicolated southern gatehouse are surely inspired by Sir Roger Fiennes's memories of his French campaigns, while the same is of course true of Lord Cromwell's Tattershall, for the tower-house at which there was no parallel in England, any more than there had been for those earlier tower-houses of returned campaigners, each highly distinctive, at Nunney, at Old Wardour, and at Warkworth.

Lord Cromwell's tower at Tattershall was not the only one he built. At his Derbyshire manor-house at South Wingfield, a great stone residential tower at the south-west corner of the inner courtyard, separated from the hall and chamber block

151 Sir John Fastolf's five-storeyed artillery tower at Caister; circular gun-ports, without sighting-slits, may be seen in the stair turret (centre) and towards the base of the wall

152 *Above* The west gatehouse at Caister, with its adjoining corner tower, both still carrying the corbels of a projecting machicolated parapet

153 *Below* The heavily machicolated gatehouse (right), with gun-ports at bridge level, of Sir Roger Fiennes's French-inspired fortress at Herstmonceux, built in the 1440s

154 *Above left* The residential strong tower in the south-west corner of the inner court at Lord Cromwell's otherwise lightly defended manor-house at South Wingfield

155 *Above right* The gatehouse at South Wingfield, furnished with the double gate becoming fashionable in contemporary France, and decorated with a display of Lord Cromwell's family heraldry

by a range of lodgings, was the main defensive element in an elaborate complex which otherwise, with the sole exception of its showy double gate, was only very lightly protected.[34] However, what made Tattershall so impressive was the scale of Cromwell's expenditure (far exceeding that on South Wingfield), and even more so the fashionable novelty of its construction. Among those influenced by Cromwell's new brick residence were, as we have seen, both Lord Hastings at Kirby Muxloe and Bishop Rotherham at Buckden (above, p. 164). Another was William Waynflete, bishop of Winchester (1447–86), whose handsomely machicolated residential gatehouse at Farnham Castle, in Surrey, must have owed something both to Tattershall and to Caister as well, for Waynflete, a Lincolnshire man himself, was well acquainted with their builders, Cromwell and Fastolf, and later served as an executor for each of them.[35]

Brick-building was still expensive. But this in itself was an attraction to the rich, while what brick offered was a surface patterning and a crispness of detail virtually unobtainable in stone. The diaper work is much more obvious and more skilled on a later building like Bishop Waynflete's gatehouse at Farnham. Yet patterning was to be a feature of Tattershall already in the 1430s and of Herstmonceux in the following decade, and if brickwork and stone were combined with discretion, the opportunities for further decoration were limitless. Very plainly, Tattershall's tower was a showpiece. Its most decorative façade, richly fenestrated even at ground-floor level, was outward-looking, facing westwards across the inner moat. Although equipped with a top-floor fighting gallery, machicolated out in the latest French fashion, even this had been broken by the insertion of corner turrets which, as formerly capped by finialed lead-covered spirelets, were certainly more decorative in purpose than military.

This is not to say that defence was neglected at Tattershall. It was Lord Cromwell who added a second outer moat and who contrived an approach, much of it commanded from his tower, across three separate bridges each protected by its gatehouse. Nevertheless, what undoubtedly impressed the treasurer's many imitators—as it was surely intended to do from the beginning—was less the military capability of the fortress he had re-modelled at Tattershall than the state he could afford to keep within it. His great residential tower, luxuriously fitted for his personal use, was an addition to the hall and chambers, kitchen and chapel of the original castle on the site. It provided him with a parlour, or perhaps a court-room, on the ground floor, heated by a fireplace richly ornamented with the treasurer's family heraldry. Above this there was a hall, communicating with the kitchen in the

156   The great tower and gatehouse at the bishop of Lincoln's palace at Buckden, built for Bishop Thomas Rotherham in the 1470s and probably modelled, at least in part, on Tattershall

157 *Above left* Bishop William Waynflete's gatehouse at Farnham: a fine example of late-medieval brickwork again probably influenced by Tattershall

158 *Above right* Ralph Lord Cromwell's tower-house at Tattershall, built as a residence within the castle for Cromwell himself and defended at the wall head with a projecting fighting-gallery very much in the current French fashion

159 *Right* Tattershall: brick vaulting with stone heraldic bosses at the intersections of the ribs

buildings to the south, and supplied with closets in the turrets and with its own garderobe in the thickness of the north wall. On the second floor, what must have been an audience chamber was approached by a long corridor, or ceremonial lobby, finely vaulted in brick with heraldic shields on the stone bosses at the intersections of the ribs. Over this again, on the third floor of the tower, Lord Cromwell's bedchamber, very similar in plan to the hall two storeys below, was well supplied with closets and with a garderobe.

Throughout the building, the quality of the brickwork and of the other fittings, especially the fireplaces, would certainly suggest the employment of foreign craftsmen at Tattershall, for which there is already independent evidence in a surviving incomplete series of building accounts.[36] The moulded brick vaults of the closets and of the second-floor lobby, although at home enough in contemporary Flanders and northern France, would be difficult to parallel in England at this date, as

160   The entrance front, as rebuilt for Napoleon III by Viollet-le-Duc, of Louis d'Orléans' Pierrefonds, showing the use of machicolated fighting-galleries and the placing of decorative sculptured panels on the walls

161 Baconsthorpe: a moated manor-house fortified by John and Henry Heydon during the second half of the fifteenth century, the main defensive emphasis being placed on a residential gatehouse (right)

would be also the fine heraldic chimneypieces, again of characteristically French elegance, or the whole elaborate contrivance of the covered and machicolated fighting-gallery for which the true models are more likely to be found at Rambures and Vitré, at Pierrefonds or at Sully-sur-Loire.[37]

Caister and Tattershall were the last playthings of notable favourites of fortune. Tricked out in the latest military dress, what had chiefly attracted contemporaries at these castles was their conspicuous exhibition of extravagance. For lesser men, experiencing a similar need for defence, the options were not, of course, so plentiful. Certainly, for most of these, fortification of a large enclosure was out of the question. What might still be done was to build a strong tower, or to concentrate defence on a gatehouse. Recalling the same solution reached almost a century before by Sir Richard Abberbury at Donnington, these were just the characteristics of a castle like Baconsthorpe, built to meet the requirements of a prospering Norfolk gentry family which had good reasons of its own for being unpopular.

162 The tower-house at Belsay (*circa* 1340), characteristically northern in plan with defence concentrated on the strong fighting-platform at roof level

John Heydon (d. 1479), the founder of the family fortunes, was a prosperous lawyer, who had picked his way successfully through the factional struggles of the Wars of the Roses, and who had made many enemies in East Anglia, among them Sir John Fastolf, in the process. It was he who assembled the better part of the estate at Baconsthorpe, in north-east Norfolk, not very far from Caister. And it was probably the jealousy he inspired in his neighbours that persuaded him, in the 1450s or perhaps a little later, to put up a new fortress to protect it. Baconsthorpe Castle, as planned by John Heydon, was no more than a fortified manor-house, laid out as a moated rectangular enclosure with square towers at the four corners (never completed during his lifetime) and with a residential gatehouse centrally placed in the south curtain. Later, under his son Sir Henry Heydon (d. 1503), the defended circuit was joined on the east and was considerably extended towards the north. However, the focus of the defences remained the great gatehouse, fully equipped (just as the gatehouse at Donnington had been) as an occasional residence for the owner and for his family. On the ground floor, on either side of the gate passage, there were two lodgings, each with a fireplace and individual garderobe. Above these, John Heydon's apartments, approached by their own stair from the courtyard, included a parlour and chapel on the first floor, with another great chamber on the second. There were further garderobes and fireplaces at each level, and handsome windows facing forward over the drawbridge as well as back into the security of the inner court.[38]

Of course, the Heydons' castle, even as improved by Sir Henry, would not have been capable of resisting a serious assault. Yet its water defences and its massive gate tower had their obvious value as a deterrent, and it was exactly this sort of fortification—enough to cause the marauder to move on, while not sufficient still to excite the suspicion of the king—that was most characteristic of the private castle in England during this (its final) period. In the North especially, the troubled condition of the Scottish border country continued to favour castle-building; nor is it surprising that the tower-house tradition, especially strong in Scotland from the late fourteenth century where it developed at such castles as Threave in Kirkcudbright-shire, should have spread southwards through the Marches in the so-called 'pele' tower and in its many local variants. The majority of these towers were never more than simple square or rectangular structures, with one room stacked on another to make an economical emergency retreat. However, there were others, including Belsay and Chipchase, in Northumberland, as well as the lesser-known Ayton, in northern Yorkshire, and Hylton, near Sunderland, where something more sophisticated was attempted. And each of these last, although on a very different scale, was a tower-house properly so-called.

Ayton, built by Sir Ralph Eure (d. 1422) at the turn of the fourteenth and fifteenth centuries, was a comparatively simple rectangular structure in the style more familiar further north in Northumberland where Sir Ralph, before his marriage to the Ayton heiress, had originally had his roots. Surrounded by its barmkin, or walled enclosure, it had all the usual characteristics of the northern pele tower. From a stone-vaulted

163 Chipchase: a late-fourteenth-century tower-house in the northern style, with a vaulted basement under three residential floors, and with a machicolated and turreted fighting-platform at roof level

Hylton

164 A conjectural reconstruction, with interpolated windows, of the west front at Hylton Castle before its late-nineteenth-century re-modelling (after Beric M. Morley)

ground floor, or basement, it rose another two storeys, with a hall and smaller solar on the first floor of the building, and the bedchambers of Sir Ralph and of his family on the second. Originally, only one small door gave admittance to the tower, entering the ground-floor kitchen from the end-wall on the north-west; there was no direct access from the kitchen to the adjoining store (which was entered by a separate stair from the hall above), and the only lighting at this level was by narrow firing-loops in each of the long sides of the rectangle. At roof level, a wall-walk ran behind the embattled parapet, with a square turret, or bartisan, corbelled out at each corner.[39]

Ayton, despite its simplicity of plan, was finely built of well-shaped ashlars, with decorative string courses on the outer wall face, and with good vaulting and other details within. It has even been suggested that John Lewyn, the master mason of Bolton Castle and perhaps of Lumley, Raby, and Warkworth as well, may himself have had a hand in its construction.[40] More certainly, Lewyn (or a man of his school) would have been responsible for the elaborate tower and gatehouse at Hylton (Co. Durham), contemporary with Ayton, and one of the most sophisticated buildings of its genre. In terms of accommodation, Ayton had been no more than adequate. In contrast, Sir William Hylton's new castle, although preserving the main characteristics of the pele tower plan, was equipped with all the elements (including separate lodgings) considered essential to a great household of this date, all within the compass of one building. Hylton Castle, indeed, with its typically northern defensive emphasis, with the comfort (even luxury) of its fittings, with its showy battlements and extravagant machicolation, and with its ostentatious display of family heraldry, brings together conveniently many of the threads of the period. More than an enlarged chamber block of the kind that Lord Cromwell would later supply to his houses at Tattershall and South Wingfield, the great tower at Hylton was fully equipped with its own kitchen, store-rooms, and well; its first-floor hall, adjoining the kitchen and sited squarely over the long entrance passage, rose through another two storeys, or through the entire remaining height of the building; completing the accommodation, a chapel, the great chamber, and a series of individual lodgings (each with its garderobe) interlocked cunningly, one of the grander of these apartments, on the uppermost level, having direct access to the wall-walk and to the turrets by which it was broken.[41]

Hylton's machicolated bartisans, its deliberately awe-inspiring battlements complete with stone soldier-figures, and its strongly vaulted and ill-lit ground floor, were all very familiar in the North. They identify it as a development on the pele-tower plan, although one of exceptional elaboration. But to see Hylton purely as a northern Marcher fortress, rooted in the limited culture of its region, would be to do its builder an injustice. Included high in the heraldry that decorates the west front are the arms of England quartered with France, as they had been since Edward III laid claim to the French throne at the opening of the Hundred Years War. With these again are the white hart badge of Richard II, the Percy lion, and the devices of many of the higher nobility of the northern frontier, including the popinjays of Sir Ralph Lumley, builder of the neighbouring castle which, especially in its crenellations, had so much in common with Hylton (above, p. 136).[42] In effect, Sir William's tower at Hylton was more than a fortress and certainly more than the comfortable residence of a man of above-average wealth. It was a celebration of chivalry and a permanent statement of a system of values which William Hylton, his kindred and his associates, in the tradition of their class, had passed their lives in upholding in the North.

Chapter 9

Last Things

There have been many explanations for the demise of the castle in sixteenth-century England. Some have seen in it the deliberate policy of the Tudors and of a government anxious that power should never again slip into the hands of the over-mighty subject. Others, with more reason, have attributed the decline to a rapid improvement in the accuracy of the gun and, above all, to the development of a highly mobile siege artillery, as first seen in action in 1494 on Charles VIII's invasion and reduction of Italy. But although it is true that the Tudors, one after the other, laid their hands on as many private castles as they could, this was more a tribute to what they believed the castle still to be than a carefully considered programme of resumptions.[1] A castle remained an instrument of war, for which there were uses especially in border territories. Nor had the debate about the respective merits of the long-bow and the hand-gun in any way run its course by the mid-sixteenth century. Upnor Castle (Kent), built in the 1560s for the protection of the queen's fleet on the Medway, was very much a fort of the artillery age. Yet there were long-bows still in the armoury at Upnor as late as the reign of James I.[2] National pride in an ancient skill would scarcely have permitted anything else.

Satisfaction with the healthy virtues of a national sport pulled in one direction; fashion tugged in another. Castellated gatehouses were to enjoy favour in England for the first half of the sixteenth century very much as they had done in the past. Towards the end of the century and at the beginning of the next, there would be a brief return to full-blooded castle-building—inspired by nostalgia, by new wealth, and by the inflation of honours under James I—in such mock-fortresses as Longford (Wiltshire), Walworth (Co. Durham), and Rhiwperra (Glamorgan). But the cold wind of reason that had blown away the superstitions of the Church at the Reformation, would lay a chill upon chivalry as well. In the sixteenth century, for the first time, a conspicuous parade of heraldry began to look just a little old-fashioned. In truth, the Tudor aristocracy, much of which was new, no longer carried with it the chivalric luggage of its predecessors. And taste, too, had swung away from the militaristic bric-à-brac of the later Middle Ages towards the revival of a vigorous new classicism. The late arrival of the Renaissance in northern Europe inevitably ensured that it should take effect there with peculiar force. Almost immediately, a sense of the past developed. In the 1560s, orders were still being given to repair inland castles 'for the defence of the country' and for their potential in suppressing rebellion. Yet it was in 1562 that Tickhill (Yorkshire) was commanded to be maintained for no better reason than its worth as an 'ancient monument'. Early in the next century, when castles everywhere were being allowed to decay, the particular purpose of preserving Pontefract, another Yorkshire fortress, was 'to prevent the ruin of a monument of such antiquity and goodly building'.[3]

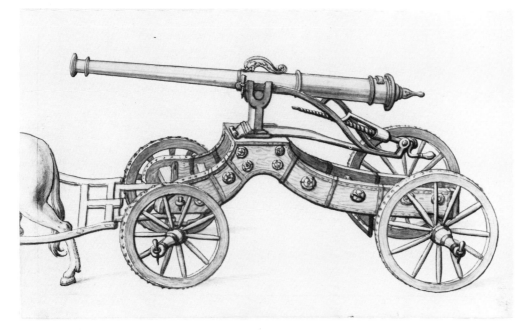

165 A mobile siege gun; Portuguese, late sixteenth century

Renaissance motifs had first become familiar in England in Henry VII's reign where they are recognizable, for example, in Henry's coinage and in the unprecedented use there of a profile portrait of the king. But there were many still, on Henry VIII's accession in 1509, who were reluctant to follow the young man into anything more than a merely token acceptance of the new fashions at court, among these being Edward Stafford, third duke of Buckingham. The Staffords had been a magnate family since the mid-fourteenth century when Ralph, a successful soldier during the earliest episodes of the Hundred Years War, had been created first earl of Stafford on 5 March 1351. However, the real expansion of their fortunes had occurred only in Duke Humphrey's time, when it had been owed to an exceptionally rich inheritance (above, p. 152). And by the time Duke Edward himself came into the title on the restoration of the forfeited Stafford estates in 1485, he was both one of the wealthiest of the great landowners of that date and also the successor, although still very young, to an unusually ancient tradition.

Only just in his thirties when Henry VIII came to the throne, Duke Edward nevertheless preserved the values of an earlier date even when these could be dangerous to himself. His lineage and great wealth had made him the natural leader of those among the old aristocracy who felt put out by Henry's reliance on new men,

166 Duke Edward's rebuilt parish church and palace at Thornbury, left incomplete on his execution in 1521 but still retaining the line of the great outer court (left), with the inner court and surviving buildings (centre), and the walled privy garden sited between these buildings and the church

among them the upstart Wolsey. And although the charges brought against him of treasonable conspiracy, which led to his execution in 1521, were certainly exaggerated and may well have been totally untrue, Henry's distrust of such a man was not unfounded so long as his claim to the throne was still mooted. Duke Edward, who considered himself a friend of the king, did nothing to calm Henry's fears. He boasted descent from Thomas of Woodstock, one of Edward III's sons, and was the son himself of Catherine Wydeville, sister to Edward IV's queen. Fond of heraldry, Duke Edward delighted in conspicuous display, among the elements of which were the maintenance of a great household and the financing of an ambitious building programme to accommodate it.

Thornbury Castle, on which Buckingham was spending as much as a fifth of his income in the years when building was most active in the 1510s, was scarcely a fortress in anything but name. Nevertheless, this great defended establishment, remote though it was in rural Gloucestershire from anything touching the court, preserved enough features of the old factious and militaristic tradition to alert and alarm the king. The prominent crenellations of its high outer walls presented a formidable front to the world, while particularly impressive was to be the projected west façade of the duke's private court, of which only the lavishly machicolated southern corner tower, at the angle of Buckingham's apartments, was ever taken to its full height. Other gestures in the direction of defence were the portcullises at the gates, the highly decorative but still efficient crosslet loopholes facing outwards on the ground floor of the duke's new works, and the gun-ports on either side of the entrances.[4]

167 Thornbury: the great bay windows on the privy garden front of Duke Edward's domestic range, sensitively restored by Anthony Salvin in 1854

However, more threatening to public order than the fortifications of Thornbury was the scale of the retinue it housed. Duke Edward's household was never as large as that of his father or great-grandfather, the second and first dukes. Yet with a following of some 150 men on his regular payroll and with a riding household usually about half that size, the duke's private forces were still sizable enough to constitute, on the most unfavourable projection, the nucleus of a rebel army such as Duke Henry had recruited in 1483 in the rising against Richard III.[5] It was with this spectre especially that the Tudors lived, prompting them to tighten yet further the existing restrictions on the retinues of their magnates and to view with a lively and continuing suspicion any household that rivalled their own. Duke Edward's lavish hospitality to the court at Penshurst (Kent) in 1519 and the extravagance of his apparel on such state occasions as the Field of the Cloth of Gold in the following year, cost him what trust the king retained in the loyalty of this most splendid of his subjects. On trumped-up charges, Buckingham was committed to the Tower on 16 April 1521 and executed just a month later. Thornbury Castle, at which he spent his last winter while the building works continued on all sides, was only half finished when he died.

Thornbury is often, and quite usefully, seen as the end of the private castle tradition in England. Its great courts and multiple lodgings had been built to meet the needs of

168   The embattled gatehouse and flanking towers at Titchfield Abbey, built for Thomas Wriothesley following the Dissolution on the site of the former abbey church

169 Hoghton Tower: a view through the inner gate arch to the outer embattled gatehouse at Hoghton, both built for Thomas de Hoghton in the 1560s in the still fashionable 'medieval' style

an old-fashioned over-inflated household, and they were out-moded even while Buckingham lived. Later building on this scale would be characterized by more integrated planning, disposing of the separate units in favour of more spacious family quarters, saloons, and galleries, and reducing fortification (where it survived at all) to the level of an expensive conceit. Nevertheless, the tradition of the strong tower and the fortified gatehouse died hard in sixteenth-century England. The ostentatious fortified front of Compton Castle (Devonshire), although thoroughly medieval in flavour, is an addition of about 1500. At Compton Wynyates (Warwickshire), the early-sixteenth-century domestic façade is broken near its centre by a great embattled stone tower, while the anachronistic gatehouses of Titchfield (Hampshire) and Hoghton (Lancashire) are works of the mid-Tudor period. At these and many more, some recollection of antiquity was clearly important in Tudor society both for reasons of status and as a method of finishing off a façade. Yet the true purpose of works of this kind was never to be left in much doubt. By far the most handsome

170 Sir Henry Marney's multi-storey gatehouse at Layer Marney, intended to be the showpiece of a great country house he never lived to complete

171 Turrets and battlements at Sir Richard Weston's Sutton Place, retaining a slight 'medieval' flavour at a fashionable mansion of the 1530s otherwise more remarkable for its high-quality Renaissance brickwork and terracottas

gatehouse of early Tudor England is Henry Lord Marney's tower at Layer Marney (Essex), built on a scale that was plainly intended to out-class anything similar before it. It is a many-windowed confection, its four turrets rising to eight storeys, topped not by battlements in the standard medieval manner but by the miniature shell-gables, with dolphin ornaments, of the dawning northern Renaissance. Before beginning on his fashionable new mansion, which was never in the event completed beyond the gatehouse, Sir Henry Marney had spent most of his adult life at court, his last office being the keepership of the privy seal to which he was promoted in 1523, just before he died. Characteristically for a man of his circle, he was attracted by the new ideas flooding in from Italy, and was ready to employ (in a way that Buckingham was not) the very latest materials in his building.

The use of terracotta in building was a short-lived fashion in England, largely confined to the 1520s and 1530s and directly attributable to imported Italian craftsmen. At Layer Marney, the shell-gables and their dolphins are of Italian terracotta, as are the scrolled window-heads and highly decorated mullions and transoms, moulded with Renaissance motifs. It was a style that would reach its apogee in England just a few years later at Sutton Place (Surrey), built in the 1530s for Sir Richard Weston, a similarly long-serving courtier and former associate of Lord Marney. Yet Sutton Place is a country mansion in the new style, with scarcely a reminder, except in some decorative crenellations, of the older traditions which had still been influential at Layer Marney. Open and undefended, it was the house of a man of high fashion, widely travelled and grown old in the service of the king. Sir Richard's brother, even more travelled than himself, was lord prior of the knights of St John in England. His son, Francis, before his disgrace and execution in 1536, was an intimate companion of the king. Sutton Place, in consequence, was as up to date as

172 Carlisle: a medieval keep and curtain wall adapted for artillery by Henry VIII's engineers

anything in England at the time, the product of the most advanced taste at court. Henry VIII came there to admire it in 1533, having himself given the manor of Sutton to Sir Richard in recognition of his services, some twelve years before, in the downfall and condemnation of Buckingham.

When Henry and his intimates gathered to plan or to applaud a new building, they saw themselves as the upholders of innovation in the arts and, less directly, of that spirit that had brought England during Henry's reign back into the forefront of European affairs. Henry's vision of himself as a Renaissance prince encouraged him in a rivalry, both artistic and political, with his contemporaries, Francis I of France and Charles V, king of Spain and Holy Roman emperor. Accordingly, much of the decorative treatment of Henry's palace at Nonsuch (Surrey) was borrowed from Francis I's re-modelling of Fontainebleau. And then again when, after years of successfully holding them apart, Henry's rivals came together against him in 1538, the threat of a joint invasion by those he most feared drove Henry into a programme of coastal fortification of a novelty and scale exceeding anything yet attempted in the West.

Henry's ambition was to complete a chain of gun-forts, blockhouses, and batteries to protect every major potential landing-point on the invasion coasts to the east and the south of his kingdom. Since early youth, Henry had been interested in guns. He had also acquired considerable experience in the design of fortifications, being himself the author of a 'device' for the re-fortification of Calais in 1532 which was both an attempt to modernize the existing defences and a programme for the development of new ones.[6] Certainly, conversions of this kind had become quite common by the 1530s. Norham (Northumberland), after its unexpected fall to the Scots in 1513, was modified—not very successfully—for artillery, its mural towers being re-designed with triangular fronts and the whole fortress re-equipped with new gun-ports.[7] Henry's own stipulations for Calais had included the cutting down in height of the Beauchamp and Dublin Towers 'as moche as nede shalbe', the latter to be 'lyned, made broder, and massied up with lyme and stone, and thereupon a platfourme to be made to bere a grete pece of ordinaunce, as well to beate over the bulwerke ther, as to scoure the contreth thereaboutes.'[8] And the levelled-off parapets, the wide gun embrasures, and strengthened wall-walks of Carlisle (Cumberland) still show the marks of a similar conversion undertaken at this important border fortress in 1541 under the direction of Stephen von Haschenperg, Henry VIII's Bohemian engineer.[9]

Yet powerful though the old fortresses could be made to be, even the best conversion was quite evidently no substitute for a building specifically designed both to carry and to resist artillery. Such buildings of their nature would be non-residential; they might house a garrison for the term of its duty, but had few of the comforts that had come to be expected in the residence of a magnate, and had as little in common with the private castle of the central and late Middle Ages as that castle itself had had nothing much to do with the communal fortifications that preceded it. Henry VIII's artillery forts were put up at a time when the medieval castle-building tradition had, for other reasons, lost much of its direction. But they had a role of their own too in the disappearance of that tradition, for they had disposed already of much that recommended the castle to the private owner, while demonstrating also in their rapid obsolescence the heavy cost of keeping up to date.

173 Bari, in southern Italy: one of Frederick II's greater fortresses, remodelled in the early sixteenth century for artillery

Perhaps the most advanced of the coastal fortifications of the previous generation, begun in 1481 and completed during the reign of Henry VII, had been Dartmouth Castle (Devonshire), the direct contemporary in its earliest stages of Lord Hastings's Kirby Muxloe (above, pp. 160–64). Dartmouth is an important building, most particularly for the rectangular gun-ports with which it was equipped, widening the field of fire of the gunners and much ahead of their time. Yet in other respects the planning of Dartmouth was medieval. It consisted of two great towers adjoining each other, one rectangular, the other circular. Both towers had their gun-decks in the basement, with two residential storeys above. At the seaward angle, a largely decorative turret rose above the crenellated parapet of the rectangular tower, giving to the whole that touch of the spectacular without which no late-medieval military building was complete.[10]

Dartmouth, with St Petrox Church immediately behind it, looks less massive than it is. Yet it is plain that, in a building of this kind and date, height was still considered to be an asset, it being exactly this characteristic of castle-building that would alter most dramatically in the next century. By the time that Henry VIII began his programme of works on the English coasts, no military engineer could have failed to heed the lesson of the crushing success of the French artillery against fortifications of conventional profile. The great fortress at Salses, in Roussillon, begun in 1497 under the direction of the Spanish engineer Ramirez, was already under siege six years later when its upper-works were almost totally destroyed by the French guns. As modified from 1503, Salses was one of the first of a new generation of artillery fortresses, half hidden in the landscape in its broad dry moat, low in profile, and massively strengthened against the gun.[11]

In effect, strongholds like Salses were to reverse the emphasis of late-medieval fortification in such a way as to deprive the castle of many of its more obvious attractions, at least for the private owner. The medieval building, always as much a residence as a fortress, had never sought to conceal itself from the public gaze but had gained, rather, from its prominence. The tower, originally defensive in intention and still retaining something of this role, had become a symbol of dominance, as essential to the façade of the late-medieval castle as was the fearsomely embattled gatehouse. Yet in the new artillery forts, as progressively refined through the sixteenth century, nothing of this would survive. Military engineering advanced faster in this period, with more obvious effect, than at any other time. But its comfortless products had little room to spare for domestic ease and still less to offer to chivalry. The many-purposed building that the castle had been, was reduced by the new technology to a fort, lightly garrisoned except during an emergency.

174 The great tower at Dartmouth, one of the earliest of the coastal artillery blockhouses, built in the final decades of the fifteenth century to include a battery at basement level

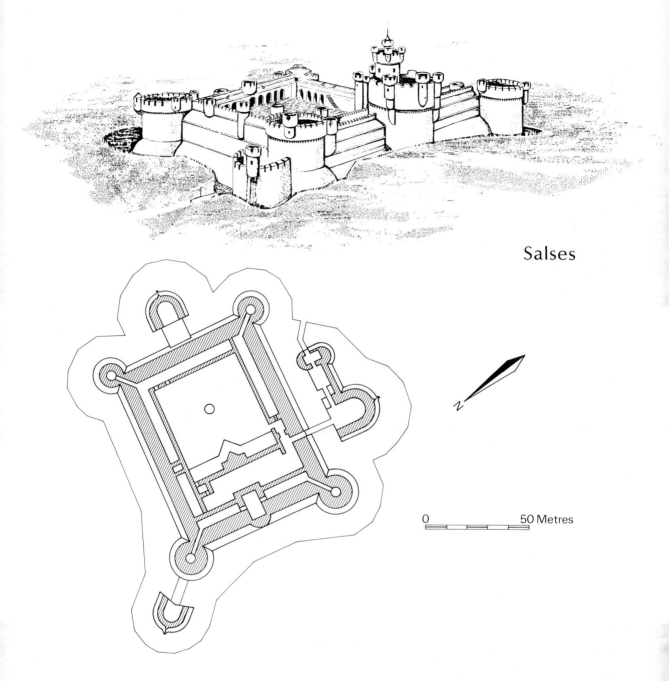

Salses

175   The pioneering artillery fort at Salses (Roussillon), re-drawn from a sketch of the early sixteenth century and showing it before later modifications did away with many of the turrets and levelled the more vulnerable upperworks; the plan of Salses (below) is of the fortress today

176 Henry VIII's coastal fort at Camber, equipped in 1539–43 with semi-circular bastions strengthening the earlier artillery tower (1512–14), which still rises centrally above parapet level

Henry's building programme, beginning in 1538 and driven on by the very real threat of invasion, was uncompromising in its modernity. Moreover, it demonstrated, in constant changes of plan, the deep concern and the personal interest of the king and his military advisers. The fort built at Camber (Sussex) in 1539–43 was already a reconstruction of the artillery tower raised on the same site in 1512–14, at the beginning of Henry's reign. Yet even while it was being built, a major change was introduced in the plan of its bastions to achieve their present semi-circular form.[12] Camber's low-lying and dumpy semi-circular bastions, overlooked by the great tower at the centre, are typical of Henrician work of this period. They are repeated, for example, at the Kentish forts of Deal, Walmer, and Sandown (now destroyed by

177 *Below left* The Henrician artillery fort at Deal, built in 1539–40 to protect the Downs, a sheltered anchorage between Sandwich and the Goodwin Sands

178 *Below right* Walmer: the companion fort to Deal and Sandown (now demolished), built for Henry VIII in 1539–40 and subsequently converted into the official residence of the Lords Warden of the Cinque Ports

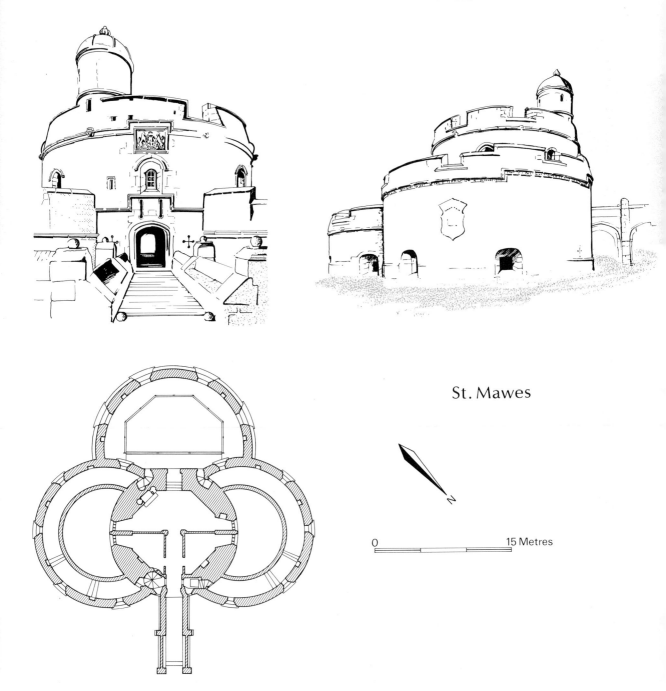

St. Mawes

0   15 Metres

179 Henry VIII's artillery fort at St Mawes, opposite Falmouth, built in 1540–43 with an aesthete's eye
for geometrical perfection of form

180 The Elizabethan fort at Upnor, built by Sir Richard Lee in the early 1560s to protect shipping lying at anchor in the Medway; the upper part of the façade, with its distinctive decorative roundels, is of seventeenth-century date; in front of the fort, palings follow the line of Sir Richard's triangular bastion

the sea), at Hurst on the Solent in Hampshire, and at St Mawes on the Roseland peninsula opposite Falmouth in Cornwall. What they offered their garrisons was a refined form of concentric defence, with guns in multiple tiers. And in this particular, as in the massing of their bastions, they were the equal of anything in Western Europe at the time. Such fortresses as these, with their appealing geometry, were the source of much aesthetic satisfaction among contemporaries. At St Mawes, the mood is caught by a series of inscriptions, specially commissioned from John Leland, antiquary to the king, and composed in Latin hexameters. One of them (in translation) urges its readers to 'Honour Henry the Eighth, most excellent king of England, France, and Ireland'; another hopes 'May the soul live for ever of Henry the Eighth who had this made in the thirty-fourth year of his reign' (1542–3); a third promises 'Henry, thy honour and praises will remain for ever'.[13]

St Mawes, a virtuoso performance in interlocking circles, is perhaps the most immediately attractive of Henry's castles. But it was not to be a model for anything else. Among the fortifications directly attributable to the king himself are those of Hull (Yorkshire) and Southsea (Hampshire), almost exactly contemporary with St Mawes. At both, triangles and rectangles replaced the cylinder shapes in favour during the earlier part of the building campaign, while there were intimations already before the end of Henry's reign of revolutionary new developments in military engineering that, just as soon as they were adopted, would make the blockhouse, of whatever plan, obsolete. The angle bastion, projecting as a salient from the main line of the defences and characteristically of arrow-head plan, had been developed in Italy from the early sixteenth century. It offered many advantages in an improved field of fire and in a greatly enlarged platform for the guns. By the 1540s, it was in use at Antwerp, in the Netherlands. At Yarmouth (Isle of Wight), not long after, Henry's new castle was already being equipped with an arrow-head bastion in the latest fashion at its most vulnerable south-east corner.[14]

Yarmouth was planned and built in 1546–7. Still essentially a blockhouse, relying on the strength of its stone walls for its security, it had much in common with the coastal forts of the next two decades, including Tresco (Scilly) in 1548–54 and Upnor (Kent) in 1559–67, at neither of which was there any real emphasis on the lowering and protection of the façade.[15] However, what might serve quite well as a defence against shipping, where the land-based gunner in any engagement must preserve a considerable advantage, was nothing like as suitable to the more static conditions of the conventional long-term siege. Sir Richard Lee, who built Upnor specifically to protect Elizabeth's warships on the Medway, knew very well what he was doing. He had begun his career as a military engineer at Calais in the 1530s, and by the 1550s had built up a reputation in this particular skill that was second to none in the kingdom. In January 1558, towards the end of Mary's reign, he had been sent to Berwick-upon-Tweed, on the border with Scotland, where any assault on that important frontier town could be expected to come not from the sea but from the land. Although never completed to Sir Richard's original plan, the fortifications of Berwick preserve today one of the most advanced defence systems of the time. In some respects even—in particular in his exploitation of the earth rampart—Sir Richard improved on the work of the Italian engineers from whom he had learnt his profession.[16]

Berwick is a great urban fortification, not a castle. Its defences were a development on those of the fortified cities of Flanders and northern Italy, and were quite obviously unsuitable for a building which, like a private residence, might be conceived on a much smaller scale. But there was another difference too in their execution. The progress of fortification at Berwick—the most expensive such enterprise in Elizabeth's reign—was punctuated by doubts and disputes. Within two years of Sir

181   The Elizabethan defences of Berwick-upon-Tweed: Sir Richard Lee's arrow-head bastions are clearly visible on the two most exposed flanks of the town, to the north and the east; the south (top) and riverside frontages continued to be protected by the medieval town walls

182 Castell Coch, rebuilt from the ground by the Victorian architect William Burges for John Patrick
     Crichton-Stuart, the wealthy and eccentric third marquess of Bute, whose other works of romantic
     antiquarianism included the reconstruction of Cardiff Castle

Richard's beginning on the works, an Italian consultant, Giovanni Portinari, was
making alternative proposals. Four years later, in 1564, Portinari was again called in,
this time with two colleagues, a fellow Italian (Iacopo Contio) and an Englishman
(William Pelham), and further imperfections in the plan were made clear. But this was
a dispute between professionals, and what moved the disputants was their purely
professional assessment of the military capability of the new works. Sir Richard had
placed two-tiered batteries (flankers) in the protected angles (orillons) of his arrow-
heads bastions to command the face of the wall, and these were criticized for their
inaccessibility and small size. Neither Italian approved of the bank with which Sir
Richard proposed to continue his walls behind the sentry walk, and both considered
the slope of the wall and of the bank too steep to remain stable under fire. On the
extent of the fortifications, and on what should be included most desirably within
them, even the consultants failed to agree.[17]

   The science of military engineering was moving forward very swiftly at the time,
and one expert's opinion was just as likely to be correct as another's. However, what
was significant about disputes like those at Berwick was that they were removed

entirely from the private sphere and had become the concern of professionals. There are parallels, of course, between the sixteenth-century border defence programmes of the Tudors and the great works, almost three centuries earlier, of Edward I in Wales. But the Edwardian castle had functions as a residence, as an administrative centre, and as a vehicle for display, which it shared with the private fortress and which, by its example, it helped to promote in a similar style in private building. Emphatically, this was not to be the case in Elizabethan England. Alphabet plans and other conceits were much favoured by the late Tudor gentry. But nobody built a country house on the plan of a star-shaped fortress, and the idea of half-hiding a new mansion in protective earth was obviously too absurd to be seriously entertained, even at a time when architectural extravagances of one kind and another were common form.

If a castle were built in late-sixteenth-century England—and some still were—it would look back into antiquity for its model, having more in common with such a self-consciously romantic nineteenth-century restoration as the Marquess of Bute's Castell Coch (Glamorgan) than with anything nearer its own time. Effectively, the thread from the past had been broken. For a full five centuries the private fortress had performed a role in medieval society that was far from exclusively military. In the final event, it was not military science alone that out-moded it, for there had been radical changes in the concepts of lordship and dominion and in how men would relate to one another. The fine points of modern fortification, as debated at Berwick in the 1560s, remained the interest of many in Elizabethan England but the preoccupation of the merest handful of professionals. Authority had found other means of self-expression.

Notes and References

Abbreviations

Antiq. J.	*Antiquaries Journal*
Arch. J.	*Archaeological Journal*
Bull. Inst. Hist. Res.	*Bulletin of the Institute of Historical Research*
E.H.R.	*English Historical Review*
Ec.H.R.	*Economic History Review*
J. Brit. Arch. Assoc.	*Journal of the British Archaeoloical Association*
King's Works	*The History of the King's Works,* H.M.S.O. (general editor: H. M. Colvin)
Med. Arch.	*Medieval Archaeology*
Proc. Brit. Acad.	*Proceedings of the British Academy*
R.C.H.M.	*Royal Commission on Historical Monuments*
T.R.H.S.	*Transactions of the Royal Historical Society*

Individual castle-guides, published by Her Majesty's Stationery Office on behalf of the Department of the Environment, by the National Trust, and by other bodies, are cited below by author (where given), title and date, thus:

R. Allan Brown, *Rochester Castle*, 1969.

Pendennis and St Mawes Castles, 1963.

Chapter 1 Castles of Conquest and Settlement

1 For the role of castles in the Conquest, see especially John Le Patourel, *The Norman Empire*, 1976, pp. 304–18; Majorie Chibnall (ed.), *The Ecclesiastical History of Orderic Vitalis*, 1969, ii: 218–19.
2 A useful general account of this process is to be found in Gabriel Fournier's *Le Château dans la France médiévale: essai de sociologie monumentale*, 1978, pp. 38–61.
3 Annie Renoux, 'Le château des Ducs de Normandie à Fécamp (Xe – XIIe S.)', *Archéologie Médiévale*, 9 (1979), pp. 5–35.
4 Pierre Héliot, 'Les origines du donjon résidentiel et les donjons-palais romans de France et d'Angleterre', *Cahiers de Civilisation Médiévale*, 17 (1974), pp. 217–34.
5 The point is well stated by Brian Davison in his 'Early earthwork castles: a new model', *Château-Gaillard III*, 1969, pp. 37–47, although I find it hard to agree with his conclusion.
6 Gabriel Fournier, op. cit., pp. 66–71; Michel de Bouard, 'Quelques données françaises et Normandes concernant le problème de l'origine des mottes', *Château-Gaillard II*, 1967, pp. 19–26.
7 Philip Barker and James Lawson, 'A pre-Norman field-system at Hen Domen, Montgomery', *Med. Arch.*, 15 (1971), pp. 58–72.
8 P A Barker, 'Hen Domen, Montgomery, 1960–77', *Arch. J.*, 134 (1977), pp. 101–4.
9 Brian K. Davison, 'Castle Neroche: an abandoned Norman fortress in South Somerset', *Somerset Archaeology and Natural History*, 116 (1972), pp. 16–58.
10 D. F. Renn, *Pevensey Castle*, 1970.
11 Charles Peers, *Richmond Castle*, 1953.
12 R. Allen Brown, *Rochester Castle*, 1969.
13 *King's Works*, i: 32.
14 Ibid., i: 32, ii: 647.
15 Stuart Rigold, 'Recent investigations into the earliest defences at Carisbrooke Castle, Isle of Wight', *Château-Gaillard III*, 1969, pp. 128–38.
16 J. G. Coad, 'Excavation at Castle Acre, Norfolk 1972–1976. An interim report', *Château-Gaillard VIII*, 1976, pp. 79–85.
17 John Clifford Perks, *Chepstow Castle*, 1967.

18   *R.C.H.M. Dorset*, ii: 57–78; *King's Works*, ii: 616–19.
19   Brian K. Davison, 'Three eleventh-century earthworks in England: their excavation and implications', *Château-Gaillard II*, 1967, pp. 40–43.
20   A. D. Saunders, 'Excavations at Launceston Castle 1965–69: interim report', *Cornish Archaeology*, 9 (1970), pp. 83–92.
21   Martin Biddle, 'Excavations at Winchester, 1971. Tenth and final interim report', *Antiq. J.*, 55 (1975), pp. 104–6.
22   *R.C.H.M. Dorset*, ii: 57–9.
23   Charles Homer Haskins, *Norman Institutions*, 1918, pp. 278, 282.
24   L. J. Downer (ed.), *Leges Henrici Primi*, 1972, pp. 108–9, 116–17.
25   Brian Hope-Taylor, 'The excavation of a motte at Abinger in Surrey', *Arch. J.*, 107 (1950), pp. 15–43.
26   For the most recent discussion of the custom of the March, see R. R. Davies, 'Kings, lords and liberties in the March of Wales, 1066–1272', *T.R.H.S.*, 29 (1979), pp. 41–61.
27   D. J. Cathcart King and C. J. Spurgeon, 'The mottes in the Vale of Montgomery', *Archaeologia Cambrensis*, 114 (1965), pp. 69–86.
28   Leslie Alcock, *Dinas Powys. An Iron Age, Dark Age and Early Medieval Settlement in Glamorgan*, 1963, especially pp. 73–93.
29   Cardiff Archaeological Society, *Llantrithyd. A Ringwork in South Glamorgan*, 1977, p. 13.
30   For the best recent discussion of the ringwork castle, see D. J. Cathcart King and Leslie Alcock, 'Ringworks of England and Wales', *Château-Gaillard III*, 1969, pp. 90–127.
31   S. E. Rigold, *Eynsford Castle*, 1964; and see also the same author's 'Eynsford Castle and its excavation', *Archaeologia Cantiana*, 86 (1971), pp. 109–71.
32   *Med. Arch.*, 5 (1961), p. 319.
33   Gabriel Fournier, op. cit., p. 59.
34   T. G. Hassall, *Oxford Castle*, 1971.
35   Brian K. Davison, 'Excavations at Sulgrave, Northamptonshire, 1960–76', *Arch. J.*, 134 (1977), pp. 105–14.
36   *Med. Arch.*, 5 (1961), p. 318; 6–7 (1962–3), p. 322; 8 (1964), p. 255.
37   Ibid., 13 (1969), pp. 258–9.
38   Ibid., 23 (1979), p. 263.

Chapter 2   The Transition to Stone

1   J.-F. Finó, *Forteresses de la France médiévale*, 1977 (3rd edition, revised), pp. 405–8.
2   M. W. Thompson, 'Recent excavations in the keep of Farnham Castle, Surrey', *Med. Arch.*, 4 (1960), pp. 81–94.
3   Martin Biddle, 'Wolvesey: the *domus quasi palatium* of Henry de Blois in Winchester', *Château-Gaillard III*, 1969, pp. 28–36.
4   E. M. Jope and R. I. Threlfall, 'The twelfth-century castle at Ascot Doilly, Oxfordshire: its history and excavation', *Antiq. J.*, 39 (1959), pp. 219–73; T.C.M. and A. Brewster, 'Tote Copse Castle, Aldingbourne, Sussex', *Sussex Archaeological Collections*, 107 (1969), pp. 141–79.
5   *King's Works*, i: 38–9.
6   Gabriel Fournier, *Le Château dans la France médiévale*, 1978, pp. 80–81.
7   R. Allen Brown, *Rochester Castle*, 1969.
8   W. Douglas Simpson, *Castles in England and Wales*, 1969, pp. 58–61.
9   J. G. Coad, 'Excavation at Castle Acre, Norfolk 1972–1976. An interim report', *Château-Gaillard VIII*, 1976, pp. 79–85.
10   M. W. Thompson, op. cit., p. 91.
11   B. Wilcox, 'Timber reinforcement in medieval castles', *Château-Gaillard V*, 1972, p. 194.
12   M. W. Thompson, *Pickering Castle*, 1958.
13   *King's Works*, ii: 561.
14   T. L. Jones, *Launceston Castle*, 1959; A. D. Saunders, 'Launceston Castle: an interim report', *Cornish Archaeology*, 3 (1964), pp. 63–9.

15 C. A. Ralegh Radford, *Restormel Castle*, 1947; *King's Works*, ii: 804–5.
16 For Totnes, see S. E. Rigold's 'Totnes Castle. Recent excavations by the Ancient Monuments Department, Ministry of Works', *Report and Transactions of the Devonshire Association*, 86 (1954), pp. 228–56, and the same author's *Totnes Castle*, 1955.
17 J.-F. Finó, op. cit., pp. 399–404.
18 For valuable recent studies of Issoudun and Villeneuve, see Jean Vallery-Radot, 'La Tour Blanche d'Issoudun (Indre)', *Château-Gaillard I*, 1964, pp. 149–60, and the same author's 'Le donjon de Philippe-Auguste à Villeneuve-sur-Yonne et son devis', *Château-Gaillard II*, 1967, pp. 106–12.
19 M. W. Thompson, *Conisborough Castle*, 1959.
20 For this, see especially R. Allen Brown's 'Framlingham Castle and Bigod 1154–1216', *Proceedings of the Suffolk Institute of Archaeology*, 25 (1949–52), pp. 127–48, and the same author's 'Royal castle-building in England, 1154–1216', *E.H.R.*, 70 (1955), pp. 353–98, with its sequel 'A list of castles, 1154–1216', ibid., 74 (1959), pp. 249–80.
21 R. Allen Brown, *Orford Castle*, 1964.
22 J.-F. Finó, op. cit., pp. 449–54.
23 For the fullest recent discussion of Pembroke, see D. J. Cathcart King's 'Pembroke Castle', *Archaeologia Cambrensis*, 127 (1978), pp. 75–121.
24 *King's Works*, i: 76–7, ii: 613, 844–5.
25 R. Allen Brown, op. cit. (1959), p. 249.
26 C. H. Hunter Blair and H. L. Honeyman, *Norham Castle*, 1966.
27 Charles Peers, *Richmond Castle*, 1953.
28 Charles Peers, *Middleham Castle*, 1943.
29 *King's Works*, ii: 830.
30 M. W. Thompson, *Kenilworth Castle*, 1977.
31 *King's Works*, ii: 783–4; Charles Peers, *Portchester Castle*, 1953.
32 R. Allen Brown, *Dover Castle*, 1974.

Chapter 3   Growing Sophistication

1 R. Allen Brown, *Dover Castle*, 1974; *King's Works*, i: 78.
2 M. W. Thompson, *Conisborough Castle*, 1959.
3 R. C. Smail, *The Crusaders in Syria and the Holy Land*, 1973, pp. 100–102.
4 Ibid., pp. 99–100.
5 J.-F. Finó, *Forteresses de la France médiévale*, 1977, pp. 377–80, 484–7.
6 R. Allen Brown, *English Castles*, 1976, p. 92.
7 J.-F. Finó, op. cit., pp. 366–70.
8 R. Allen Brown, op. cit. (1974).
9 J. D. K. Lloyd and J. K. Knight, *Montgomery Castle*, 1973; *King's Works*, ii: 739–41.
10 Armin Tuulse, *Castles of the Western World*, 1958, pp. 57–61.
11 C. A. Ralegh Radford, *Grosmont Castle*, 1946.
12 O. E. Craster, *Skenfrith Castle*, 1970.
13 C. A. Ralegh Radford, op. cit.; *King's Works*, ii: 657–8.
14 C. A. Ralegh Radford, *Tretower Court and Castle*, 1969.
15 O. E. Craster, *Cilgerran Castle*, 1957.
16 A. R. Myers (ed.), *English Historical Documents 1327–1485*, 1969, pp. 1138–8; for the castle itself, see John Clifford Perks, *Chepstow Castle*, 1967.
17 Dorothea Oschinsky, *Walter of Henley and other Treatises on Estate Management and Accounting*, 1971, p. 407.
18 For a general discussion of this and related points, see P. A. Faulkner, 'Castle planning in the fourteenth century', *Arch. J.*, 120 (1963), pp. 215–35.
19 *King's Works*, ii: 868–9.
20 Ibid., i: 113–14.
21 For a fuller discussion of these, see my own *Medieval England. A Social History and Archaeology from the Conquest to A.D. 1600*, 1978, in particular pp. 47–61.

22   Charles Peers, *Carisbrooke Castle*, 1948; *King's Works*, ii: 591.

Chapter 4   A Time for Professionals

1   *King's Works*, i: 308–18; J. Goronwy Edwards, 'The building of Flint', *Flintshire Historical Society*, 12 (1951), pp. 5–20; R. Allen Brown, *English Castles*, 1976, pp. 110–11.
2   A. J. Taylor, *Rhuddlan Castle*, 1956; *King's Works*, i: 318–27.
3   For a brief discussion of this very close and intimate group, see Michael Prestwich, *War, Politics and Finance under Edward I*, 1972, pp. 42–9.
4   A. J. Taylor, *Caernarvon Castle and Town Walls*, 1972, p. 21.
5   Ibid., p. 29.
6   For some details of the career of Master James of St George, see *King's Works*, i: 204–5.
7   Ibid., pp. 395–406; R. Allen Brown, op. cit., pp. 105–6.
8   J.-F. Finó, *Forteresses de la France médiévale*, 1977, pp. 471–4.
9   Armin Tuulse, *Castles of the Western World*, 1958, pp. 87–8, 99–100, 102.
10   Stewart Cruden, *The Scottish Castle*, 1960, pp. 65–8.
11   C. A. Ralegh Radford, *Goodrich Castle*, 1958.
12   J. M. Lewis, *Carreg Cennen Castle*, 1960.
13   C. N. Johns, *Criccieth Castle*, 1970; *King's Works*, i: 365–7.
14   C. A. Ralegh Radford, *White Castle*, 1962.
15   *Denbigh Castle and Town Walls*, 1943; *King's Works*, i: 333–4.
16   *King's Works*, ii: 685–7; C. A. Ralegh Radford, *Kidwelly Castle*, 1975.
17   For Caerphilly, see especially Douglas B. Hague's account of the castle in T. B. Pugh's *Glamorgan County History. Volume III. The Middle Ages*, 1971, pp. 423–6.
18   R. Allen Brown, op. cit., p. 114.
19   For Gilbert, earl of Gloucester's income and other circumstances, see especially Michael Altschul's *A Baronial Family in Medieval England: the Clares, 1217–1314*, 1965, passim.

Chapter 5   Castles of Law and Order

1   For these, see the writings of R. H. Hilton, in particular 'Peasant movements in England before 1381', *Ec.H.R.*, 2nd series, 2 (1949–50), pp. 115–36; 'Lord and peasant in Staffordshire in the Middle Ages', *North Staffordshire Journal of Field Studies*, 10 (1970), pp. 1–20; and *Bond Men Made Free*, 1973, pp. 85–90.
2   N. Denholm-Young, *The Country Gentry in the Fourteenth Century*, 1969, pp. 34–8.
3   The best informed estimate puts the true cost of the royal castle-building programme in Wales, incurred between 1277 and *circa* 1340, at about £100,000, or many millions of pounds in our money. Of this figure, some 80 per cent is thought to have been spent before 1301 (*King's Works*, i: 406–7).
4   This is certainly the view of Richard W. Kaeuper, 'Royal finance and the crisis of 1297', in *Order and Innovation. Essays in Honour of Joseph R. Strayer* (eds. William C. Jordan, Bruce McNab, and Teofilo F. Ruiz), 1976, pp. 103–10.
5   The most recent discussion of the crisis of 1297–8 is included in Michael Prestwich's introduction to his edition of *Documents Illustrating the Crisis of 1297–98 in England*, Camden Fourth Series, 24 (1980), pp. 1–37, but see also the same author's more general study *The Three Edwards. War and State in England 1272–1377*, 1980, in particular pp. 27–32.
6   Isabel S. T. Aspin, *Anglo-Norman Political Songs*, Anglo-Norman Text Society, 11 (1953), pp. 105–15.
7   J. R. Maddicott, *The English Peasantry and the Demands of the Crown 1294–1341*, Past & Present Supplement 1, 1975, pp. 64–5.
8   Naomi D. Hurnard, *The King's Pardon for Homicide before A.D. 1307*, 1969, in particular pp. 311–26.
9   J. R. Maddicott, 'The birth and setting of the ballads of Robin Hood', *E.H.R.*, 93 (1978),

pp. 276–99; for the criminal gangs, see the summary in chapter 3 of John Bellamy's *Crime and Public Order in England in the Later Middle Ages*, 1973, pp. 69–88.

10   Richard W. Kaeuper, 'Law and order in fourteenth-century England: the evidence of special commissions of oyer and terminer', *Speculum*, 54 (1979), pp. 734–84.
11   Isabel S. T. Aspin, op. cit., pp. 71, 74.
12   See, for example, J. R. Maddicott, *Law and Lordship: Royal Justices as Retainers in Thirteenth- and Fourteenth-Century England*, Past & Present Supplement 4, 1978, p. 14.
13   H. R. T. Summerson, 'The structure of law enforcement in thirteenth-century England', *American Journal of Legal History*, 23 (1979), in particular pp. 325–7.
14   Ralph B. Pugh, 'Some reflections of a medieval criminologist', *Proc. Brit. Acad.*, 59 (1973), p. 83.
15   Ian Kershaw, 'The Great Famine and agrarian crisis in England 1315–1322', *Past & Present*, 59 (1973), pp. 3–50.
16   Barbara A. Hanawalt, *Crime and Conflict in English Communities, 1300–1348*, 1979, pp. 238–60.
17   For the development of this practice already under Edward I, see Michael Prestwich, *War, Politics and Finance under Edward I*, 1972, pp. 61–6; and for the follow-up in the next reigns, see G. A. Holmes, *The Estates of the Higher Nobility in Fourteenth-Century England*, 1957, pp. 78–84.
18   Michael Altschul, *A Baronial Family in Medieval England: the Clares, 1217–1314*, 1965, pp. 236–7.
19   J. R. S. Phillips, *Aymer de Valence, Earl of Pembroke, 1307–1324*, 1972, pp. 254–7.
20   Ibid., pp. 260–67.
21   P. A. Faulkner, 'Castle planning in the fourteenth century', *Arch. J.*, 120 (1963), in particular pp. 216–18 (Chepstow) and 221–5 (Goodrich).
22   J. R. Maddicott, *Thomas of Lancaster 1307–1322. A Study in the Reign of Edward II*, 1970, pp. 23, 45.
23   For a description, with sketch plans and elevations, of the gatehouse at Tonbridge, see Sidney Toy, *The Castles of Great Britain*, 1963 (3rd edition), pp. 243–4. For Dunstanburgh, see J. R. Maddicott, op. cit. (1970), passim, and C. H. Hunter Blair and H. L. Honeyman, *Dunstanburgh Castle*, 1955.
24   J. R. Maddicott, op. cit. (1970), pp. 31–5.
25   For the grant to Huntingdon of 1,000 marks in lands and rents, see G. A. Holmes, op. cit., p. 4 (note); for the general circumstances of these promotions, see Michael Prestwich, op. cit. (1980), pp. 148–9.
26   For the most recent comprehensive description of Maxstoke, see N. W. Alcock, P. A. Faulkner, and S. R. Jones, 'Maxstoke Castle, Warwickshire', *Arch. J.*, 135 (1978), pp. 195–233.
27   For further discussion of the phenomenon of the moated site at this period, see my own *Medieval England*, 1978, pp. 111–15.
28   Ibid., p. 113 and figs. 75 and 76; see also the interim reports on this work published in *Med. Arch.*, 12 (1968), pp. 195–6; 13 (1969), pp. 273–4; 14 (1970), p. 194; and 16 (1972), pp. 195–6.
29   Adrian Oswald, 'Interim report on excavations at Weoley Castle, 1955–60', *Transactions and Proceedings of the Birmingham Archaeological Society*, 78 (1962), pp. 61–85.
30   E. Clive Rouse, *Longthorpe Tower*, 1964.
31   For a comment on both Stokesay and Acton Burnell, see R. Allen Brown, *English Castles*, 1976, p. 126.
32   C. A. Ralegh Radford, 'Acton Burnell Castle', in *Studies in Building History, Essays in Recognition of the Work of B. H. St J. O'Neil* (ed. E. M. Jope), 1961, pp. 94–103.
33   W. G. Thomas, *Weobley Castle*, 1971.
34   C. A. Ralegh Radford, *Llawhaden Castle*, 1947.
35   *King's Works*, ii: 838–9.
36   Ibid., ii: 930–37; also D. E. Strong, *Eltham Palace*, 1958. For the text of the agreement of 1315 concerning Queen Isabella's retaining wall at Eltham, see L. F. Salzman, *Building in England down to 1540*, 1967 (2nd edition), pp. 422–4.

Chapter 6   Castles of the Hundred Years War

1   Gabriel Fournier, *Le Château dans la France médiévale*, 1978, pp. 229–33.
2   *King's Works*, ii: 842–4; and see my own *Medieval Southampton*, 1973, in particular pp. 127–9.
3   *King's Works*, ii: 792–3.

4 Ibid., i: 237 (footnote); William Anderson, *Castles of Europe from Charlemagne to the Renaissance*, 1970, p. 237.

5 *King's Works*, ii: 793–804.

6 Ibid., ii: 659–66; for the recent excavations at Hadleigh, including a useful reconstructed plan of the castle, see P. L. Drewett, 'Excavations at Hadleigh Castle, Essex, 1971–1972', *J. Brit. Arch. Assoc.*, 38 (1975), pp. 90–154.

7 For this judgement, see the almost identical words of R. Allen Brown, *English Castles*, 1976, pp. 144, 146, and P. A. Faulkner, 'Castle planning in the fourteenth century', *Arch. J.*, 120 (1963), p. 230.

8 Catherine Morton, *Bodiam Castle*, 1975, pp. 8–10.

9 Ibid., pp. 9, 18.

10 P. A. Faulkner, op. cit., pp. 230–34.

11 W. Douglas Simpson, '"Bastard feudalism" and the later castles', *Antiq. J.*, 26 (1946), pp. 159–61.

12 For a comment on Marienburg (Malbork), see William Anderson, op. cit., pp. 246–8.

13 Margaret Wood, *Donnington Castle*, 1964.

14 W. Douglas Simpson, 'The castles of Dudley and Ashby-de-la-Zouch', *Arch. J.*, 96 (1939), in particular pp. 153–4.

15 J.-F. Finó, *Forteresses de la France médiévale*, 1977, pp. 333–7. Examples of French tower-houses without this difference include Bours (Pas-de-Calais) and Sarzay (Indre).

16 S. E. Rigold, *Nunney Castle*, 1957.

17 *Farleigh Hungerford Castle*, 1975.

18 R. B. Pugh and A. D. Saunders, *Old Wardour Castle*, 1968.

19 K. B. McFarlane, *The Nobility of Later Medieval England*, 1973, pp. 92–3.

Chapter 7   Castles of Chivalry I: Before 1400

1 G. A. Holmes, *The Estates of the Higher Nobility in Fourteenth-Century England*, 1957, pp. 38–9.

2 R. R. Davies, *Lordship and Society in the March of Wales 1282–1400*, 1978, pp. 194–5.

3 A. Hamilton Thompson, *The History of the Hospital and the New College of the Annunciation of St Mary in the Newarke, Leicester*, 1937, passim.

4 L. F. Salzman, 'The property of the earl of Arundel, 1397', *Sussex Archaeological Collections*, 91 (1953), p. 34.

5 Llinos Beverley Smith, 'Seignorial income in the fourteenth century: the Arundels in Chirk', *Bull. Board of Celtic Studies*, 28 (1979), p. 450.

6 M. Cherry, 'The Courtenay earls of Devon: the formation and disintegration of a late medieval aristocratic affinity', *Southern History*, 1 (1979), pp. 71–97. For a brief account of the Courtenay rise to power, see G. A. Holmes, op. cit., pp. 32–5.

7 For the early history of the Percy family, see J. M. W. Bean, *The Estates of the Percy Family 1416–1537*, 1958, pp. 3–11.

8 For a plan of Alnwick as it was before the nineteenth-century and other re-modellings, see Jill Rathbone, 'Alnwick Castle', *Arch. J.*, 133 (1976), p. 149.

9 For Largoët and Pierrefonds, see J.-F. Finó, *Forteresses de la France médiévale*, 1977, pp. 421–5, 444–8.

10 C. H. Hunter Blair and H. L. Honeyman, *Warkworth Castle*, 1954; and see also the descriptions of Warkworth in W. Douglas Simpson, 'Warkworth: a castle of livery and maintenance', *Archaeologia Aeliana*, 15 (1938), pp. 115–36, and Peter Curnow, 'Warkworth Castle', *Arch. J.*, 133 (1976), pp. 154–9.

11 For a well-illustrated description of the surviving medieval defences at Raby, see Alistair Rowan, 'Raby Castle, Co. Durham', *Country Life*, 10 July 1969 (pp. 78–81) and 17 July 1969 (pp. 150–53).

12 Charles R. Peers, *Middleham Castle*, 1943.

13 Gabriel Fournier, *Le Château dans la France médiévale*, 1978, p. 234.

14 James Raine (ed.), *Testamenta Eboracensia I*, Surtees Society, 4 (1836), pp. 272–8.

15 L. F. Salzman, *Building in England down to 1540*, 1967, pp. 454–6.

16 P. A. Faulkner, 'Castle planning in the fourteenth century', *Arch. J.*, 120 (1963), pp. 225–30.

17 George Jackson, *The Story of Bolton Castle*, 1956.
18 L. F. Salzman, op. cit. (1953), pp. 46–52.
19 J.-F. Finó, op. cit., p. 437; for another reproduction, in full colour, of the same miniature, see my own *Atlas of Medieval Man*, 1979, p. 165.
20 M. W. Thompson, *Kenilworth Castle*, 1977.
21 *King's Works*, ii: 936–7.
22 Ibid., i: 163.
23 Ibid., ii: 870–82.
24 J.-F. Fino, op. cit., pp. 475–9.
25 The words are those of the continuator of Higden's *Polychronicon*, as quoted in *King's Works*, ii: 881.
26 Ibid., i: 184–5.
27 For a description of the towers, with plans and a section of Caesar's Tower, see Sidney Toy, *The Castles of Great Britain*, 1963 (3rd edition), pp. 204–5.

Chapter 8   Castles of Chivalry II: The Fifteenth Century

1   A. R. Bridbury, 'The Black Death', *Ec.H.R.*, 2nd series, 26 (1973), pp. 584–5.
2   R. I. Jack, *The Grey of Ruthin Valor*, 1965, passim.
3   John Hatcher, *Rural Economy and Society in the Duchy of Cornwall 1300–1500*, 1970, chapter 7 ('The Fifteenth Century').
4   A. J. Pollard, 'Estate management in the later Middle Ages: the Talbots and Whitchurch, 1383–1525', *Ec.H.R.*, 2nd series, 25 (1972), pp. 564–5.
5   Ibid., pp. 560–61.
6   Rodney Hilton, *Bond Men Made Free. Medieval peasant movements and the English rising of 1381*, 1973, pp. 156–7.
7   G. A. Holmes, *The Estates of the Higher Nobility in Fourteenth-Century England*, 1957, pp. 117–19, 126.
8   M. G. A. Vale, *Piety, Charity and Literacy among the Yorkshire Gentry, 1370–1480*, Borthwick Papers 50, 1976, pp. 24–5.
9   R. H. Hilton, *The English Peasantry in the Later Middle Ages*, 1975, pp. 66–7.
10 For a discussion of such strikes, in particular as experienced on the bishop of Worcester's estates, see Christopher Dyer, 'A redistribution of incomes in fifteenth-century England', *Past & Present*, 39 (1968), pp. 11–33.
11 For this argument, see R. R. Davies, 'Baronial accounts, incomes and arrears in the later Middle Ages', *Ec.H.R.*, 2nd series, 21 (1968), pp. 211–20.
12 Llinos Beverley Smith, 'Seignorial income in the fourteenth century: the Arundels in Chirk', *Bull. Board of Celtic Studies*, 28 (1979), pp. 454–5; Carole Rawcliffe, *The Staffords, Earls of Stafford and Dukes of Buckingham 1394–1521*, 1978, p. 106.
13 G. A. Holmes, op. cit., pp. 101, 104.
14 J. M. W. Bean, *The Estates of the Percy Family 1416–1537*, 1958, p. 41.
15 Carole Rawcliffe, op. cit., pp. 18–19.
16 Quoted by K. B. McFarlane, *The Nobility of Later Medieval England*, 1973, p. 152.
17 For these and other alliances, see Carole Rawcliffe, op. cit., pp. 21–4.
18 J. R. Lander, 'Marriage and politics in the fifteenth century: the Nevilles and the Wydevilles', *Bull. Inst. Hist. Res.*, 36 (1963), p. 120.
19 For the more severe view of the Wydeville influence, see M. A. Hicks, 'The changing role of the Wydevilles in Yorkist politics to 1483', in *Patronage, Pedigree and Power* (ed. Charles Ross), 1979, pp. 60–86.
20 Ibid., p. 67.
21 A. J. Taylor, *Raglan Castle*, 1950; for a convincing revision of Dr Taylor's dating of the keep and other buildings at Raglan, see Anthony Emery, 'The development of Raglan Castle and keeps in late medieval England', *Arch. J.*, 132 (1975), pp. 151–86.
22 Anthony Emery, op. cit., pp. 174–5, 185–6.

23   T. L. Jones, *Ashby de la Zouch*, 1953; and see also W. Douglas Simpson, 'The castles of Dudley and Ashby-de-la-Zouch', *Arch. J.*, 96 (1939), pp. 142–58.

24   A. Hamilton Thompson, 'The building accounts of Kirby Muxloe Castle, 1480–1484', *Trans Leicestershire Archaeological Society*, 11 (1919–20), pp. 193–345.

25   For Rambures, see J.-F. Finó, *Forteresses de la France Médiévale*, 1977, pp. 455–8.

26   Charles Peers, *Kirby Muxloe Castle*, 1957.

27   Terence P. Smith, 'Someries Castle', *Bedfordshire Archaeological Journal*, 3 (1966), pp. 35–51.

28   W. Douglas Simpson, 'Buckden Palace', *J. Brit. Arch. Assoc.*, 3rd series, 2 (1937), pp. 121–32.

29   Roger Virgoe, 'William Tailboys and Lord Cromwell: crime and politics in Lancastrian England', *Bull. John Rylands Library*, 55 (1972–3), pp. 459–82.

30   Roger Virgoe, 'Some ancient indictments in the King's Bench referring to Kent, 1450–1452', in *Documents Illustrative of Medieval Kentish Society* (ed. F. R. H. Du Boulay), Kent Records, 18 (1964), p. 255; quoted also by Carole Rawcliffe, op. cit., p. 178.

31   For these measures, see my own *Medieval England*, 1978, p. 177, quoting A. D. K. Hawkyard's unpublished Keele M. A. thesis *Some late-medieval fortified manor houses* (1969).

32   H. D. Barnes and W. Douglas Simpson, 'Caister Castle', *Antiq. J.*, 32 (1952), pp. 35–51; also the same authors' 'The building accounts of Caister Castle, A.D. 1432–1435', *Norfolk Archaeology*, 30 (1947–52), pp. 178–88. For the circumstances of its building and a suggestion that work at Caister had already begun as early as 1430–31, see K. B. McFarlane, 'The investment of Sir John Fastolf's profits of war', *T.R.H.S.*, 5th series, 7 (1957), pp. 91–116.

33   H. D. Barnes and W. Douglas Simpson, op. cit., pp. 44–50.

34   Michael Thompson, 'The construction of the manor at South Wingfield, Derbyshire', in *Problems in Economic and Social Archaeology* (eds. G. de G. Sieveking, I. H. Longworth, and K. E. Wilson), 1976, pp. 417–38.

35   M. W. Thompson, *Tattershall Castle*, 1974, p. 16.

36   For these accounts, accompanied by a useful discussion of the castle itself, see W. Douglas Simpson (ed.), *The Building Accounts of Tattershall Castle 1434–1472*, Lincoln Record Society, 55 (1960); and for another earlier discussion of Tattershall, frequently repeated verbatim in the later, see the same author's 'The affinities of Lord Cromwell's tower-house at Tattershall', *J. Brit. Arch. Assoc.*, 40 (1935), pp. 177–92.

37   M. W. Thompson, op. cit., pp. 15–16.

38   S. E. Rigold, *Baconsthorpe Castle*, 1966.

39   F. C. Rimington and J. G. Rutter, *Ayton Castle, Its History and Excavation*, 1967, passim.

40   Ibid., p. 28.

41   Beric M. Morley, 'Hylton Castle', *Arch. J.*, 133 (1976), pp. 118–34.

42   Ibid., pp. 131–4.

Chapter 9   Last Things

1   H. M. Colvin, 'Castles and government in Tudor England', *E.H.R.*, 83 (1968), pp. 225–34.

2   Ibid., p. 226.

3   Ibid., pp. 232–3.

4   A. D. K. Hawkyard, 'Thornbury Castle', *Trans Bristol and Gloucestershire Archaeological Society*, 95 (1977), p. 57.

5   Carole Rawcliffe, *The Staffords, Earls of Stafford and Dukes of Buckingham 1394–1521*, 1978, pp. 88–9, 99–101.

6   Published by John Gough Nichols (ed.), *The Chronicle of Calais*, Camden Society, 35 (1846), pp. 125–9; and see also *King's Works*, iii: 346–7.

7   C. H. Hunter Blair and H. L. Honeyman, *Norham Castle*, 1966, pp. 8–9.

8   John Gough Nichols, op. cit., p. 127.

9   G. H. P. Watson and Geoffrey Bradley, *Carlisle Castle*, 1974.

10   For a full description, see B. H. St J. O'Neil, 'Dartmouth Castle and other defences of Dartmouth Haven', *Archaeologia*, 85 (1936), pp. 129–57; also A. D. Saunders, *Dartmouth Castle*, 1965.

11   For Salses, see J.-F. Finó, *Forteresses de la France Médiévale*, 1977, pp. 459–62.

12   H. S. Ames, 'A note on the results of recent excavations at Camber Castle, Sussex', *Post-Medieval Archaeology*, 9 (1975), pp. 233–6.

13   *Pendennis and St Mawes Castles*, 1963, pp. 24–5, 28.

14   S. E. Rigold, *Yarmouth Castle*, 1959; for Henry's fortifications in general, see B. M. Morley, *Henry VIII and the Development of Coastal Defence*, 1976.

15   T. J. Miles and A. D. Saunders, 'King Charles's Castle, Tresco, Scilly', *Post-Medieval Archaeology*, 4 (1970), pp. 1–30; A. D. Saunders, *Upnor Castle*, 1967.

16   Iain MacIvor, 'The Elizabethan fortifications of Berwick-upon-Tweed', *Antiq. J.*, 45 (1965), pp. 64–96; and see also the same author's *The Fortifications of Berwick-upon-Tweed*, 1972.

17   Iain MacIvor, op. cit. (1965), pp. 84–7.

Index